"This book is truly inspirational. I am not usually drawn to memoirs, but this one drew me in. Through *Unexpected Destinations* Wes, a remarkable church leader and friend of mine, shares experiences that will inspire readers to respond faithfully to their own callings by our Lord Jesus Christ. Readers will glimpse the deep impact of the author's leadership and ministry on people in many countries around the world and across denominational lines. . . . A must-read for all ministers and laypersons."

— SETRI NYOMI
General Secretary, World Communion
of Reformed Churches

"*Unexpected Destinations* bears witness to a life journey committed to discerning the way of Christ. The journey is personal but not solitary. Wes finds his bearings on this journey in community — in the community of marriage to Karin, in the community of family and church. It is a story not only of unexpected destinations but also of unexpected companions in diverse Christian churches and communities in every country and region around the world. Readers will meet an American Christian pilgrim who is faithful to Christ, committed to global Christian mission and evangelism, inspired by the vision of Christian unity, and determined both to encounter the world with an open mind and to engage it with the truth of the gospel."

— FR. LEONID KISHKOVSKY
Director of External Affairs and
Interchurch Relations,
Orthodox Church in America

"Inspiring, reflective, intimate, and visionary — vintage Wes. From reading his memoir I learned so much about his journey through life — his agonies and ecstasies, his disappointments and dreams — and throughout I recognized the ecumenist that he is. . . . An important contribution to the exercise of discerning what ecumenically yet needs to be done."

D1445714

Unexpected Destinations

An Evangelical Pilgrimage
to World Christianity

Wesley Granberg-Michaelson

Foreword by
Jim Wallis

William B. Eerdmans Publishing Company

Grand Rapids, Michigan / Cambridge, U.K.

Published 2011 by

Wm. B. Eerdmans Publishing Co.

2140 Oak Industrial Drive N.E., Grand Rapids, Michigan 49505 /

P.O. Box 163, Cambridge CB3 9PU U.K.

Printed in the United States of America

17 16 15 14 13 12 11   7 6 5 4 3 2 1

Library of Congress Cataloging-in-Publication Data

Granberg-Michaelson, Wesley.

Unexpected destinations: an evangelical pilgrimage to world Christianity /

Wesley Granberg-Michaelson; foreword by Jim Wallis.

p.   cm.

ISBN 978-0-8028-6683-7 (pbk.: alk. paper)

1. Granberg-Michaelson, Wesley.

2. Reformed Church in America — Clergy — Biography.   I. Title.

BX9543.G73A3   2011

284′.273092 — dc22

[B]

2011015857

www.eerdmans.com

To Cliff and Marge Michaelson,

my parents,

whose love and faith began my journey.

Contents

Contents

Foreword

———————

"Mission comes first." That radical declaration, as the author calls it, is at the heart of both this book and the life and vocation of my dear and long-time friend Wes Granberg-Michaelson.

I didn't peruse this book, as I confess I sometimes do before writing a comment, or even a foreword for a book. I read this one, carefully, cover to cover. It traces Wes's journey, but also the most hopeful vision of Christian faith that has been emerging over these last four decades. It's a pilgrimage that I have been blessed to share with Wes as a fellow traveler, friend, and brother. This book is really many things: a moving personal and spiritual memoir, an exciting documentary on the cutting edge of the church's life over these forty years, an engaging theological reflection on the best ideas and the controversies of our generation, and a ringing and persistent call to the social and racial justice at the heart of the gospel message. Reading *Unexpected Destinations* was both inspiring and encouraging to me, just as it has always been when I am with Wes. The book is more than a chronicle of Wes's story; it is also the story of our generation as we have sought not just to stay in the church but to transform it *and* the world outside of the church. Isn't that the reason for being the church? Wes keeps calling that our mission.

My earliest contact with Wes was when he was a young legislative assistant calling me urgently on behalf of a senator named Mark Hatfield, who was excited to find some fellow evangelicals (even young ragtag seminarians with beards and long hair) who agreed with the Oregon Republican's biblical protest of the war in Vietnam. When Wes then came to visit us in Chicago (his hometown and where we were going to seminary), I quickly sensed an easy and deep kindred spirit and suspected we would have a long and fruitful relationship. And it has been a great ride together. Wes got me my first meeting in Washington, a lunch with Hatfield in the Senate Dining Room, but neglected to tell us how to dress, as he describes our comical debut encounter with official Washington in this book.

Wes was, of course, one of the early "sojourners," part of both our magazine and our community in Washington, D.C. Together we wrote, spoke, and mobilized on the relationship between the church and public life, faith and politics — a conversation that we have been having together over all these years, and still are. All the while, Wes has chosen to root his deep and abiding call to mission in the authentic experience of Christian community, first at the Church of the Saviour led by Gordon Cosby (a deep influence on both of us), then at Sojourners, then at the Community Covenant Church of Missoula, Montana, and, for almost two decades, in the Reformed Church of America.

From Sojourners, Wes went on to pioneer Christian leadership on the environment, then to lead the World Council of Churches on critical issues of church and society, and then to provide what I consider the most exemplary leadership of a denomination that I have ever seen. Wes's leadership has helped forge the RCA as a bridging church that is both evangelical and ecumenical (often opposing spirits and energies), issuing a "Call" to itself and the wider church to revitalize existing congregations or create new ones, with a bold commitment to a multicultural future for the church.

In Wes's own words to his General Synod, "The church is formed in response to God's mission in the world." He describes the relationship between the "founding" church at Jerusalem and the first "missional" church at Antioch when he says, "My conviction is that it's the journey from Jerusalem to Antioch that defines the church's life today. Our most critical challenge is continuing the transition from being a settled denomination to becoming a missional church." I believe Wes's clear and key demarcation between *settled* and *missional* churches is the real division of the church today — more than liberal and conservative, or any other distinction. And be sure to read his enlightening description of the heartland and frontier churches of the north and the south, the latter being where literally all the growth of the church is now taking place. This book also contains a definitive history of the two most important new ecumenical ventures in the United States and internationally — Christian Churches Together and the Christian Forum, respectively. In both of these unique and extraordinary projects Wes has been a behind-the-scenes servant leader, as everyone involved in them, including myself, will attest.

Over all these years of knowing Wes, I have always been impressed with how he has always kept a personal journal, has always found a place of regular retreat wherever he is, and has always sought out wise spiritual directors. That concern for grounding and anchoring his life and decisions in a regular and deep contemplative practice and discipline has shaped Wes's life. And the book intersperses some of those fascinating journal entries throughout his story.

Wes and I both come from a very similar evangelical background. His was in Park Ridge and mine in Detroit, but they were quite similar in many ways. And his description of that background as something he had to overcome but also as a solid foundation almost moved me to tears because it is so true: "The evangelical subculture in which I was raised was infiltrated by pernicious racism, captured by right-wing nationalism, absorbed with rampant materialism, and defended by haughty self-righteousness. But it taught me to ask the right question. What about Jesus?"

In an epilogue that is really a call to a Christian faith for the next generation, Wes says that we must follow Jesus to the frontiers of the world, to the poor, the marginal, the young, and, yes, the currently unbelieving who label their religious preference as "none of the above." Only a church that sacrifices everything else for the mission of Christ is ready for that future.

JIM WALLIS

Acknowledgments

Time to write is a precious commodity. The Reformed Church in America gave me the gift of a three-month sabbatical in spring of 2010 that provided the time to write a good portion of this memoir. My friends Phil and Nancy Miller helped provide the space where I could do this concentrated writing. Mark Van Oss, my wife's cousin and an insightful reader, provided discerning comments and encouragement early in the process. Sharon Van Gelderen, my executive assistant, compiled and saved the chapters as I wrote them. Jim Wallis, my friend of four decades, has encouraged and affirmed my writing consistently, and accepted without hesitation my request to write the foreword. His generous words reflect a long and treasured journey of common Christian witness. Throughout this time, my wife Karin has believed in this project and encouraged me to make the sacrifices necessary to see it completed. I am so grateful for her gracious love and her abiding conviction that I needed to tell this story.

This book would not have been possible without the patient, generous, persistent support of Jon Pott, editor in chief at Eerdmans Publishing. He encouraged me to write this memoir of my journey, and accompanied me in exploring publishing possibilities with an honesty and unselfish commitment that are all too rare in this industry. As Jon quietly explained over lunches at Rose's by Reeds Lake, Eerdmans is evangelical, ecumenical, and Reformed. So am I. This is a good fit, made possible by a highly gifted, faithful, and committed editor and friend. Thank you, Jon.

Introduction

On Wednesday evening, August 25, 2010, I was in the Filadelphia Church in Stockholm, Sweden, with about four thousand others from around the world attending the Pentecostal World Conference. It was one of the most unexpected destinations in my life's journey. I was there representing the Global Christian Forum at the invitation of Bishop James Leggett, president of the Pentecostal World Conference, whom I had gotten to know well through Christian Churches Together in the USA.

Barely a month earlier, I had announced my decision to finish my service as general secretary of the Reformed Church in America after seventeen years. That decision came to me with clarity on a personal retreat at a Benedictine monastery, Christ in the Desert, in New Mexico. I had a compelling sense that this was the right step to take, but I had no idea where it was leading. Further, my spiritual experiences as a Protestant church leader were stretching from contemplative prayer in the Catholic monastic tradition to contemporary Pentecostal worship.

High-octane music rocked the Filadelphia Church that evening, and then Brian Houston came to speak. Houston is the leader of the Hillsong Church in Australia, a Pentecostal megachurch with global partner congregations around the world, including in Stockholm. Its music, much of it composed by Darlene Zschech, is sung by millions in congregations everywhere around the globe.

Houston began with a story of being on a moving walkway in an airport. There was a commotion at the end, with people bumping and pushing into one another. A woman unfamiliar with such walkways had simply stopped when she got to the end, and the walkway was carrying others into her.

"What I want to say to you tonight is this," Houston preached. "Just because something is over, don't stop."

He went on to say he was preaching to all those who had come to the end of a season or an era in their ministry.

"The end of an era is not the completion of a destiny," he proclaimed. "Every end is an opportunity for God to do a new thing."

I was sitting in the front row of the congregation with my hosts and other guests. Houston was giving examples of those in times of endings, and said, "You may have just completed service as heading a denomination and are wondering what comes next." We had never met. Suddenly it became one of those times when I had the sense that this sermon was being preached directly to me. It was as if I had been brought to Stockholm to hear these words.

My journey has been filled with that sort of thing. Endings of chapters have yielded surprising new beginnings. I've gone down pathways previously unimagined and arrived at destinations totally unexpected. And all this seems beyond me. It's certainly no course that I have charted.

That's what I've tried to write about in this memoir. My hope is that it might encourage others in their journey of faith. I'm told that Søren Kierkegaard once said, "Faith is walking as far as you can in the light and taking one step more." All of us find ourselves in places where we ponder whether and how to take that one step more. Sharing our stories gives us courage to do so.

But writing a memoir is not without dangers, especially for a Calvinist. The story is not supposed to be about us, but about the providential grace of God. I'm reminded of lines from the hymn "How Deep the Father's Love," by Stuart Townsend: *"I will not boast in anything, no gifts, no power, no wisdom. But I will boast in Jesus Christ, his death and resurrection."*

Such a self-emptying posture becomes even more difficult since we live in a time and culture where glorified individualism and the cult of personality seem to reign triumphant. Even the American Psychiatric Association recently considered whether or not to maintain the DSM category for severe narcissism as a behavioral disorder. (They did.) I don't want to contribute to the kind of egomania that seems to run rampant in entertainment, politics, sports, and even religion.

When Edmund Morris, the masterful biographer and admirer of Theodore Roosevelt, commented on Roosevelt's flaws, he identified "an almost erotic love of the personal pronoun." That's a chilling reminder of the temptation to place one's own experience at the center of all reality. A grace-filled Christian pilgrimage understands that it's a theocentric life, rather than an egocentric life, that reveals one's deepest purpose and truest destination.

Yet, the personal story of how such a pilgrimage unfolds can be revealing and instructive. The foundation of Christian faith is the startling claim that God took on flesh in Jesus. Those who follow him live in the expectation that God's grace and love intersect their own flesh and blood in a journey of transformation. Our faith can never remain abstract; it finds concrete expression, and takes on form, in the crucible of our lives. Describing how that happens matters.

My hope is that this memoir chronicles that mysterious, grace-filled process in my own inward and outward journey. Certainly my telling of this is filled with flaws; the compulsion toward self-justification dies hard in any of us. But I trust that enough truth seeps out to mark an authentic sharing of this pilgrimage.

Gore Vidal wrote that *"a memoir is how one remembers one's own life, while an autobiography is history, requiring research, dates, facts double-checked."* While I've recounted a pilgrimage of some sixty years, this is certainly more memory than history. My own fascination, and I trust that of the reader, is how one's interior journey shapes and molds the exterior events that constitute one's history. The attempt is to explore why things happened, rather than merely recount what happened.

For more than four decades I have kept personal journals of my inward journey and its various destinations. I first learned this practice as a spiritual discipline while being a member of Church of the Saviour in Washington, D.C. I've quoted often from these journals in the pages of this memoir because they reflect more accurately than even my present memory the inward feelings, questions, experiences, and insights during critical points of my life. They help keep me honest about my inner dialogue in the midst of external events, and I trust they illumine the personal struggles and yearnings behind my public persona.

As Brian Houston completed his sermon that night in Stockholm, he explained, "The story of our lives has to do with the themes of our hearts." Houston urged us to "Live life going forward. . . . This is called faith." I trust that what my memory recounts from the past in these pages is a testimony to how God persistently desires to call us into a grace-filled future.

Jesus and the Dentist

――――――

IT WAS FEBRUARY 11, 1950, and I was talking to my mother about God. As a four-year-old, I was full of questions about Jesus and the stories from the Bible that filled my young mind. Why did God let Jesus die if he was God's Son? Why does Jesus love me, and all the little children?

My mother sensed that I was ready to understand the plan of salvation. So she explained that God sent Jesus, his Son, because God loved us. It was a paraphrase of John 3:16, the first Bible verse I ever memorized. We all sin — even a four-year-old. Jesus died on the cross to pay for our sin. What we need to do is to ask Jesus to come into our hearts. That will make us a new person, and when we die we will go to heaven. Would I like to ask Jesus into my heart?

I thought about this. Maybe I was trying to figure out the part about Jesus needing to die because of my not liking my older brother, Ron, when he teased me. Perhaps, in this simple way, this was about the meaning of "substitutionary atonement" — a doctrine that, more than sixty years later, still seems to raise as many questions in me as answers. But I remember thinking this over.

We were about to leave for a dentist appointment with Dr. Cartright. Moments of eternal destiny often come in the midst of mundane circumstances. And from what I remember, I was much more worried about what would happen when I sat in Dr. Cartright's dentist chair than whether or not I would go to heaven.

1

So I said to my mom, "Can I ask Jesus to come into my heart when we get back from Dr. Cartright's office?"

My mother was worried. She didn't want to lose the eternal significance of this conversation. So she said, "Well, Jesus could come again while you are at Dr. Cartright's office. And if you haven't asked Jesus to come into your heart, you won't go to heaven."

I'm not sure what went through my mind. Later, after learning more about the second coming, I guess I could picture my mom being swept up into heaven while I stayed behind in the dentist chair. I'm not sure what would have happened to Dr. Cartright. We went to him for his price, not his theology.

In any event, that sealed the deal. I agreed to ask Jesus to come into my heart right then. And I prayed the prayer to do so. So from that day, my mother, and then I, would explain that I was born again at four.

This stayed with me. At Roosevelt (Theodore, not FDR) Elementary School in second grade, I thought I had fallen in love. But I was worried. On the playground with its swings and jungle gym, I explained to the object of my affection that she really couldn't be my girlfriend unless she accepted Jesus as her Savior. All she had to do was say this prayer.

She walked over to the side of the playground and stood alone for a few moments while I nervously waited. Then she came back and announced that she had done it. I was happy because now she could be my girlfriend. At dinner that evening I proudly told this whole story to my parents. I'm sure they were just praying that I'd do the same thing twenty years later.

For the evangelical subculture of that time, everything depended upon the moment when one made that decision to accept Christ as one's personal Savior. The radio broadcast of Billy Graham's crusades was called *The Hour of Decision*. His monthly magazine, which came to our home in a newspaper format, was called *Decision*.

A few years after that day in February, we sat in the living room of my grandfather's summer home — the "Big House" — at Lake Geneva, Wisconsin, with family and visiting missionaries. My grandfather, "Big Daddy," suggested that we go around the circle and share the story of the moment when we each had decided to accept Christ. Some of the stories were dramatic. Although just a young boy, I was included in the circle, and shared what Big Daddy was delighted to hear again — that I had accepted Jesus when I was four, after my mom explained how to be saved. The part about Dr. Cartright didn't come up.

But my grandmother said something I never forgot. "I can't really name a specific time or place. I feel like I've always been a Christian. But what's important is that I know Jesus lives in my heart, and I talk to him every day." Others nodded and added strong "Amen's." Years later I figured out she had been baptized by her parents in the state Lutheran church in Norway. Her Christian faith wasn't marked from a moment of dramatic decision. That seemed, at the time, odd, yet no less valid.

Happy Second Birthday

———

M Y MOTHER always remembered the date February 11, 1950, when I asked Jesus into my heart. This was called my "second birthday," the day I was born again, while June 14, 1945, was the day I entered the world at Swedish Covenant Hospital in Chicago.

When she was ninety, my mother-in-law, Carol Granberg, told me about her conversion as a four-year-old. She was in the bathtub, talking with her mother about what to expect on her forthcoming birthday, just a few days before Christmas. Her mother said, "And do you know whose birthday it is on Christmas?" She wasn't quite sure, but then figured out that it was the birthday of Jesus.

"I'd like to give Jesus a present for his birthday," Carol said.

Her mother replied, "Well, the only present you can give Jesus is your heart," an echo of the last line of Christina Rossetti's beautiful carol "In the Bleak Midwinter." So my mother-in-law, guided by her mother, prayed a prayer to do so.

Faith can be described as giving all you know about yourself to all you know about God. Certainly that's possible for a four-year-old. Many can trace their pilgrimage of faith to moments and memories of experiencing as a child the reality of God's love. Often those encounters are mediated by mothers.

Yet, even a novice in child psychology recognizes the emotional and intellectual dependence of young children on their parents. Ascribing "free will" to a four-, or six-, or eight-year-old in the decision of whether or not to accept the parents' invitation to accept Jesus is highly problematic, to say the least.

Other Christian traditions are simply more honest about how a family and a committed religious community shape and form the spiritual experience of one's early childhood in ways far beyond one's choice or control. But the evangelical subculture in which I was shaped and formed insisted that it was necessary to make a free choice for Jesus — or not — even when one was bound for kindergarten.

So it's no surprise that my mother was increasingly concerned when my younger sister, Marcia, had not yet made her decision to accept Jesus into her heart. When she was in the first or second grade, it became a crisis. This was no time to rest in providence of God's grace. Rather, it called for some Arminian creativity.

When February 11 rolled around, Mom unveiled her plan. After we had finished dinner on that cold February evening, Mom placed on the kitchen table a birthday cake with, I think, five candles. She, Dad, and Ron began singing happy birthday to me.

Following the desired script perfectly, Marcia said, "What's this? Wes's birthday is in June."

"Well," my mother explained, "this is Wes's second birthday."

"What do you mean?"

"This is the date, five years ago, when Wes asked Jesus into his heart. He was born again. That's why there are five candles on the cake."

I think Marcia was tempted by the prospect of another birthday cake every year.

So Mom popped the question. "Wouldn't you like to have a second birthday too?"

But even at that age, Marcia had an independent streak. This had nothing to do with the eternal state of her soul. Rather, it was more like her stubbornness a few years later when she resisted Mom's pleas to get her hair cut shorter. So, although tempted, she didn't take the bait of a second birthday cake.

Major theological debates swirl around the understanding of free will and God's sovereign grace in determining one's salvation. I've come to embrace a tradition that declares that the initiative always comes from God. My early understandings of free will and existential decisions determining eternal destiny were shaped, I think, far more by an American political culture founded on "rugged individualism" than by more biblical understandings of lives being shaped and formed through the relationships, and the intrusion of God's grace, in sacred communities.

Yet, I also know and respect what my mom prayed for. Decisive moments come in our lives that present us with the opportunity to respond to God's beckoning love and grace, or not. I don't think that takes the form of offering five-year-olds a second birthday, with a cake and a party. But we do have to decide, and keep deciding, what we will do about Jesus. Will we follow him, and forget about him?

Some years ago John Mulder, a college friend who went on to become president of Louisville Seminary for several years, compiled a book simply titled *Conversion*. In it he shared the stories of well-known persons, from long ago to the present day, who experienced dramatic and life-transforming conversions. The book is a strong, documented reminder that lives can be dramatically and decisively changed through an encounter with God's love, as expressed in Jesus. That's the hope that mature evangelical faith always desires to uphold.

Even then, we are warned by none other than Jesus to remember how this all happens. In John's Gospel, speaking to his disciples shortly before his death, Jesus reminds them, "You did not choose me, but I chose you." Beyond confessions and professions of faith that come at four or ninety-four, love has reached out to claim us in ways too mysterious and grace-filled to ever fully be known, but which we can fully trust.

A Missionary on Bonnie Avenue

I N 1950, Park Ridge, Illinois, was a newly emerging suburb on the north-west corner of Chicago's city limits. My grandfather, Carl A. Gundersen, was an immigrant from Norway who started a construction company, and he built our house on Bonnie Avenue. The backyard ended with a rectangular-wired fence, including a string of barbed wire at the top, separating the yard from the truck farm behind us. Using the wire rectangles as footholds, I could climb over the fence, as long as I was careful not to get my pants caught on the barbed wire at the top. That was a needed skill to retrieve the baseballs and footballs that ended up in the farm.

A few homes dotted the block when we first moved in. One was the LaBoy household with two children, Allan and Lenny; Allan was a year older and Lenny a year younger than me. We became best friends. We explored Park Ridge on our bicycles, daring to venture farther away than our parents ever knew.

We'd often play in our backyard. I had a swing set, and there was always the fence and the farm. And as young kids, we'd talk about everything, including Jesus. I was born again, with Jesus living in my heart. So I'd tell them about this.

My mom, as she worked in the kitchen with the window open, overheard some of these conversations. One evening she took me aside and said, "I heard you talking with Allan and Lenny about God. Do you know that you can be a missionary to them?"

Park Ridge Gospel Church, where my parents were loyal, committed members nearly since its founding, supported missionaries. Some of them came with slide shows. Every New Year's Eve we had major presentations from missionaries before the Watch Night communion service ending at midnight. Abe Vander Poy, with HCJB radio somewhere in South America, Don Hoke in Japan, and several others had their names on a large wooden map of the world, with lights that lit up at the point where they served.

But now my mom was talking to me about being a missionary to my friends, Allan and Lenny.

"Missionaries are simply people who tell others about Jesus," she explained. "I've heard you start to do that. So you can be a missionary to them, and ask if they would want to accept Jesus into their hearts, just like you did."

I took my mother's encouragement seriously. Much of my childhood, for longer than I would like to imagine, seemed to revolve around meeting my parents' expectations. And since their faith was the most important thing in their life, I certainly wasn't going to disappoint them on that front. So I thought more carefully about how to be a missionary to my friends.

But there was one complicating issue. Allan and Lenny were Catholic. Yet, from what my mother had explained, to be a Christian one had to accept Jesus into your heart. It didn't matter if you went to church. And Catholics believed differently; they thought you could get to heaven by trying to be a good person and going to their church services.

So on one of our exploratory bike rides, I began talking more directly to them about God and Jesus. I really wanted to be a good missionary to them. I explained about God sending his Son to the world, and Jesus dying for our sins on the cross. I told them how they could accept Jesus and be saved.

This was one of several missionary conversations. I reported back to my mom, and I assume Allan and Lenny began reporting this to their mother. They took my sharing with boyhood seriousness — we were best friends, after all — but told me that they too believed in God. Yes, they agreed that Jesus died for their sins. In their church, they even had big statues on the wall of Jesus dying on the cross — something missing from Park Ridge Gospel Church, I noted. They believed what I did.

I reported this back to my mom, with both excitement and some puzzlement. I really didn't have to be a missionary to my best friends. But I wondered whether my mom would agree, and why she sent me off on this missionary journey in the first place.

Allan and Lenny did share about some things they believed that were different. One was about Mary. My mom had already mentioned this. They prayed to Mary, which I really couldn't figure out. But I also couldn't understand how that could mean they weren't Christians.

And then there were the medals. For me, that was the biggest deal. In one of our bike-riding theological discourses, Allan and Lenny showed me medals that were fastened permanently onto their Schwinn, three-speed bicycles just below the handlebars. These were Saint Christopher medals, they explained. He was a saint who protected them. It meant they'd be safe riding their bikes.

I was envious. Why couldn't I have one of those? My mom tried to explain that we didn't pray to saints or Mary like the Catholics, but prayed directly to God through Jesus. But what I knew was that Allan and Lenny had a cool medal on their bikes that gave them extra protection, and I couldn't get one. That was the upshot of my first evangelical-Catholic encounter.

Selling the Farm to the Pope

———

CARL A. GUNDERSEN — "Big Daddy," as all the family called my grandfather — was a true patriarch. He was born in a house in Moss, Norway, on the Oslofjord, and immigrated to America.

Beginning as a bricklayer, he eventually started his own construction company, Gundersen and Sons. After achieving considerable success, he suffered serious losses in the Great Depression, which drove him into his own personal depression. But he recovered emotionally, and then financially.

Fundamental to his life was his personal, evangelical faith in Jesus Christ. Deeply involved as a lay leader in Salem Free Church in Chicago, a congregation made up primarily of Norwegian immigrants, he also set a model of stewardship as a successful Christian businessman.

Our family moved to Park Ridge when his home construction business was expanding. After a few years he set his eyes on the farm behind our house. One day while walking to Roosevelt Elementary School, I remember looking up at the sound of a commercial jet airplane flying low overhead toward the airport.

O'Hare Field had been a military base for the air force. Special hangars were constructed there, and I was told they housed powerful jets that were always on alert, ready to take off the moment the Russians attacked us. But then a new commercial airport was established there, with almost unlimited space to expand, compared to Chicago's existing Midway Airport.

Few could imagine how that would change Park Ridge and the surrounding area. But Big Daddy saw at least some of the vision. So he bought the farm. It was a rectangular-shaped piece of land, stretching from Cumberland Avenue on the east into a forested area on the west. His plan was to fill it with new, well-designed, and well-built homes by Gundersen and Sons.

The Catholic Church was also alert to changes — at least demographic ones. The nearest Catholic church, St. Paul's, was some distance away in downtown Park Ridge, while significant growth was happening where we lived, on the southern edge of the suburb and beyond. They needed to build a new church and school. So they approached Big Daddy.

Evangelical attitudes toward Catholicism in the 1950s were dominated by social suspicion, historical animosity, and theological rejection. By and large, Catholics weren't considered Christians. Despite my friendship with Allan and Lenny, the Catholic Church seemed like a mysterious, protected cult.

Our family would watch Notre Dame football games on our black-and-white Westinghouse TV — and root for them to lose. When a Notre Dame player lay immobile on the ground, one of us would say, "He's just faking injury to save time on the clock. That's what they do."

But once in a while, when for instance we'd watch a midnight mass on Christmas Eve and hear a bishop or cardinal talk about Jesus Christ in glowing ways, my dad or mom would say, "He almost sounds like an evangelical!" So a glimmer of hope was held out for a few who might really know Jesus, despite being trapped in a rigid, theologically mistaken, authoritarian system.

Therefore, I've always wondered what it was like for Big Daddy to receive word that the Catholics wanted to buy a section of the farm he now owned, bordering on Cumberland Avenue, in order to build a school and a church. It took him some time to decide. Meanwhile, word got around. Allan and Lenny's parents learned that my grandfather owned the land that the church wanted to buy. The school would be only a five-block walk away.

To this day, I don't really know what went on in Big Daddy's head and heart during that time. Certainly it felt like he was being asked to sell a part of his farm to the pope. I'd like to think that some early, pre–Vatican II gestures of ecumenical fellowship may have registered in his heart as he prayed about what to do. But maybe the Catholics were offering such a good price that he could turn a nice profit, and have more money to give to evangelical missions around the world who believed Catholics were not Christians.

But for whatever reason, he sold the parcel to the Catholics. For several decades Mary Seat of Wisdom Church and its school have stood along Cumberland Avenue, right where the farmhouse and barn used to be. And my friendship with Allan and Lenny was preserved.

Big Daddy and Billy Graham

S ITTING IN the family room of our home, I was looking at a map of the
world on the wall. The map had lines drawn on it, beginning in Chicago, and pins indicating various stops, marking a route that was zigzag-
ging around the world — through Tokyo, Taiwan, India, Ceylon, Abu
Dhabi, Africa, and onward. It was chronicling the journey of my grandparents, who were traveling around the world in 120 days.

It was no typical sightseeing tour. Rather, they were visiting missionaries. Big Daddy, still in the construction business, was now chairman of
the board for TEAM (The Evangelical Alliance Mission) missions. As a
committed evangelical layman, he had a heart for missions, and as board
chair, he decided he and his wife should go and personally visit many of
the TEAM missionaries who were serving in remote areas throughout
the world, to offer them support and spiritual encouragement, as well as
to learn of their challenges and opportunities.

My grandmother wrote letters, constituting a diary of their experience, using a small typewriter she carried with her. About every week an
epistle would arrive — one of several carbon copies sent to family members and friends. We would read her account and then look at the map to
see where they were. I have never forgotten that map, or those letters.

My grandfather's impact, as a committed layman, on the evangelical
world in the 1950s and 1960s was far more significant than I ever realized
growing up as his grandson. He loved to make home movies, and mem-

bers of the clan — six children, all of whom married and had families — would gather to watch them.

One movie was from someplace in the Caribbean. Big Daddy was at a swimming pool with Billy Graham, Cliff Barrows, and other members of the Billy Graham team. I don't know quite how it happened, but they were on a vacation together. He supported Graham's ministry financially, and years later, when I had the opportunity to meet Billy Graham, he spoke affectionately about my grandfather.

Youth for Christ was just beginning in the 1950s as a new evangelical parachurch ministry with the purpose of sharing the gospel with high school students. Billy Graham was involved in its early years, working with Ted Engstrom, its founder. My grandfather was an early and strong supporter of Youth for Christ, forming relationships with many evangelical leaders of that time.

In 1962, he and his wife Valborg, my grandmother, got on the train from Chicago heading to Denver, Colorado, for the twentieth annual convention of the National Association of Evangelicals (NAE). Twenty years earlier he had attended a meeting in St. Louis to organize evangelicals into one body, which became the NAE. Carl Gundersen was a member of its first board, and then was its treasurer for many years. When new office space was needed, Big Daddy donated the land in Wheaton, Illinois, on the corner of Main Street and Gundersen Drive, raised the funds, and then constructed its headquarters building.

At the convention at the Denver Hilton, however, he was both surprised and honored to receive the NAE's award as the 1962 Layman of the Year. The presentation read, in part, "For his 33 years as member of the board of the Evangelical Alliance Mission . . . for his years of unstinting service as treasurer and member of the finance committee of the NAE . . . for his dedicated service as board member and vice-chair of the National Association of Christian Schools . . . as a member of the board of Trinity College and Seminary; for his sacrificial giving of himself as the past chairman of the Chicagoland Christian Businessmen's Committee . . . and chairman of the finance committee for the 1962 Billy Graham Crusade in Chicago. . . ." When he went to the rostrum to receive the award, his only response was to recite, by memory, Psalm 34.

My grandfather never finished high school. He started working as a contractor, and built his first home when he was seventeen. Later he got a degree by taking night courses at the Moody Bible Institute. But he spent countless hours memorizing Scripture. He could recite some complete epistles by heart — like Ephesians and Colossians. When guests would gather in the evening at the summer house on Lake Geneva, Wisconsin, they would often ask him to recite passages of Scripture that he had memorized. I would listen in amazement.

Carl A. Gundersen reflected evangelical attitudes of his time. In 1960, John F. Kennedy was running against Richard Nixon for president. The United States, of course, had never elected a Catholic president, and many were concerned — particularly evangelicals. I remember clearly my parents worrying about the pope telling a president what to do — sentiments also expressed by the famous preacher Norman Vincent Peale.

One day at Lake Geneva late that summer, Big Daddy had some visitors. They met and talked on the side porch of the Big House. My grandfather didn't talk much, certainly with his grandchildren, about his various involvements. But I learned that those visiting were printing and distributing literature about the dangers of electing a Catholic as president of the United States. They wanted Big Daddy's support. And, despite his willingness to sell land for Mary Seat of Wisdom, he gave financial support to their campaign.

My grandfather expressed and embodied so much of the evangelical world that was emerging in the 1950s and early 1960s. Its entrepreneurial spirit, its conservative American patriotism, its passion for evangelical mission, its deep distrust of wider Christendom, its foundation in the words of the Bible — all were reflected in Big Daddy's life and legacy. I reacted strongly against some of these traits and embraced others, but my life's trajectory, in one way or another, was shaped by them all, and the legacy of this man of faith.

Will Sid Luckman Be Saved?

S ID LUCKMAN played quarterback for the Chicago Bears from 1939 to 1950. He was the first outstanding quarterback to run the T-formation, popularized by Bears owner and coach, George Halas. Many regard him as the finest Bears quarterback of all time, accumulating 14,686 yards in passing with 137 touchdowns. Luckman led the Bears to four National Football League championships during his tenure, including the famous 73-0 championship victory over the Washington Redskins in 1940. In 1943 he was named the most valuable player in the league, and after his playing career ended he was voted into the Pro Football Hall of Fame.

But to our family, Sid was just a friend of Dad's. My father, Cliff Michaelson, was the purchasing agent for Reed's Candy Company. Reed's made hard candies in rolls, like Life Savers. Butterscotch was their most famous flavor, and unlike Life Savers, each piece in a five-cent roll of Reed's candy was individually wrapped in cellophane. That's how we got tickets to the Bears games.

Unlike today, when lavish playing salaries set up pro football stars for life, retired players in the 1950s had to make a living. Luckman went into business, soon heading up the Cellu-Craft Products Company. They made cellophane, and my dad began buying all the cellophane that wrapped up each piece of Reed's candy from Sid Luckman.

So Sid was known well to our family. My dad once took me on a trip to the Cellu-Craft factory, where Sid led us on a tour, and I learned how cellophane was made. It took a lot of cellophane to wrap all those pieces of candy, so I'm sure Reed's was one of Cellu-Craft's more important accounts.

George Halas also kept Luckman on board with the Bears as a part-time quarterback coach even while Sid was running his company. Early every September, an envelope would arrive for my dad with three tickets for every home game of the Chicago Bears, which Dad kept in the top drawer of his dresser.

Dad was choir director at the church. Every Sunday when the Bears had a home game, my brother Ron and I would sit at the rear of the church. After the sermon and last hymn, but before the benediction, my dad would slip out the choir door to the side of the pulpit while Ron and I headed out the main door of the sanctuary. We met at the car, where our parkas, sandwiches, and thermos full of hot chocolate were waiting. It was about a forty-minute drive to 1245 Fletcher Avenue, the offices and factory of the Reed's Candy Company, where we parked for free. From there, a half-mile walk following the railroad tracks led to Wrigley Field.

In those years, the Bears played their home games at Wrigley (this continued through 1970). The field ran from the first base dugout to the left field wall, and just barely fit. Planks covered the entrance to the dugout in order to complete the back of that end zone, and the opposite end zone ended at the brick left field wall covered with dormant vines. This meant, however, that a huge section of bleacher seats could be erected in right to right-center field of the baseball park.

That's where our seats — or Sid's seats — were located, at about the 35- or 40-yard line, above the Bears bench. We could see Sid on the sidelines talking to the quarterbacks, like Billy Wade and Ed Brown, and to Coach Halas. From when we ducked out of the morning service, which ended at noon, until we got into our seats, it took about an hour, and we arrived just before the 1:05 kickoff.

Going to those games is one of my fondest memories of time with my dad. On cold Chicago November and December Sundays, we'd be huddled together with hot chocolate and a blanket, watching Willie Galimore, number 28, called the most elusive runner of all time, break away for touchdowns. We saw Mike Ditka's 1961 rookie of the year season with fifty-six receptions. And on December 29, 1963, with the temperature at 10 degrees, we witnessed the Bears beat the New York Giants, 14-10, for the national championship. I still remember Larry Morris intercepting a screen pass from Y. A. Tittle, the Giants' famous quarterback, and returning it sixty-one yards to set up the Bears' first touchdown.

Sometimes after the games we'd make our way to the catwalk where the Bears players would pass on their way to the locker room. We'd look for George Connor, their famous linebacker, and try to get his attention. Even when a player, Connor was doing some off-season sales work for the Hoerner Box Company, and Dad began buying some boxes from him for Reed's. On one Sunday after the game, Dad, Ron, and I were taken into the locker room to meet the players.

Sid Luckman and his wife, Estelle, were social friends with my parents in ways typical for business relationships of that time. At dinner in a fancy restaurant one December with the Luckmans and Jerry Markoff and his wife, my mom asked how their Christmas preparations were coming. An awkward silence ensued, and then Estelle explained, "Well, Marge, we're Jewish. We don't celebrate Christmas."

My mother was mortified. I still remember her talking about how embarrassed she was. But, she said, it led to an interesting discussion about Hanukkah (Chanukah), as Mom learned about this Jewish celebration occurring in the Christmas season. Plus, Mom wondered whether this mistake might have opened the door for future witnessing to the Luckmans about Jesus Christ.

Dad and Mom also worried about how to reciprocate for the expensive dinners the Luckmans would treat them to. They just didn't travel in the same economic and social circles. Apart from these business friends of my dad, virtually all my family's social life revolved around friends from the church — fellow evangelicals whose men held midlevel white-collar jobs with Chicagoland companies.

But Mom had an idea. She invited Sid and Estelle to our home at 1015 Bonnie Avenue for dinner. She cooked as nice a meal as she knew, and had it prepared by the time they came. Ron and I served as waiters, or servants. We were each dressed in black pants, a white shirt, and a bow tie. We served them the dinner. Sid and Estelle never forgot this. Years later, when I'd see Sid, he'd bring up this story about how "cute" Ronny and I were that evening.

But as Mom and Dad deepened their friendship with the Luckmans, this central question remained. How to witness to them about Christ? My parents actually had few non-Christian friends. It was fairly typical for evangelicals of that time to live in social enclaves with like-minded friends usually from church. The world was dangerous, and we needed to keep ourselves protected and pure. Having good non-Christian friends was unusual, and the obligation to "witness" to them always overshadowed these relationships.

Billy Graham provided a solution. In September 1959 he conducted a crusade in Wheaton, Illinois. Why was not clear. Earlier that year he had been to Australia and New Zealand and later he'd be off to Ghana and Nigeria. But he was holding an evangelistic crusade in the citadel of evangelicalism, Wheaton.

So after a lot of prayer and reflection, Mom and Dad took a bold step. They invited Sid and Estelle Luckman to go with them to the Billy Graham Crusade. And they accepted. Maybe they were genuinely curious. Or perhaps Sid was thinking, "Anything for Cellu-Craft."

This day was much anticipated. My parents worried about all the logistical arrangements — parking, seating, etc. And of course, my grandfather was very helpful, and also thrilled. Big Daddy was chair of the finance committee for the crusade, and sat on the platform with Billy Graham. Their home on Gary Court in Wheaton was an informal headquarters for the Billy Graham team. Cliff Barrows put together the tape recording for the *Hour of Decision* from Big Daddy's study.

The evening came, and my parents and the Luckmans joined the thousands gathering to hear Dr. Graham's message and invitation. "Just as I Am" was sung. My parents were praying. But Sid and Estelle Luckman remained seated.

I was only nine at the time, but I remember how earnest my folks were about the salvation of their friends. My recollection is that Sid and Estelle simply explained that they were Jews — and they were observant Jews. My parents certainly hadn't dealt seriously with the issues Paul wrestles with in Romans 9–11. They simply wanted Sid and Estelle to accept that the Messiah longed for by the Jews had already come in Jesus.

But this did lead my folks into deeper dialogue about how to understand the beliefs of their Jewish friends.

Sid Luckman remained a faithful friend. Gifts came every Christmas. When Karin and I were married in 1974, we received an onyx clock from Sid Luckman. When Carl A. Gundersen died in May 1964, Sid Luckman came to the funeral at Wheaton Evangelical Free Church. He was probably the only Jew present, and told my folks how moved he was by the service. Especially memorable, I'm sure, was the tape recording Big Daddy made to be played at his funeral, saying if he could rise up out of his casket, he would ask anyone there who had not accepted Christ to do so at that moment.

My family's relationship to Sid Luckman was like a window to the world beyond evangelicalism when I was growing up. It was a portal through which to watch my parents try to navigate between different subcultures, and struggle with the meaning of their faith for others who were their friends. It also provided the first context to hear evangelical understandings of Jews and the emerging state of Israel.

Independent, Evangelical, Nondenominational

P ARK RIDGE Gospel Church had followed the migration of people like
my parents to this emerging suburb of Chicago. One of its founding
stories is that Billy Graham, while still a student at Wheaton College in
the 1940s, served as a guest preacher to this new, young church. My parents and family became members in its early days.

Our whole life was centered on the church. Sundays included
Sunday school and the morning service, and Sunday evenings — once I
was in junior high — involved the youth group plus the evening service.
When the Bears played home games, that fit neatly into the remaining
time of the day.

My best friends, like Jim Nelson and Warren Patterson, were the kids
of my parents' best friends at church. We lived according to the mores of
the evangelical subculture of that time. No one smoked, drank alcohol,
went to movies, used playing cards, spoke profanity, or danced. We didn't
even talk about sex. We believed in Jesus, and we believed in America —
the Republican version.

Sometimes church families even took vacations together. The most
memorable one was when several families went together to Silver Cliff
Ranch, in Buena Vista, Colorado, a facility owned at the time by Young
Life, a parachurch organization working with high school students that
later became deeply formative in my spiritual journey.

During this period in American history, the evangelical subculture was largely invisible to the wider society. For instance, when Billy Graham would appear on the *Tonight Show* with Jack Paar, it created a stir among our family and friends. We'd want to be sure to watch it, in part because the wider, secular culture was giving some recognition to evangelicals. But even this was not without controversy. Some argued that Billy Graham should not appear on such a secular and worldly TV program. But others, including my mom and dad, felt he was right to use this opportunity to make a witness for Christ to this TV audience.

Being an evangelical in those days felt something like being in the closet. Rumors would spread about prominent public figures who were, in fact, "strong evangelicals." One of them was Bobby Richardson, a star defensive second baseman for the New York Yankees from 1955 to 1966. He was known to "give his testimony" in public, and was involved with the Fellowship of Christian Athletes. Casey Stengel once said of Richardson, "Look at him. He don't drink, he don't smoke, he don't chew, he don't stay out late, and he still don't hit .250!" He actually did hit an average of .305 in three World Series for the Yankees.

"Evangelical" was not a term used or understood in the mainstream press of that day. Being one was like being in a secret cult. We had our leaders, most notably Graham, we had our proscribed behaviors, and we had a network of institutions and organizations, like Wheaton College, Westmont College, Taylor University, Youth for Christ, InterVarsity, World Vision, Young Life, and many others. But apart from the fame of Billy Graham, this whole world functioned beneath the radar of the secular, mainstream culture.

That really didn't change until Jimmy Carter became president in 1976, and then shared in an interview that he was "born again." The mainstream press puzzled over what this meant, and in the process began to discover the evangelical subculture in America. For instance, a while later Ken Woodward, religion correspondent for *Newsweek* magazine, wrote a cover story titled "The Evangelicals." It was as though a foreign country had been discovered by the press. He called Jim Wallis and me frequently when writing it to be sure that he, as a Catholic, was getting the picture right about the evangelical community.

So in the 1950s and 1960s, churches like my own, Park Ridge Gospel, were struggling with the tension of how to be "in the world, but not of the world." Our church changed its name to South Park Church. A new shopping area had been built on the south end of Park Ridge called South Park (decades before the irreverent TV show of the same name). Church leaders thought that to be "relevant," they should rename their church just by its particular location, like churches in the New Testament — the church at Ephesus, the church at Corinth, etc.

South Park Church also wanted to reach out more effectively to youth. So in 1971 they hired a new, creative youth pastor, Bill Hybels. He joined Dave Holmbo, the new assistant music director, and began a creative outreach ministry to young people, focusing on music and activities that were relevant to their tastes, and teaching Scripture with direct and practical application to their lives. The program, called Son City, exploded, growing to 300, 600, and even 1,200 kids.

By then, twice as many kids were participating in Son City as there were members of the church. Conversions were happening continually and lives were being transformed. But Son City's rapidly expanding ministry was literally taking over every facility in South Park Church. Lynne Hybels, Bill's wife, recalled this in the book she and Bill wrote, *Rediscovering Church:*

> Another memory comes to mind. I walk back into the elegant sanctuary and see hundreds of kids in muddy shoes come in from outdoor competition and stomp down the carpeted center aisle to the rock and roll music screaming from oversized speakers. Strobe lights flash wild patterns on the pristine walls. The pulpit is nowhere to be seen, and I know the communion table has been stuffed into a closet somewhere. A team scoreboard has been set up on top of the white organ. I see a freshman boy, a little too zealous, forget to remove his shoes before he jumps onto the organ to write in the scores.

Scenes like these increased the tensions between Son City and adult members of South Park Church, who rejoiced in kids' lives being transformed but thought it could be done without trashing the church building. In the ensuing conflict, Bill left South Park Church. He went on to found Willow Creek Church, which has frequently been listed by pastors as the most influential church in America.

I was already out of college when Hybels first came to South Park. But my parents continued as key lay leaders in the church. Many years later I was with Bill Hybels at the Crystal Cathedral. Robert A. Schuller, Bob Schuller's son, was being installed as senior pastor. Hybels was preaching the sermon, and I was presiding at the installation ceremony.

At the Crystal Cathedral before its services, you don't gather in a lounge with the elders; you go to the Green Room for makeup. I had only met Hybels casually, and didn't really know him. He was in one chair getting makeup applied for TV while I was in the other.

"The only thing you need to know about me," I said, "is that Cliff and Marge Michaelson were my parents." My dad had died several years earlier.

"You're kidding! Cliff Michaelson was one of my strongest supporters at South Park. He was with me to the very end. I was so grateful to him, and will never forget it."

I had never known until then how my dad had dealt with the Hybels controversy at South Park. And I was proud to learn.

Will Wally and Sid Move to Israel?

LIKE MOST of the evangelical world of its time, South Park Church had a premillennial theology of the future. Here's what that means. Like most of Christianity, premillennialists believe that human history as we know it will culminate and end with the return, or the "second coming," of Christ and God's final judgment. Premillennialism, however, believes that with the second coming, a thousand-year reign on earth by Christ will be established. Peace and righteousness will be established, and at the end of that millennium God's final judgment will take place.

This theology was popularized by writings such as Hal Lindsey's *Late Great Planet Earth,* and more recently through the Left Behind novels by Tim LaHaye and Jerry Jenkins. Accompanying this theology is usually the view that conditions in the world will deteriorate as the second coming approaches. So famines, earthquakes, and wars all indicate that Christ's return is imminent. For many this can translate into a belief that efforts to improve conditions on the earth are futile.

Naturally, one might ask about all the biblical passages proclaiming the prophetic calling of God's justice in the world, with the injunctions to alleviate poverty and suffering and to seek righteousness and peace. Another doctrine called dispensationalism takes care of those problems. Originated in the nineteenth century by John Darby, this view interprets many Old Testament prophets as giving predictive keys to help explain how contemporary events are leading to Christ's return. Furthermore, passages dealing with peace, justice, and the coming kingdom of God are all understood as applying to the millennium — this thousand-year period after Christ's return — rather than having any direct relevance to today.

Happily, such views have fallen out of favor and emphasis in much of mainstream evangelicalism today and never had much credence in other branches of Christianity. But it's important to understand how deeply they influenced much of the evangelical culture in the second half of the last century. Part of the reason for the lack of any clear evangelical witness to issues of social justice and peace in the 1950s and 1960s was the assumption that conditions in the world would inevitably get worse until Christ returned, so our only hope was to save people "out" of the world.

Premillennial dispensationalism also shaped the attitudes of evangelicals during that time to the newly emerging state of Israel — and those attitudes and biases continue to exert a strong pressure on millions of evangelicals to this day. This interpretive framework asserts that Jews would return to Israel before the second coming of Christ, and that the land of Israel would play a decisive role in events leading to the end of time and the fulfillment of history. Those views flow easily into forms of evangelical, or Christian, Zionism, assuming biblical sanction for the Jewish claims on contested real estate in Palestine.

In the lower-level Sunday school rooms of South Park Church, I'd look at complex charts exploring the hidden meanings of the book of Daniel, or Revelation, and drawing connections to contemporary events in the world. The imminence of Christ's second coming seemed to be assumed. I'd gaze at dramatic sunsets, or startling cloud formations in the Midwestern sky, and think, maybe that's what it will look like when Christ comes again.

Sid Luckman was not my dad's and our family's only Jewish friend. As Dad kept searching for good deals, Wally Stolkin became his key contact for all the boxes Reed's Candy needed, replacing Bears linebacker George Connor somewhere along the way. Wally became a great family friend. He, Dad, Ron, and I would play golf together at Wally's country club. We knew his kids, who attended New Trier High School in Winnetka. His daughter Patti began attending the Young Life Club at

New Trier, which opened the door to conversations about Christian faith.

But at one point when I was younger — probably about ten — my mom was explaining to me all the various signs that pointed to the prospect of Christ's return. One of the main ones, she said, was that the Jews were returning to the land of Israel.

"So when will Wally and Sid be moving there?" I asked.

She didn't have a clear answer. This was the first time in my memory that the theology of evangelical Zionism began colliding with actual facts and relationships in my experience. That would happen many more times in the future.

When Billy Graham would meet with President Eisenhower, and then with President Kennedy, we'd hear evangelical rumors, probably with some basis, that they were talking about the "end times," the meaning of history, and also the role of Israel. The connection between the evangelical community and Israel seemed like an umbilical cord. The Jews were fulfilling the evangelicals' view of biblical prophecy — it was as if they were making the Bible's words come true.

The full scenario of this view has the Jews either coming to see Christ as their Messiah and Savior, or else being subject to God's judgment. But Israeli political leaders have been content to overlook this uncomfortable fact for them, as they have exploited this evangelical kinship for Israel for their nation's own political purposes.

I was out of college before I began to realize that there was another prism, other than evangelical Zionism, to view the Arab-Israeli conflict. Only later did I meet the small but ancient and faithful Christian community within Palestine and other Arab lands, who give witness to another narrative of persecution and hope. Today, as a peaceful solution to the Israeli-Palestinian conflict still eludes patient diplomacy, the Israeli settlements on the West Bank and in East Jerusalem remain one of the most intransigent roadblocks. Many continue to support the rights and righteousness of those settlements with theological convictions spawned by the views I first learned in the basement of South Park Church.

Baptism and the Cubs' Strikeout Record

I FIRST ASKED Jesus into my heart when I was four years old. But that wasn't the only time. As a kid, I worried about whether it really "took" or not. How could I be sure? Maybe something went wrong. What if I didn't say the words right? Or, how could I really be sure that God didn't change his mind?

So I'd ask Jesus into my heart again, just to cover my bets. My main preoccupation was that I had to get it right, and act right, to be sure the deal was secured. And whenever I'd do something "wrong," my confession would be almost like praying for another conversion experience.

South Park Church was sacrament-lite. Communion was periodic — I'm not sure how often, maybe monthly, and certainly every New Year's Eve — and consisted of Welch's grape juice and Wonder Bread. But even then, I always felt it was special. Infants were dedicated to God, with references to Hannah giving her son Samuel to the Lord. Infant baptism was inconceivable.

Because South Park Church was "nondenominational" and proud of it, its theology and practice were its own responsibility. Certainly they were informed by the broader evangelical subculture, but there wasn't any point of reference beyond themselves to which they bore any direct accountability. That's one of the features of my home church that I came to firmly reject.

An "independent, Bible-believing" church is, to my way of thinking, an oxymoron. The biblical view and picture of the church is one of deep connection and accountability between each expression of the church and the whole. A congregation simply can't live unto itself, with no framework of a shared, interdependent relationship with others, and expect to be a faithful expression of the church as inherited from the New Testament.

Denominations are simply one way of giving concrete form to this relationship of sharing and accountability. Total independence, despite its resonant American-sounding rhetorical appeal, should simply not be an option for a congregation that wishes to abide by the biblical understanding of the body of Christ.

South Park Church's view of baptism in 1957 was a mixture of Baptist and Free Church ideas. Baptism could happen only after one accepted Jesus, and it was more or less a public sign of this. It wasn't generally viewed as necessary for salvation but could serve as a testimony to the change that had happened in one's life.

My church had no baptismal font, as Reformed and Lutheran churches do, and no baptistery, as Baptist churches have. The font, of course, was not needed because there were no infant baptisms. And adult baptisms were so rare — the church was made up of Christians — that a baptistery would have had little use. It's an irony that in a church so thoroughly evangelical, I have barely any memories all the way through my high school years (and before Hybels) of any who were actually converted to Jesus Christ and joined the church, either as adolescents or adults.

My pastor, H. Leroy "Pat" Patterson, was congenial, easygoing, humorous, and winsome. He taught a "catechism" class to seventh-graders. I think this was an innovation on his part. We seventh-graders would meet on Saturday mornings and he'd take us through basic doctrines and teachings. The issue of whether to be baptized came up, at least for me, when the class was completed. It wasn't expected, but was an option, and I desired it.

We talked it all over, and made arrangements to use Edison Park Baptist Church and their baptistery on a Sunday afternoon, May 26, 1957. In retrospect, this all seems strange. I thought of myself as being "saved" and accepting Christ when I was four, but now I was being baptized eight years later. But in a setting where baptism was regarded more like a good idea than a serious sacrament celebrated by the whole church community, it seemed to make sense.

My dad, brother, and I were avid Cubs fans, and on that Sunday, May 26, 1957, the Cubs were playing the Milwaukee Braves behind a rookie pitcher, Dick Drott, the "Hummer." We listened on the radio at home, and were happy that Drott was pitching well, striking out many Braves. But we had to leave for my baptism.

We listened in the car too, and Drott was getting better and better, the closer we got to Edison Park Baptist Church. The announcer on WGN, Jack Quinlan, was saying that Drott was now within range of the all-time strikeout record for a Cubs pitcher in one game — and this as a rookie. The excitement was contagious — too contagious for some.

It was the seventh inning when we parked the car. I wanted to listen just a little longer to WGN — one more batter. My mom was totally frustrated — I was fixated on the Cubs on one of the most important spiritual days in my life. My dad was resigned to missing the end of the game. I know my brother would have found any way possible, if he could, to not go into the church until the game was over.

We entered the church and met Pat. (I'm sure he would have understood; he was a football star at Wheaton College.) I put on a white robe. And Pastor Patterson read some words from Scripture and baptized me, dunking me under water three times, "in the Name of the Father, and of the Son, and of the Holy Ghost," as reads my certificate.

A few family friends were present from church. But it was more a personal act than a community celebration. That reflected, I think, the understanding of baptism in my church. It was an act that reaffirmed one's personal faith, and gave witness to it, rather than a sacramental covenant marking one's entry as a member of a Christian community, with promises made before God to one another.

Today I think quite differently. It was actually when my wife Karin and I were members of the Sojourners Community that I first began to grasp the deep connection between the sacraments — communion and baptism — and life in the Christian community. The baptism of infants makes sense because they are being accepted and nurtured as part of a covenanted Christian community. The way we say it in the liturgy of the

Reformed Church in America is this: "You are engaged to confess Christ." That step of confession still needs to happen, and it often does after catechism. The whole sequence, compared to my experience, is reversed.

Much more could be said, especially about the way infant baptism can become little more than a social, family observance that is detached from its theological and spiritual significance. But the key, I believe, is recognizing that baptism takes place in the context of a covenanted, Christian community, extending God's grace and promises to those who would share in its life.

Dick Drott struck out fifteen batters on May 26, 1957. He set a new Cubs record at that time. Five decades later, in May, I was in my study at our Grand Rapids condo, listening to a Cubs game through my computer, on WGN. Pat Hughes and the late Ron Santo were doing the broadcast, and suddenly Hughes said, "On this date, in 1957, Cubs pitcher Dick Drott set a new record, striking out fifteen batters." And I remembered my baptismal vows.

"Watch Your Car, Mister?"

———————

P ARK RIDGE was lily-white. I took that for granted. Segregation and the problems around civil rights were in the South. The fact that Chicago and its environs were, de facto, one of America's most segregated regions never entered my mind.

When Chicago's expressway system was built with the Northwest Expressway (renamed the Kennedy following JFK's assassination), the Eisenhower Expressway, and the Dan Ryan Expressway, we passed swiftly through inner-city neighborhoods and the concentrations of black populations on the south side of Chicago. We never stopped. And my parents did not have to tell us to make sure our car doors were locked.

My experience of Chicago as a kid consisted of the Loop, where we'd go to see the windows of Marshall Field and Company on State Street every Christmas, the Field Museum (boring), the Museum of Science and Industry (an amazing wonderland), Reed's Candy Company on the north side, and of course, Wrigley Field. Other areas seemed nearly as remote as the Congo.

That even included Comiskey Park, the home of the Chicago White Sox. It was on the south side, and we didn't go there. My family grew up on the northwest side and went to Wrigley, in a largely white neighborhood of Chicago. Nearly all my friends were Cubs fans. This wasn't just about geography; it was also about race.

The one inconvenient exception was Chicago Stadium. It was built on the near west side of Chicago, and by the 1950s and 1960s the population there was mostly black, and fairly poor, as I recall. But the Chicago Blackhawks hockey team played there, and it was also the site for the Ice Follies, a circus-like show of figure skaters, clowns, and other acts on the ice that my family loved to see.

My early memory of going to Chicago Stadium stayed with me. Dad — always looking to save money — didn't want to pay the five dollars to park in the lot, but instead found a space somewhere on a nearby street. When we got out of the car, a couple of black teenagers approached us.

"Watch your car, mister?"

"Sure," Dad said, and he gave them a dollar.

This was probably one of my first direct encounters with an African American. I didn't fully understand the transaction.

"Why did he want to watch our car?" I asked.

"Well, he will make sure that no one damages it," my dad explained. He wanted me to take that at face value. But it reinforced perceptions of such a neighborhood being a strange and dangerous world.

The routine repeated itself most every time we'd go to Chicago Stadium. Once inside, I marveled at this arena. They could play basketball here one night, my dad explained, and then hockey the next. An organ, which accompanied the national anthem and played at dramatic moments during the Blackhawks games, was at one end, by the first balcony. But a second, upper balcony circled the upper reaches of the stadium. I remember some referring to it as "nigger heaven."

When I entered Maine Township High School, four thousand classmates filled its halls, from Park Ridge, parts of Niles, and Des Plaines. There was no African American student, and I don't recall any person of color. Diversity consisted of some kids with Polish last names from Niles.

Lake Geneva, Wisconsin, where we spent many summer vacation days at my grandparents' "Big House" and "Little House" near Williams Bay, was also a white enclave for the well-to-do from Chicago. For a while, Big Daddy also owned a farm in the hills a few miles from the lake. We'd go there to pick sweet corn, and sometimes I'd feed sugar cubes or carrots to the farm's black horse. Its name was Nigger.

The racism woven into the evangelical subculture of my childhood, and amplified by the wider white, suburban subculture of America's

northern cities, was largely unconscious, which made it all the more pernicious and evil. Experiences that simply introduced the reality of racial
diversity were few. The underlying attitudes and the social, economic
constructs that reinforced personal and institutional racism were barely
acknowledged and never confronted.

Before leaving Park Ridge for college, my friends Jim and Warren and
I got jobs at a Fred Harvey restaurant on the Illinois Tollway, at the Des
Plaines Oasis. The restaurants were famous because they were built over
the tollway, from one side to the other. You could eat watching the cars
and trucks pass by underneath.

We worked the night shift, from 11:00 P.M. to 7:00 A.M. Most of our
work was cleaning and mopping, and then setting up the breakfast buf-
fet. Sometimes I'd get to help in the kitchen, and do some short-order
cooking.

Two African American men, Percy and Ramsey, worked with us.
They lived on Chicago's south side, so it was a drive — maybe forty-five
minutes to an hour — for them to get to the Des Plaines Oasis. I enjoyed
getting to know them, sharing stories, and working together.

One early morning around 5:00, we were in the freight elevator together with our buckets and mops, and we all were tired.

"These two jobs are gettin' me down," Percy said.

"Yeah," I replied, thinking of how hard I was finding it to sleep during
the day. "But what do you mean about two jobs?"

"Well, you know," Percy explained, "when we leave here, we go over
to the Big Boy nearby and work the day shift."

"What?" I asked. I was incredulous. "You work during the day?"

"Yup. Our shift is from 8:00 to 4:30. Then we drive home."

"When do you sleep?"

"Well, when we can, before we have to get up and come back here.
But we need the money."

It was one of those early moments when the perceptions and stereotypes that had shaped my attitudes and formed my own deep racism were
first beginning to be challenged. Fifty years later, on a Sankofa racial reconciliation bus trip from Park Ridge to Selma, Birmingham, Jackson, and
Atlanta, I realized how deeply this is an ongoing, lifelong journey.

Can Christians Be Cool?

FOLLOWING MY BAPTISM and my entrance into junior high, I was ready to confront the major ethical challenges to a life of Christian discipleship. Like dancing. It's amazing to realize what issues could cause ethical fault lines in the evangelical community of that period. In the midst of deep racial divisions, and enduring poverty trapping millions in urban centers as well as Appalachian hollows, the issues of ethical significance were drinking, dancing, and smoking.

In seventh grade, optional square dancing lessons were offered once a week. You had to sign up, pay a small fee, and then learn to swing your partner to the call of the square dance teacher. It was fun. I'd try to get in a square (four couples) with Margie Olsen as my partner. She lived four houses up the street from me, and we'd often walk home from school together.

In eighth grade, similar classes were offered for ballroom dancing. I asked my parents for the money to sign up. But they said no. They wouldn't allow me to take ballroom dancing.

I was perplexed and crushed. All my friends were taking the class — including Margie. I couldn't imagine not being with them. And they had already allowed me to take square dancing. What was the difference?

We sat in the living room and argued.

"Just what is so wrong with dancing?" I demanded to know.

"We just don't think its right to put your arms around different

35

women who aren't your wife," my mom tried to explain. It's about the closest she or Dad could come to actually talking about sex.

It was hard to know how to respond. I did put my arms around girls when I square-danced, but there seemed to be some mysterious ethical distinction between square dancing and "real" dancing. My parents had both attended Wheaton College, with its famous pledge to refrain from dancing, drinking, smoking, card playing, and going to movies. They didn't even know how to dance with each other.

My main worry was not being accepted by my peers. Not being able to dance made me feel out of it. But my folks were stressing how I had to be a strong witness for Christ. Sometimes, they said, this meant not being popular, and not doing some things just because everyone else was. Their worry was that the "world" would contaminate me, and they wanted me to stay pure.

This became even more anxiety-producing for me when I was sick on the day that the gym teacher showed a film and gave a talk for the annual sex education class. Convinced that I was missing out on life's deepest secrets, I kept pumping my friends to tell me all about it, but wasn't satisfied. There was no expectation of any discussion at home — I was embarrassed when my mom washed my jock strap.

So here I was as an emerging teenager, desiring to be a good Christian witness — and please my parents — but also wanting to be "cool," not knowing how to dance, and worried that I didn't know the real truth about the facts of life. In eighth grade I learned the date when the sex education class would be taught again, and circled it on my calendar. Nothing would keep me away from school that day. But the class consisted of a cartoon about sperm and eggs, an explanation about how they got together, which I had already figured out, and then the gym teacher holding up a jock strap and telling the boys why it was important. I was underwhelmed, but relieved to know I hadn't missed much, after all.

At heart, I was caught in a microcosm of the greater tension beginning to grip the larger evangelical world. Should our calling be to maintain a faithfully ethical and pious witness that would separate us from the fallen world — "come out from among them and be ye separate"? Or should we discover creative ways to engage the culture evangelistically with the truth of Christ, and not be defined by what seemed like "legalisms"? In some ways this was the struggle between a more classic "fundamentalism" and a more thoughtful, modern evangelical movement represented by emerging institutions like Fuller Seminary in California.

For me, as I entered Maine Township High School, with its four thousand students, it was a question of whether to carry the Bible on top of my other books as a witness, whether to learn (secretly) how to dance, and whether to run for election as a class officer or student council member. Could I be a Christian and also be "cool"? Just what was I supposed to do with Jesus?

No one helped me answer that question more during that time than Bill Starr, the leader of the Young Life club for kids at Maine. Young Life is a parachurch organization, meaning it exists outside the formal, denominational structures of the church but is designed to assist in the broader work of the whole church. Often, people found such organizations because they perceive the formal church to be failing in some part of its ministry, and an outside initiative is required to meet the need. That is how, for instance, Sunday schools were established in American churches — initially by an independent "Sunday school" movement.

Young Life's founder, Jim Rayburn, saw the church failing pitifully to relate in meaningful ways to high school students. He understood that such young people needed to be listened to in their own settings, and they desired to find young adults whom they could trust. The point wasn't to try to get such kids to come to a church, where they'd probably just be bored. Rather, the gospel had to be brought to where they hung out, through people who genuinely took the time to know and care about them.

Thus, Young Life is committed to "incarnational evangelism." The phrase they use, which I still repeat today, is, "You have to win the right to be heard." Meetings take place once a week in the home of one of the students, and consist of fun stuff, skits, singing, and a short talk by the Young Life leader. Summer camps, which began with Star Ranch and Frontier Ranch in Colorado, provide exhilarating experiences for high school kids, sharing through words and relationships the good news of Christ.

Bill Starr became the person I could talk to about all my questions, doubts, struggles, aspirations, and feelings. The faith he shared and lived didn't revolve around a set of legalisms, or an anxiety about keeping separate from the world. Rather, following Christ engaged one in the world. Relationships were what mattered because they mediated the love of Jesus.

All this was in stark contrast to my experience at South Park Church. I still attended, and in fact was president of the church's youth group. But it seemed dull by comparison. At one point a new youth leader, Al Bishop, challenged me when our high school prom was coming.

"We'll have our own event," he explained, "a dinner at the Mile Race Inn, entertainment, and good Christian fun. We need leaders like you to take a stand, and set an example by not dancing."

I thought he was out to lunch.

Meanwhile, Young Life was a blast. I went to camp at Frontier Ranch, and then went back for a month to serve on the "work crew," cooking the wrangler's breakfast every morning. Back in Park Ridge, we met early in the morning at "campaigners" with other high school students to study the Bible — using the modern J. B. Phillips translation — and pray. This was with classmates who didn't go to South Park Church. A book we read by J. B. Phillips seemed to sum up my previous experience of faith: *Your God Is Too Small.*

Bill became my counselor, pastor, and mentor. He was the only one I could talk to about my adolescent sexual tensions. He actually told me what masturbation was — I didn't even know what the word meant, and was overburdened by teenage confusion and guilt.

Adolescence, of course, is a primary time of dealing with the challenges of beginning to form one's own identity and taking the first steps toward self-differentiation. Young Life provided those early opportunities to begin internalizing the Christian faith I had inherited, discovering a pathway to follow Jesus that led me into the world, instead of fleeing from it.

So I jumped into student life at Maine, was elected as class vice president, and then to the student council. I ran for student council president, and a pattern began that would stay with me throughout my vocational life: seeking leadership in order to revise organizations so they would function better. The school paper described my working on the Student Council Revision Plan, Election Week Revision, and Representative Election Revision Committee, plus being director of a thirty-two-school Leadership Conference.

Then I'm quoted as saying, "The lack of understanding and cooperation between the Student Council and the Administration must be cor-
rected if council is ever to gain any noteworthy purpose, effectiveness, or
worth." I have no idea why, as a sixteen-year-old, and still as a sixty-five-
year-old, I've been focused on how to reform and renew organizations
and institutions.

But my reform-minded candidacy wasn't appealing enough, and I
lost to my friend Bob Beart, who established the unofficial record for
balls hit over the fence for home runs at Roosevelt Elementary, and who
went on to become the director of the Scottsdale, Arizona, branch of the
Mayo Clinic. I settled for vice president.

My senior year I was president of the Young Life club, and I made a
bet with Bill Starr that I could get 150 kids to club one night. If I did, he
would swallow a live goldfish. And if not, I would. I narrowly lost, and the
story of the live goldfish going down my throat circulated throughout
Maine.

Student politics continued that year as I was campaign manager for
Carol Craigle, who was running for student council president. A female
student was always elected as secretary, but we wanted to break that tradition. Plus, Carol was from Niles, which was like the other side of the
tracks. We worked hard, but didn't win. One of the sophomores who
helped us was Hillary Rodham.

Like me, Hillary Rodham grew up in Park Ridge as a Goldwater Republican. She was smart and likable, and we served together on the student council. But while I was involved in Young Life, Hillary was deeply
involved in her youth group at the Park Ridge Methodist Church. Her
youth pastor, Don Jones, was known for driving a sports car, and he
worked to get his group engaged in current issues.

Don Jones took Hillary and others to hear Dr. Martin Luther King Jr.
speak when he was in Chicago. Hillary tells this story, and it was part of
her journey out of the white, homogeneous cultural reality of Park Ridge.
Her faith propelled her, and continues to do so. At the National Prayer
Breakfast in 2010, Secretary of State Hillary Clinton testified to the ongoing relevance of her faith, nurtured in the Methodist tradition from those
early years.

In 2007 the emerging presidential candidates spoke at a Faith, Poverty and Values Forum sponsored by Sojourners/Call to Renewal. As a board member and chair, I received a thank-you letter from Hillary, and at the bottom she wrote, "It's a long way from Park Ridge." It has been for both of us.

A Modest Rebellion

ELIZABETH O'CONNOR, the late author of books emerging from the Church of the Saviour in Washington, D.C., bought my wife Karin and me a book she said we had to read: *The Drama of the Gifted Child.* We were close friends from our time together in this church, and were eager to read what "Betty O" recommended. This insightful book basically described the psychological dynamics of a young child who is gifted and learns at an early age to find psychic security through fulfilling and even exceeding the expectations of his or her parents. But in the process, one's inner and true sense of self can be submerged and nearly lost.

The book rang true, deeply, for me as well as for Karin. From my time of being "born again" at four throughout my childhood, and then through high school, it felt like I did most everything right in my parents' eyes. My parents and others praised my accomplishments, my grades, and my outward behavior. At church and in Young Life, I was looked to as a model Christian, and the Park Ridge Jaycees named me the city's outstanding junior citizen.

It would take years, however, to discover an internal sense of self, rather than one based on pleasing others. But a defining moment early in that journey came around my choice of a college.

Wheaton College felt almost like part of a large, extended family. Park Ridge was about forty minutes from Wheaton, and we would go there constantly. Its basketball stars were heroes, like Mel Peterson, whose turnaround, fadeaway jump shot seemed impossible to stop. It was unforgettable when they played for the NCAA small college championship in Evansville, Indiana. On fall Saturday afternoons we'd watch the Wheaton Crusaders football team, and our pastor, Pat Patterson, was often there as well.

Both my parents were Wheaton grads. Nearly all my aunts and uncles went to Wheaton. We knew coaches, like Harv Crouser and Lee Pfund. And when my older brother Ron was thinking about college, Wheaton was the only alternative. He was an excellent baseball player — catcher and captain of the Maine High School team that won the state championship — and looked forward to athletics as well as the course work at Wheaton. The Pledge didn't bother him; he'd always find ways to have fun.

I also went to Honey Rock Camp as a kid, a camp in northern Wisconsin, near Eagle River, that was owned and run by Wheaton College. Some of its coaches were there, and the counselors were mostly Wheaton students. Wheaton was simply a focal point for much of my early life.

So, sitting in Bill Starr's office off of Main Street in downtown Park Ridge, I was surprised and interested when he said, "I really wonder whether you should go to Wheaton College."

Bill himself was a Wheaton grad. But he had some clear and different ideas.

"I think you'd spend a lot of energy rebelling against things that really aren't that important," he explained. He had in mind the various expressions of legalism that were woven into the cultural fabric of Wheaton College.

We had been studying some of Paul's epistles, and his own fight against "legalisms" of his day contrasted to the freedom known in Christ. Bill seemed convinced that I would grow more in an atmosphere that was less parochial and less familiar than Wheaton. I asked if he had someplace in mind.

"Why not take a look at Hope College in Holland, Michigan?"

My only knowledge of Hope College came from Wheaton basketball games. Once in a while, Hope would play Wheaton, and I thought they had the most bizarre name for a sports team that I had heard — the

Flying Dutchmen. Their players, I remembered, were tall, with unusual Dutch names.

In my senior year at Maine, I was also getting interested in psychology. This was mostly through reading *The Meaning of Persons,* a book by the Swiss Christian doctor and psychologist Paul Tournier. It had a deep impact on me. I went on to read *Guilt and Grace.* In sync with Young Life's deep emphasis on mediating the gospel through human relationships, Tournier's writings were opening new windows of understanding into how the human personality was shaped, and what this had to do with Christian faith.

Bill told me about one particular professor at Hope College, Dr. Lars Granberg. He taught psychology, and had taught for several summers at the Young Life Institute at Fountain Valley, Colorado. This was the training center where Young Life staff would take courses taught by professors like Lars Granberg; Paul Jewett, a theologian from Fuller; Dr. Bernard Ramm; and many others.

In light of my interests, Bill offered to take me on a trip to Hope to meet Dr. Granberg and others. We arrived for dinner at Dr. Granberg's home. One of his daughters, Karin, was just going out on a date. We had a wonderful dinner and conversation, and the next day I toured the campus. It all seemed unfamiliar, intriguing, and very inviting.

My parents weren't sure what was happening. They had great respect for Bill, but couldn't understand his nudging me away from Wheaton, and they resented it. But I don't think they believed anything serious would come of it. Yet, it was by now all becoming clear within me.

The showdown happened in the dining room. We'd had previous uncomfortable talks about college, but this was the hour of decision. I was deeply anxious, yet an inner determination had formed within me.

"I've decided to go to Hope College."

I rehearsed all the arguments.

"I'll have more freedom to explore my faith and the things that really interest me. I won't just be reacting to legalisms at Wheaton and fighting battles that aren't worth it. Besides, Hope is a Christian college. It's not like I'm going to Cornell University." I had gotten Cornell's literature and was intrigued for a short time with the idea of going to an Ivy League school.

But nothing I said seemed to make any difference. They were completely distraught, shaken, and even angry. They had never imagined nor intended such an outcome. I'd always done things right. Now, in one of my adolescent life's most crucial decisions, I was rejecting their wishes, and even their hopes and dreams for me.

Finally, in exasperation, I said, "You've always told me that I could go to any college I wanted to!"

"That was so when you went to Wheaton, you wouldn't feel that you were forced to go there," my mom replied honestly.

It seems strange, and almost pathetic, to confess that my major act of rebellion as a teenager was choosing what college to attend. But given my psychic history, this marked a critical early passage in my journey of self-differentiation. My faith would now find a new, and largely unknown, context in which it could be tested, shaped, and matured.

That fall, my parents drove me to Holland in their Pontiac Bonneville. I had a couple of suitcases full of clothes and belongings, and we pulled up to Taylor Cottage on Tenth Street, across from Durfee Hall. It would be my home for the next year.

I unloaded my things and went back to say good-by. My parents were both crying — a rare sight. I tried to console them.

"Don't worry. It's not that long until Thanksgiving, and I'm planning on coming home then. Don't be so sad."

"No, it's not that," I remember one of them saying to me. "It's because you're not going to Wheaton."

Years later all this would change. My parents came to appreciate Hope and love what it did for me. Further, some of my cousins in the Gundersen clan began to follow, as well as a nephew, plus our kids and others. At one point, more of my generation from the extended family and their kids had gone to Hope than to Wheaton.

But on that fall day at Taylor Cottage, when my parents' Pontiac pulled away, I felt like I was walking alone and naked into an unknown future.

Grace Wins

———————

IT DIDN'T TAKE ME long to figure out that I was probably the only freshman who was entering Hope College as an act of rebellion. The student body was about 1,600, less than half the size of my high school. I knew only two people on campus — Dean Overman and Neal Atkinson, upperclassmen who also had Young Life connections.

This Dutch and Reformed environment had its own parochial cohesiveness; it was just different from what I had known. So in many ways it was a liberating experience. My first Sunday, during freshman orientation, I decided to go to one of these Reformed churches, and picked a redbrick church not far from the library. The service was formal, rather dull, and most of the hymns sung were psalms. No Fanny Crosby songs here. I also did not spot other students.

That evening an outdoor reception was held for the incoming freshmen. I went up to the dean, Jim Harvey, and asked, "Where do students here go to church?"

"Oh, they mostly go to various Reformed churches nearby," he replied.

"Well, I didn't see any at the church I was at this morning."

"Which one did you attend?"

"The one over there," I responded, pointing toward the church, which was visible a couple of blocks away.

"Oh," said Dean Harvey. "That's a Christian Reformed Church."

Puzzled, I looked at him and said, "What do you mean?"

And so I heard for the first time the story of the split between the Reformed Church in America and the Christian Reformed Church about a century earlier. In Harvey's version, the dispute was over whether or not church members could join the Masons, a fraternal order. Those opposed finally came to the one church building — now Pillar Christian Reformed Church — and defended it at gunpoint against their adversaries. The story seemed humorous, shameful, and ludicrous, all at once. This was my introduction to the Dutch Reformed culture of West Michigan, and its two competing Reformed denominations.

Forty-six years later, Jerry Dykstra, then executive director of the Christian Reformed Church, and I, serving as general secretary of the Reformed Church in America, traveled together to Israel and Palestine. In Jerusalem, we had a meeting with the patriarch of the Greek Orthodox Church.

His Holiness said, "Can you please explain to me the differences between your denominations, and why you are separate?"

I felt like crawling under the table. In that setting, any honest answer would have seemed as humorous, shameful, and ludicrous as when I first learned this story as a freshman at Hope.

As I began at Hope College to absorb the Reformed voice in the broad understanding of Christian faith, it felt clarifying and liberating. The emphasis on seeking an integrated "world and life view," for instance, taught me not to fear the process of seeking truth, but to embrace it. Christian faith had the potential to provide an integrating framework for understanding the world and its discoveries. Biblical insights and perspectives are in dialogue with the economy, politics, ecology, literature, science, philosophy, and the arts in the belief that in the end, all truth is one. This was a refreshing change from a view that focused Christian faith primarily on one's personal experience and viewed the wider world from a stance of suspicion and defensiveness.

But perhaps most significant was the broader and deeper understanding of God's grace that rests at the bedrock of the Reformed tradition. In the religious climate in which I was nurtured, so much depended on me. It was *my* decision — even at four years old. My faithfulness. My purity. My commitment. Of course I memorized the verse, from the Navigators Scripture memorization cards that we used around the kitchen table after every dinner, that "all had sinned and fallen short of the glory of God," and that we were saved "by faith, and not by works, lest any man should boast." Yet, the responsibility for maintaining that commitment and striving toward a kind of spiritual perfectionism seemed to be mine.

The understanding that God's grace takes the initiative, and does so in ways that precede my knowledge, awareness, and action, was comforting. Further, the sense that I am held securely by grace that is stronger and more trustworthy than anything I can achieve was and is profoundly freeing. In the contest between me and God, grace wins. It provides the basis for the full relinquishment of one's self into God's love — and that is the pathway to radical discipleship.

It would be some years after leaving Hope before I could articulate all this in a compelling way. But, at Hope, I felt, sensed, and absorbed these truths largely through key professors who became mentors and even friends, and certainly through the college chaplain, Bill Hillegonds. He also helped change my understanding of the church.

Like most evangelicals, my emphasis was on my spiritual union with Christ, and I knew I had an automatic union with anyone else who shared this experience of Christ. This "invisible" belonging together with other Christians was the "real" church or body of Christ. Congregations and denominations were just organizations that provided a place where such fellowship might happen. But of course, this fellowship could occur anywhere two or three were gathered.

A valuable thread of truth is of course woven through that view. But it also can easily "spiritualize" the understanding of the church and thus remove it — and one's life — from the concrete reality of people physically gathered together in the ongoing life of a community in ways that make the message of the gospel take on flesh.

In one of our many conversations in his office in the basement of Dimnet Chapel, Hillegonds challenged me in words I remember to this day: "Wes, you've got this nice spiritualized ideal of the body of Christ. But the thing is, it's got to get concrete. It has to translate into a group of people together in a place on a corner somewhere who are actually being the church, trying to live as Christ's body."

We tried to put that into practice right at Hope. Hillegonds and a group of students were discontented that area congregations, plus required morning chapel, were the only options for "church." Why couldn't we have a real church, on campus, made up of interested students and any faculty who might wish to join?

Twenty-two student "trustees" came together to form the Board for the New Student Church. I was the president, and we drafted a brochure that went out to the student body. Some of its language is still relevant: "Worship is not entertainment. Perhaps it's where the self stops long enough to glance at God, only to find that God has been staring him (her) down, with a smile, for quite some time." And this: "If people are drawing close to the One who knows their lives more intimately than any other, then they should be more fully exposed to their true selves. Christianity cannot remain a system of thought. It must, like Christ, become incarnate."

We developed a creed for those who would be "communicants," but opened the service and learning activities of the church to any who wished to participate. Opportunities for engagement in the world were stressed: "The Student Church believes that the problems of the jobless Appalachian coal miner or the starving, neglected four-year-old girl in India are the concern of the Hope College student. A church without a sense of mission doesn't take its beliefs seriously."

This was the first time I was engaged with others in thinking through what the church should be and then working on a model to implement it. Over the coming years, my participation in other alternative, emerging church communities would follow. The consistency in the themes and values throughout these alternative models of the church — Church of the Saviour, Sojourners Community, Community Covenant in Missoula, Montana — in retrospect, is striking.

Even at Hope, I seemed to vacillate between the church and politics. As in high school, I jumped into student politics, became class president, and then in my junior year was elected student council president. In 2010 Bruce Neckers, a friend and a distinguished lawyer in Grand Rapids who had served as student council president the year before me, sent me a copy of my campaign brochure that he had found in some old papers.

As in high school, there was a list of things I proposed to change. But the brochure also stressed more opportunities for involvement off campus: a "Hope College Peace Corps," participation by students in voter registration drives like those sponsored by the Southern Christian Leadership Conference, and a student exchange with schools like Talladega College, a black college in the South.

But as I think back to those years, and the drama going on in the nation at the time, what stands out is the isolation of Hope College, and my life, from the movements of social change. These years were the high point of the civil rights movement. The march from Selma to Birmingham, the voter registration drive, the killings of the civil rights workers in Mississippi, the March on Washington, and the signing of the civil rights bill — all this was happening. Any awareness and involvement from the Hope College community were minimal.

Further, President Johnson's massive troop buildup in Vietnam was under way in 1966-67. My response was to set aside arguments for or against the war, and focus on humanitarian needs. We started the Hope-Holland-Hamlet campaign, to raise funds for a village in South Vietnam. Eventually we got the funds transferred there through John Marks, then a foreign service officer who later resigned to protest the war. We met again in Washington when we both were working against the war — me with Senator Hatfield, and John with Senator Case of New Jersey.

Hope College introduced me to the Reformed theological tradition that expanded my more narrow evangelical background, and convinced me of the need to connect my personal faith in Christ to the external realities of the world. But I had little idea of how those connections would actually get made, and the impact that would have on my life's journey.

How Would Jesus Vote?

———————

THE FLOOR of the Chicago International Amphitheater was filled with the Republican delegates from every state for their 1960 national convention. Reporters roamed the aisles, and excitement filled the air. It was time for the band to play the "Star-Spangled Banner" for the opening of the evening session. Vice President Richard Nixon would be giving his acceptance speech as the GOP's nominee for president of the United States.

I was wearing a red, white, and blue striped vest and an Uncle Sam hat, carrying an American flag. Other identically dressed young people were lined up, and we all marched down the aisles as the band played, stopping at our assigned spots. It was a good photo shot on the black-and-white TV picture: the arena filled with young people carrying American flags as the national anthem was played.

Once on the arena floor, I adroitly found a way to stay there, standing to the side, and listened to Vice President Nixon give his speech to thunderous applause. A minority of conservatives had pushed for their emerging hero, Barry Goldwater. It would take them four more years to capture the party and nominate Goldwater, in 1964, with disastrous results in that election. And Governor Nelson Rockefeller, a "liberal Republican," had a following, but the evening and the nomination belonged to Richard Nixon.

I was fifteen, and had just finished my freshman year at Maine Township High School. A friend, Danny Hayes, and I had gone downtown a couple of days before to get close to the events surrounding the GOP convention. We'd responded to a gathering of "young Republicans," and an organizer quickly enlisted us to carry flags on the convention floor a couple of nights later.

Somehow, my parents agreed to let Danny and I get a room at the YMCA Hotel. We didn't even have driver's licenses. But we were going to be part of the Republican National Convention — something so special that it probably overrode my parents' anxieties.

With new credentials as young Republicans, we got into various events. One was a reception for a young and upcoming governor from Oregon, Mark O. Hatfield. I had heard about Governor Hatfield because he was "rumored" to be an evangelical. We met at the reception, and I told him my brother, Ron, was attending Wheaton College.

"That's a fine school," the governor said. It was like code language in those days for people to identify themselves in public settings as evangelicals. Eight years later our lives would intersect in ways that would shape much of my future, and engage both of us in a challenging relationship with the evangelical community, and then in a conflictive, confrontational relationship with the person being nominated in 1960 for president.

At the time, my family was thrilled with my part in the GOP convention. Some got a glimpse of me on TV. We went up to Lake Geneva, and I took my vest and hat along to show my grandparents, aunts, uncles, and cousins. There's a picture of me on the lawn in front of the Big House proudly wearing my outfit.

By the time I graduated from Hope College in 1967, I was fascinated with the question of how my faith related to politics. I had read Reinhold Niebuhr's *Moral Man and Immoral Society,* as well as Bonhoeffer's *Ethics,* and had written a major senior paper offering a Christian critique of Marxism. I was intellectually intrigued by these subjects. My thinking was shifting beyond the marriage of evangelicalism and conservative Republicanism that so deeply defined my family, church, and white suburban culture.

My faith also beckoned me toward theology. I was reading more of people like Niebuhr and Bonhoeffer. At that time the Rockefeller

Brothers Foundation had a "trial year" fellowship that would pay all costs of attending seminary for one year. The idea was to provide promising students who might not automatically think of seminary the opportunity to see what it was like. I called it a fellowship for those who couldn't make up their minds, and it fit me. I applied for it and received it.

Selecting Princeton Seminary allowed me to also take some courses at the Woodrow Wilson School of International Affairs, a graduate school of the university. I signed up for "The Structure and Strategy of Communist and Revolutionary Movements," taught by James Billington. An expert on Russian history and culture — he wrote *The Icon and the Axe* — Billington opened me further to the world of political theory and practice in a time when the globe was filled with revolutionary movements. Further, James Billington became a mentor and friend; he went on to become the Librarian of the Congress.

I chose to write my research paper on the Vietnam War that was raging. Reading many books about the history of the country and the current conflict — including Cornell scholar George Kahin — convinced me that the war was both a foreign policy disaster and a moral travesty. I still clung to my evangelical roots, but now I was firmly rejecting the conservative, nationalistic political ideology that had seemed wedded to the evangelical world.

Meanwhile, the theological environment at Princeton Seminary was in ferment. I took a course from Richard Shaull titled "Models of Missionary Theology." My first surprise was that some of the books on his reading list were used in my course with Dr. Billington — books by Regis Debray and Frantz Fanon, for instance, both revolutionary theorists from the Third World. Shaull, it turns out, was teaching liberation theology before it had a name. Out of his own missionary experience in Latin America, he became convinced that the message of the gospel translated into a revolutionary paradigm for societies that were holding people in economic, political, and social oppression.

I was challenged, even though I disagreed with what seemed like a simplistic faith in the outcome of Marxist and revolutionary movements. But all this was pushing me to think critically and carefully about my own background. The final paper for Shaull's course called for reflections on the "cultural theology of my past." What I wrote then I can still affirm today:

> I often infer that it has been my great misfortune to have matured in middle-class, conservative suburbia. Add to this religious training in a church which belongs to the National Association of Evangelicals, and surely I am burdened with a tragic flaw.... Yet, I choose to appreciate my background rather than to limit God's grace. I am neither defensive, proud, nor hostile to my formative environment; I try to be grateful.
>
> To speak of its limitations ... Meaningful social insight barely exists. Slums are seen only from the expressways. Naturally a relevant social ethic becomes impossible, and not because of theological confusion, but because of the inability, failure, or perhaps refusal to look carefully at the world's complexion.
>
> Since my earliest years in Sunday School I can remember the American flag standing on one side of the pulpit, the Christian flag on the other. Now it seems that most of the faithful regarded those flags as being at least equally important....
>
> A combination of social forces typical of conservative suburbia and theological beliefs inherited from the Fundamentalist movement created the cultural theology of my past. Its expression in form and word gave witness to a class and a culture, but rarely to a theology which was not conditioned and enslaved by those forces.
>
> Yet I am continually drawn to an affirmation of faith. If my past consisted solely of a cultural theology I would have cynically attempted to reject it all long ago. But the redeeming fact of my past was that in the midst of this religious morass, I occasionally was exposed to a saving remnant and saw, primarily through them, glimpses of a theology that challenged my life rather than rationalizing its present form. A few were convicted of their own prosperity as they let themselves be exposed to human need. Gradually I began to see the differences between the two flags on either side of the pulpit. Once in a while the Bible would become the Word.

My theological youth and adolescence, despite all of the burdens and blindness, enabled me to grow rather than regress. There was some health — enough to sustain me. I can only be thankful.

Admittedly, those words contain some of the existential flourish one might expect of a twenty-two-year-old seminarian. But they point to a basic experience of coming to terms with the formative years of my youth that would free my future journey in proactive, rather than reactive, ways.

The Vietnam War overshadowed seminary life in 1967-68. Antiwar sentiment was growing. Senator Eugene McCarthy entered the New Hampshire primary, and McCarthy buttons were seen on many seminarians. In dorms or over pizza and beer at the King's Inn, we'd struggle with the ethics of the war and the draft. We had seminary deferments; yet, I knew that if drafted, I could not in good conscience obey and go.

Taking another course at the Woodrow Wilson School, this time from Richard Falk, a well-known expert in international law, I focused more on Vietnam. My antiwar convictions deepened, while in seminary classrooms I focused on theology and ethics, continuing to relate my political convictions to my understandings of faith. I felt like asking, "How would Jesus vote?"

Then I received an invitation to the National Prayer Breakfast in Washington, D.C. As a student leader at Hope, I had in previous years been invited to this annual event, held each February. It was originated by the "fellowship movement" and brings together the president, many members of Congress, governmental officials, and public leaders to affirm the role of prayer and the guidance of God in the affairs of the nation. Prayer groups meet weekly in both the House and the Senate, and Doug Coe, the quiet leader (with a Young Life connection), worked to extend this model in other countries around the world.

A separate program during the day was scheduled for student leaders, and Senator Mark O. Hatfield would be speaking at a student luncheon. Hatfield was well known as a dove on Vietnam, casting the sole vote against the war at the 1965 and 1966 national governors' conferences. In 1967 he began serving as Oregon's junior senator, and he was an evangelical. I wanted to meet him — again.

As he finished his luncheon remarks to the student group, I waited to speak with him as others left.

"Senator Hatfield," I began. "I want you to know how much I respect your views opposing the war in Vietnam. And I also know you're an evangelical Christian. I'm also an evangelical, and I'm deeply opposed to the war. I'm studying at Princeton Seminary."

The senator was intrigued. His luncheon talk hadn't focused on Vietnam. It was about leadership, fellowship, and faith. But he wanted to know more about my views. The fact was that in 1968, the number of evangelicals who were clearly and publicly opposed to the Vietnam War was minuscule. He didn't meet many.

"Where are you going from here?" Hatfield eventually asked.

"Over to Capitol Hill," I said. We were at the Washington Hilton.

"Would you like a ride?" he asked.

I could hardly believe it. We went to the parking lot and got into his red Mustang. His car had a phone in it — something I had never seen — and he called his secretary, Marilyn Fernandez, to say he was on his way back.

Then we talked more about the war, Christian faith, and my own journey. By the time we got to the parking lot of what is now called the Dirksen Senate Office Building and started toward his office, I bravely asked a question that had just been formulating in my mind.

"Do you ever accept any interns from a seminary to work with you for a year?"

"Well, that might be possible. Why don't you write me a letter? And also get in touch with Eric Lindauer on my staff."

I got back to Princeton and immediately found John Mulder, my best friend there — we had been at Hope together — to share the news. I could hardly believe it. So I worked on the letter, sending it to Senator Hatfield and Eric, and enclosing, as I remember, one of the papers I had written on Vietnam.

Eric invited me back for a visit. We talked over the arrangements; they could provide just a small stipend but would welcome my coming. I met other staff, and didn't even see the senator again. But the offer was set, and I would show up in the fall of 1968.

At Princeton I talked to President James McCord. He looked and talked like Broderick Crawford, the cop on the TV program *Highway Patrol* — a large body, a direct, no-nonsense manner, and a gravelly voice. But he was enthused, and arranged to give me $500 of support from some fund.

More important, I talked to the Field Education Department. I wanted to know whether this could meet the requirement of an intern year for my field education. Normally that happens in a church. But in the late 1960s, the whole definition of ministry was up for grabs. Anything seemed to qualify — including work in a senator's office. That meant I could keep my student deferment, and not be drafted. I was headed for Washington, D.C.

Journey Outward, Journey Inward

WHILE I WAS TRYING to chart my journey to D.C., the historical drama of 1968 began to unfold. President Lyndon Johnson shocked the political world with his announcement of not running for reelection, following Senator Eugene McCarthy's unexpectedly strong showing in New Hampshire. Martin Luther King Jr. was assassinated while standing on a hotel balcony in Memphis, Tennessee, on April 4. Several cities were engulfed in anger and violence, and a heavily armed National Guard patrolled Washington, D.C.

Bobby Kennedy entered the presidential race. Some called him an opportunist, but I favored him over McCarthy. He had the political skill and experience, I reasoned, to actually end the war and achieve the goals he was articulating. Plus, the response of so many groups of people to his charismatic style was creating hope. I watched all this from the sidelines with no idea that, four years later, I'd be assisting the Democratic nominee in trying to reach the evangelical community.

Home from a year at Princeton Seminary, I was in bed, but the portable TV in my room was on as I was staying up late to watch the returns from the California primary. Kennedy had won. And then in the confusion of the Ambassador Hotel in Los Angeles came the report that he had been shot. I watched in disbelief.

It was late, and my dad, hearing the TV, wandered in wondering why I was still awake, just like he often did when I was younger. I told him the news, and we watched the unfolding tragedy silently. No one even in my extended family had ever supported a Kennedy, except for my uncle Ralph. But this was hard to comprehend. When Frank Mankiewicz emerged with the news that Robert Kennedy had died, it felt like the whole nation was coming unglued.

By the time the Democratic National Convention came to Chicago, with Vice President Hubert Humphrey's nomination a certainty, antiwar protestors were angry and desperate. A friend from Czechoslovakia, Pavel Spivak, whom I had met there during a European Young Life trip, was visiting in Chicago. We went down to Grant Park together to see what was happening.

We watched police, anxious and mad, charge the antiwar protestors with methods Senator Abe Ribicoff called "Gestapo tactics" the next day on the convention floor, to the utter disgust of Mayor Richard J. Daley. Pavel watched all this happen, having also seen police and tanks crush a rebellion in his home country. He said to me, "Police are the same everywhere."

The next day I got in touch with Jim Lord, another friend from Young Life. His dad was a federal judge in Minnesota, and a friend of the Humphreys. Jim got me on a special bus with his family and other Humphrey friends, which had a police escort to get through the demonstrations and into the hall for the evening program. It was a long way from carrying the flag at the Republican convention eight years earlier.

A few weeks later I began my internship with Senator Hatfield. A basement, one-room apartment on Capitol Hill was home; I called it a "deficiency" apartment. I threw myself into my work, enjoying exciting times with a small staff most of whom were previous associates from Oregon. But I was spiritually homeless.

Senator Hatfield, his wife Antoinette, and their four children attended Fourth Presbyterian Church in Bethesda, Maryland, not far from their home. Eric Lindauer and his wife were also members. The pastor was Dick Halverson, a white-haired, dynamic preacher with a baritone voice. A Wheaton grad, he had dated my mom in college. Later Dick became chaplain of the Senate, largely through Mark Hatfield's influence.

The services were predictably evangelical, with solid preaching. A young adult group provided fellowship; it included some who had Young

Life connections. But no one talked about Vietnam or, for that matter, about any of the burning social issues of the day. It was an evangelical co-coon, comfortable but confining.

So I started wandering into other congregations close to my apart-ment on Capitol Hill. At St. James Episcopal Church, the rector actually preached about Vietnam, as well as urging members to be involved in ef-forts addressing poverty and social needs. I was encouraged. Yet, the more I listened, I began to say, "Yes, but where is Jesus?" It began to seem like I was hearing well-motivated social concern that was bereft of any spiritual depth. And my soul needed to be fed.

At Hope College, Jim Malcolm, a faculty member and friend, had shown me a copy of *Call to Commitment.* We read it when we were form-ing the student church. It was the story of an experimental church in Washington, D.C., that stressed a high personal commitment, spiritual disciplines, and a fascinating involvement in the community. It met in a redbrick row house off of Dupont Circle, at 2025 Massachusetts Avenue. After being caught in the ecclesiological gulf between evangelism and social action for almost a year, and frustrated by absence of a church that could both feed my soul and support a relevant witness in the world, I showed up at Church of the Saviour.

Gordon Cosby's preaching was real. He talked about the "inward journey" of faith with fresh language and insights that I simply had not heard. The spiritual life involves a disciplined task that continually opens up all parts of one's life to the rigorous work of transformation through God's love. Gone were the pious spiritual platitudes of my up-bringing. Life in Christ requires focused inner attention, listening prayer, attuned exploration of God's work in my life, and the discovery of gifts in-tended to build up the body of Christ for strengthening its witness in the world.

This intense inward journey has to find outward expression. God's work is the transformation not only of lives, but also of communities, so-cieties, and the world. And each of us is "called" into a particular role in that work of God. Few things are more important than discerning this call. It will propel us into missional work addressing unjust structures and social needs with the vision of God's kingdom.

This takes place within the crucible of mission groups, functioning like a microcosm of the church. That's where one finds accountability for the disciplined work of one's inner journey. Gifts are discovered and exercised here. But all this happens around a common, outward missional calling. *Koinonia,* or fellowship, doesn't exist for its own sake, but rather to undergird corporate participation in some aspect of God's mission.

The fruitfulness of this approach was obvious. The Potter's House — probably the first coffeehouse started by a congregation — provided an ongoing place of hospitality and outreach in the Adams Morgan neighborhood of D.C. Jubilee Housing was working on renewed places to live. A vision for a new school — the Dag Hammarskjöld University — was being pursued. Outreach to children without parents had been long established.

Church of the Saviour was my first experience with a church deeply committed to living out the whole gospel. It began to ground, deepen, and enliven my personal faith in Jesus Christ as never before. In that congregation the gospel was whole. To journey with Christ was serious, risky, and demanding, but fruitful. Evangelical faith was not severed from social justice. Fellowship was not separated from mission. The Word was not isolated from the world. This was the most "missional" congregation I had ever encountered.

Yet, entering more fully into its life was costly, by design. You didn't just join. A whole process of discipleship and formation was required. That began with the School of Christian Living — courses taught in the evenings sharing the theology and practice of the church. I began attending.

The "spiritual disciplines" were the most difficult part to accept. Church of the Saviour's experience convinced them that one's "inner journey" could happen only with daily, committed times of prayer, Scripture reading, reflection, and journal writing. They got specific — forty-five minutes each day. Initially this just sounded to me like another legalism. One evening Mary Hitchcock, a longtime member, compared it to the way a good pianist had to practice, or an accomplished athlete had to train. Finally, I began to try.

On June 29, 1969, scrawling a first journal entry on white typing paper, I wrote this:

To begin the disciplines — To respond to the call.
  I decided today that in order to fortify my inner self and to be-

come the sort of person that I am called to be, I must enter into the disciplines outlined by the group at the Church of the Saviour. 45 minutes each day — reading, meditating, and writing.

This all came through a preliminary reading of the material (at the School of Christian Living). Bonhoeffer's part about living with the present — including unfilled desires — and mastering the circumstances, which is a sign of maturity — this especially struck home with me. It describes what I *must* do and what I want to do and gives a hint of what I am called to be. So tonight I dedicate myself, for this week, to the fulfillment of this discipline, which has come to me as "good news," so that I may become the sort of person I am called to be. This will have an effect on all areas of my life. It is the re-entry into my inner self; it is the point of embarkation for a new pilgrimage, for a journey inward, for an encounter with God. I welcome it.

Four days later, it was clear this would not be easy, but could be fruitful:

July 3, 1969

It is difficult to keep this discipline, especially the writing aspect, as witnessed by the long time between these entries. My thoughts today have centered around an incident at work, namely, it appeared as though Senator Proxmire was lifting MOH's (Mark O. Hatfield) material on military spending. As the evidence of this became clear in this regard, I grew *furious*. The day consisted of plots to protect MOH's work and unmask Proxmire. But now, this evening, I am doubting all I did. Reading in Romans about "forsaking self-assertiveness," "never pay back a bad turn for a bad turn," "let the other fellow have the credit" — all this has made me conclude that today's actions perhaps were not wise, and not in love.

The tension continued, and would for some time. I was trying to respond to the pressures of work with Hatfield and find time for this new commitment. Ten days later:

July 13, 1969

"Springs of living water."

This again is my deep, heartfelt desire — to nurture my inner spiritual life, to receive the waters of the spirit, flowing forth so I will never thirst again. Out of the *depths*. This is the issue — what is at the depths of my being? I fear there is little. Distracted by the demands of work each day, my life revolves around only the responsibilities of such external activity. There is no chance to truly develop the inner, lasting qualities of love, concern, long-suffering, etc. That is the real point — these qualities must be developed from within; at present they have no opportunity to grow.

It didn't take long to realize the difficulty of maintaining such disciplines alone. I began looking for a mission group to join as an intern member, but had difficulty imagining how to fit this into a schedule that already seemed so crowded. But by the end of the year, I had joined the Potter's House group that met on Friday evenings, thinking that this had the best chance of fitting with the pressures from my work. I'd rush from the Hill, without supper, to get there for our group meeting at 6:00, for our time of prayer and sharing. We opened the doors of the Potter's House at about 7:30, and I'd serve coffee, tea, cheesecake, and carrot cake to those who wandered in, praying for them and trying to create an atmosphere of hospitality.

The group had a "spiritual director" to whom we all were accountable for reporting on how faithful we were, or not, in keeping our disciplines, as well as sharing ongoing concerns about our journey. I'd never heard the term before; only later did I discover that spiritual directors were a common practice within models of faith formation in the Catholic tradition.

I'd give written reports, usually typed out hurriedly at the office, in the blue-colored type of official Senate correspondence.

January 31, 1970

In the two weeks since joining the Mission Group I have had an extremely hard time even coming close to meeting the minimum requirement of the spiritual discipline. . . .

February 6, 1970

I have not been very much more successful in fulfilling my disciplines this week than I was the last. . . . The pressures on my time from work have been particularly severe. I did read Jeremiah . . . and I must establish some definite routine for meeting with God, meditating, and writing in my journal.

March 13, 1970

During the week I was able to be relatively faithful to certain of my disciplines — particularly writing in my journal. However, I've not been as faithful in regular prayer. . . . Yet, things have definitely improved from when I started.

March 20, 1970

It has been a week of escalated pressures, demands, and tensions. Long nights, weary days, hectic activity, and a depressed composure has resulted. . . .

March 27, 1970

This week has been a mix of experiences as far as my inner and outward journeys are concerned. I was able to spend an evening at Dayspring meditating on my forthcoming Easter sermon; this entire time was one of real renewal. . . .

A quote I read that month and entered into my journal, from William May's book *A Catalogue of Sins,* seemed to express and critique how I often felt during those days: "His life is a lonely struggle between himself and a job that seems too much. . . . He is tempted to faintheartedness, worrying about his coming days as though life were a solitary struggle between his own pitiful resources and the monstrous obligations of the morrow."

My inward journey had begun in earnest, and was beginning to take root. But external events would intervene. When I wrote my spiritual autobiography as the last step in joining the Church of the Saviour a couple of years later, I described what happened in April 1970 and the months thereafter as follows: "The internal life and regular prayer and reading I was developing that year was disrupted, and nearly eliminated, by the President's invasion of Cambodia. In June I found time to write, 'I don't know how seriously I have been affected personally, but it is clear that the growing sensitivity to things of the Spirit has suddenly been thwarted.' I was not yet at that point of seeing that the evil in the world demands the response, not just of action, but also of prayer."

The Evangelical Dove

THE Republican National Convention in 1968 was in Miami. Richard
Nixon had the nomination. The question was the choice of his running mate. Senator Mark O. Hatfield was frequently mentioned. Billy
Graham urged Nixon to make Hatfield his choice. But southerners, now
being courted by the GOP as part of their emerging "southern strategy,"
were lukewarm, especially given Hatfield's outspoken record on civil
rights as well as his antiwar views.

For Hatfield, the primary issue was the Vietnam War. Few knew that
the senator had actually been approached to enter the New Hampshire
primary as a peace candidate before Eugene McCarthy agreed to do so,
and Hatfield was very supportive privately of McCarthy's efforts. He had
also talked with Nelson Rockefeller, who had been a candidate for the
GOP nomination. But Hatfield was convinced Rockefeller would be a
hawk on Vietnam, particularly because of the views and influence of
Rockefeller's foreign policy adviser at the time — Henry Kissinger.

Nixon's view was less clear. He spoke of a "secret plan" to end the war.
The Democratic nominee, Hubert Humphrey, was hopelessly linked to
Lyndon Johnson's war policies. So Hatfield calculated that he'd at least
have a chance to influence Nixon's views and actions on Vietnam. He
gave a seconding speech at the convention to Nixon's nomination. But
even in negotiating his speech with Nixon's high command, Hatfield began to question Nixon's true intentions.

Despite Billy Graham's efforts, and because of the views of southerners like Strom Thurmond, Nixon didn't choose Hatfield, and instead turned to the relatively unknown Maryland governor, Spiro Agnew. When I arrived in Senator Hatfield's office in the fall of that year, Hatfield still held out hope that Nixon would offer a better chance than Humphrey to bring an end to the Vietnam conflict, and had argued so publicly in an article in the progressive publication *Christianity and Crisis*. But his private feeling toward Nixon seemed tepid.

I was just a seminary intern. But as projects were given to me, my writing and work were valued. Moreover, a rapport was established with the senator revolving around both his Christian faith and his antiwar convictions. By 1969 the senator's chief speech writer on Vietnam and foreign policy, Gayle Debruyn, told me that she and her husband wanted to return to Oregon. Now that we had worked together, she was confident I could take over her tasks, so she was going to leave. Sometime later, Sam Mallicoat, a grandfatherly figure and longtime associate of Governor, and now Senator, Hatfield, took me on a walk down the sixth-floor hallway of the Dirksen Senate Office Building, where our offices were located.

"Wes, there may come a time when 'the boss' [as he always called the senator] will run for president. You never know when lightning might strike. And if that should happen, and if he'd end up in the White House, you could be with him. You understand how he thinks, and you capture his thoughts so well in writing. You could end up like Ted Sorensen [President Kennedy's famous speech writer]. But in any event, we'd like you to stay on board," Sam told me, using as always language from his former time in the navy.

These were heady words for a twenty-four-year-old kid. But I also knew I wouldn't be returning to Princeton Seminary. My work and role grew. Now I was in charge of all the senator's efforts dealing with Vietnam as well as other policy issues such as his campaign to reduce military spending. Plus, I was preparing the material, and writing the speeches, for all his appearances before various Christian groups, conferences, and colleges — and these were growing. This was the same time when I was trying, with difficulty, to step deeper in the life of the Church of the Saviour with its rigorous expectations.

With my future on Senator Hatfield's staff now clear, including the responsibility for advising him on foreign policy issues, I arranged for a trip to the Soviet Union that fall. I had taken Russian in high school and college, and though rusty, I could get by in conversation. Ever since studying with James Billington, my interest in Russian culture had increased. Hatfield had tried, unsuccessfully, to persuade the Nixon administration to appoint Billington as U.S. ambassador to the Soviet Union.

Hatfield wrote to Soviet ambassador Dobrynin, whom he knew through Washington social circles, about assisting me, as the senator's executive assistant, with appointments in Moscow. That opened doors. Meetings were set up with officials in the foreign ministry and other government officers that surprised staff in the U.S. embassy; they insisted on accompanying me. The range of issues concerning U.S.–Soviet relations was discussed, including Vietnam and the Soviet invasion of Czechoslovakia.

Russian tanks had cruelly crushed the "Prague Spring" led by Alexander Dubček a few months before (August 20, 1968). Prior to arriving in Moscow I had gone to Prague and rendezvoused with my friend Pavel. He was deeply depressed, describing how totalitarian rule had closed back in on his society. The official Soviet justification of their actions was lamentable.

In the evenings in Moscow I'd break away from officialdom and find my way to jazz clubs where young people flocked. Striking up conversations, I learned of their fascination with the West and alienation from the structures of official authority. Worshiping at the one Baptist church in Moscow, and talking with its pastor and members, gave me a glimpse of religious life struggling under an oppressive system. Even more, a visit to an Orthodox seminary, and participation in its worship liturgy, gave at least a sense of Orthodoxy's deep, historical connection to the soul of Russian culture, even after its massive repression by communist rule.

In Tashkent and Samarkand, in Uzbekistan, I got a sense of those areas of the Soviet Union populated by non-Russian ethnic groups; several broke away decades later after the fall of the Soviet Union. But then I boarded the Trans-Siberian Railroad. Conversations, usually with vodka, flowed freely when those in my compartment recognized an American was with them. It always seemed an occasion for a celebration.

In Novosibirsk, Irkutsk, and Khabarovsk, I often managed to evade the Intourist guides assigned to me and find occasions to speak informally with people. Often younger people would talk in terms of a spiritual search for meaning. At the people-to-people level, I discovered amazing points of connection beneath the ideological hostility and military confrontation of the Cold War.

Those lessons stayed with me as I yearned to understand how my Christian faith should view the rigid animosities of U.S.–Soviet relations, with their massive nuclear capabilities of "mutually assured destruction."

With Richard Nixon's election, Senator Hatfield decided to give him a year to see if he would make progress in changing Vietnam policy and ending the war. Throughout 1969 Hatfield restrained his direct criticism, still pressing his case for why our involvement was strategically and morally wrong, but seeing whether there really was an effective "secret plan" to end the war.

As 1970 began, in Hatfield's mind, the jury was in. Nixon talked about "Vietnamization" of the war — trying to equip more South Vietnamese to carry more of the burden — but in Hatfield's view, that would simply mean "changing the color of the corpses." There was no fundamental change in policy.

Senator William Fulbright's Foreign Relations Committee had held famous hearings on the war. But in Senator Hatfield's view, serious opposition should use the one clear Constitutional power in such matters given to the Congress — the "power of the purse" to fund and pay for war. In fact, Hatfield was convinced that the executive branch — both Johnson and Nixon — had vastly overreached its authority vis-à-vis the Congress in carrying out the war.

Senator George McGovern, Democrat of South Dakota, was also a staunch opponent of the war. He believed it was time to draft and offer a bill that would cut off funds for the Vietnam War by a date certain in the future. Hatfield agreed, and I worked with McGovern's legislative aide, John Holum, on how to proceed. By mid-April 1970 the bill was introduced with speeches on the Senate floor and a press conference. It received modest attention; most senators even opposed to the war regarded it as too radical an idea.

Then, on April 30, 1970, President Nixon announced that U.S. troops had invaded Cambodia. The war was now being expanded to another country. People reacted in disbelief. Spontaneous protests erupted. When Senator Hatfield drove in from Bethesda to the Capitol the next morning, the traffic circle near American University was flooded with demonstrating students. This was the pattern across the nation.

Then, on May 4, four students protesting at Kent State University were shot and killed by the National Guard. Shock and outrage galvanized millions. Antiwar sentiment was spreading way beyond students, throughout many segments in society.

Suddenly, the focus turned to the McGovern-Hatfield legislation introduced in the Senate just a few days before. Congress had to act to stop Nixon's policies, and this was the way. Senators Hatfield and McGovern, and their staffs, were thrust into the legislative center of the antiwar movement.

With three other senators, Hatfield and McGovern went on television, buying the time to plead their cause, and asked for financial support. Money poured in. A coordinated effort to lobby senators was begun. TV and radio ads were produced and played. Gordon Weil, another key assistant to McGovern, John Holum, myself, and a few other staffers found ourselves coordinating an emerging national campaign.

The White House tried to play for time, believing the intensity of protest would subside. Further, Senators John Sherman Cooper and Frank Church brought forth an amendment to circumscribe and limit the incursion into Cambodia, and debate got drawn out. It was September by the time the McGovern-Hatfield amendment reached the Senate floor. The White House was pressuring and alleging that the measure would cut off money for troops in the field — untrue, but effective.

Before the vote, in the GOP cloakroom off the Senate floor, I overheard a phone conversation between Senator George Aiken of Vermont, a Republican dove whose vote we thought we might get, and Bill Timmons, Nixon's key legislative contact in the White House. If the administration would just be sure to shore up price supports for milk, helping Vermont's dairy farmers, Aiken said he would vote with the administration against McGovern-Hatfield. I was still idealistic enough to be stunned — more deaths in Vietnam in exchange for good milk prices.

We received thirty-nine votes.

Senator Hatfield was disappointed. He and Senator McGovern had worked very hard. They said their effort would continue as long as the war went on, and the measure would be brought back to the Senate the next year.

But what most deeply discouraged Mark Hatfield was the nasty and mean criticism he received from fellow Christians. Letters would come addressed to "Dear Former Brother in Christ." Some Christian groups disinvited him from scheduled speaking engagements. He could understand differences among Christians on the Vietnam War. But he couldn't comprehend how fellow evangelicals would challenge the validity of his faith, or otherwise express such hostility, based simply on his opposition to the war.

Plus, the Republican leadership in Oregon was angry with him for not supporting the president on a variety of issues, and his reelection in 1972 seemed questionable. He asked me at one point to find examples of legislative issues where he had supported the president. I did some research and told him there wasn't much, but he did favor an administration proposal to explore converting the United States to the metric system.

Feeling rejection from the evangelical Christian community, and political vulnerability from opposing Nixon, he thought about leaving the Senate. Riding to National Airport one day, he told me that if he had to make the decision then, he'd be gone. But he hung on, still working against the war and trying to shore up his political base at home.

With the senator's support and encouragement, I decided to visit Vietnam and Cambodia. I needed to see it firsthand. The U.S. embassy in Saigon gave me their briefings, but then I set off to meet other contacts. The Mennonite Central Committee, with Earl Martin, was doing amazing humanitarian work in Quang Ngai Province. A tour by motor scooter demonstrated how difficult it was for foreign troops to control the remote countryside. I met antiwar activist Don Luce, who put me in touch with South Vietnamese student leaders who opposed the war.

Official and unofficial contacts convinced me even more that the military solution we were seeking, with the South Vietnamese regime in Saigon, would never happen. And the echoes from that time resound when I watch the news of our present war in Afghanistan.

In Cambodia it was even worse. When my Air France Caravelle jet landed, I was met by a government delegation. The invasion and bombing had installed the Lon Nol regime, and apparently I was one of the first congressional staff to visit since that time. A squadron of about two dozen Cambodian soldiers was assigned to accompany me around Phnom Penh, the capital, and its immediate environs. That's how bad the security situation was. An evening conversation over drinks at the hotel with longtime Indochina war correspondent François Sully — who was a tragic war casualty himself a few months later — gave me the most valuable, and depressing, perspective on Cambodia's situation.

In 1971 Hatfield and McGovern kept pressing their measure for withdrawal of troops by a certain date, and were getting closer to passage. Now the Nixon administration was arguing that such a measure would not get our prisoners of war home. Logic here didn't seem to matter; POW issues get settled when wars end. But the administration's allies were, in effect, arguing that we had to continue fighting in order to bring home our POWs.

But in a crucial Senate debate, the measure almost passed. One political problem by now was that George McGovern was preparing his race for the Democratic nomination for president, and his political opponents didn't want to approve anything that could assist him. So after the McGovern-Hatfield measure was narrowly defeated, Senator Lawton Chiles of Florida brought up essentially the same amendment, but with his name on it.

As the clerk called the roll, and Senator Hatfield and I were counting, it got to the fifty votes necessary for passage (with a vacancy, there were ninety-nine senators at the time). But Senator John Stennis of Mississippi, chair of the Armed Services Committee and leading defender of the war policy, raced over to Senator B. Everett Jordan of North Carolina, an old friend of his. I watched as Stennis convinced Senator Jordan to change his vote before the tally was completed and announced. The amendment lost by one vote, 49-50.

All this, however, was generating increasing political pressure on the administration. Technically, even if the measures proposed by Hatfield and McGovern had passed both houses, Nixon could have vetoed them. But rising public pressure was having its effects.

Yet, we worried about the way the POW issue was being used and manipulated by the administration. Senator Hatfield had received some evidence that a couple of Christian Missionary and Alliance missionaries thought to have died could actually be POWs. We couldn't verify it, but the senator had an idea. What if the North Vietnamese could be persuaded to release any civilian POWs, and even do so through his intervention? Wouldn't that help defuse the POW issue?

Another thought was shared. Could that provide support in the event that Hatfield would enter the presidential primary race as an antiwar candidate against Nixon? That wasn't likely, but many were remembering McCarthy's challenge of Lyndon Johnson four years earlier.

So Hatfield proposed that I accompany Gerry Frank, his longtime friend who ran his political operation in Oregon, to Paris and talk to the North Vietnamese delegation there. It would have to be private and secret. I had colleagues at the American Friends Service Committee make the contacts and word came that a meeting was arranged.

Gerry was independently wealthy — the Meier and Frank Department Stores were formerly in his family. In December 1971 we flew to Paris, stayed in a fancy downtown hotel, and he even took me to the Follies. On a Friday afternoon we went by taxi to Choissy-le-Roi, a suburb, where the North Vietnamese compound was, hosting their delegation at the ongoing, and so far fruitless, Paris Peace Talks.

We were received by a leader of their delegation, Mr. Vy, and a deputy. For three hours we had an extensive discussion about the war, prisoners, and policies. They did not acknowledge having any civilian prisoners, but emphasized that all prisoners would be returned at the war's conclusion. A few weeks after our visit, they began explicitly and publicly emphasizing this commitment.

Senator Hatfield's work as an evangelical dove would continue, as would my service with him. He finally decided to run again for reelection to the Senate in 1972. The nation's antiwar energy would now be directed into the presidential elections, and McGovern's race for the nomination. I remained a part of Church of the Saviour as an intern member, but I longed for more balance. The inward journey that I had begun, which was disrupted by the intense, antiwar efforts, still beckoned me.

The Politics of Jesus

A N ODD-LOOKING, newsprint magazine was delivered to my desk in Senator Hatfield's office in early fall 1971. Called the *Post-American,* the magazine had on its cover a picture of Jesus with a crown of thorns, wrapped in an American flag. I began to read. With evangelical fervor, articles lambasted what they called the "cultural captivity" of the church, calling for a "de-Americanization" of the gospel.

The Vietnam War was not just a strategic blunder, but a colossal moral failure demanding from the church prophetic denunciation in the manner of the Old Testament prophets. The silence of the evangelical church made it complicit in the horrors of the war. Recovering a truly biblical faith in today's setting would produce a radical, countercultural witness to the gospel of Jesus Christ.

The words I read were fresh and compelling, articulating what I had been feeling and trying to say. The critique I read was not just of the Vietnam War, but of the overall materialistic and militaristic values of the culture that had also captured the church. Rediscovering the radical message of Jesus, and recovering a truly biblical faith with its prophetic power, was the urgent need of the day.

I tried to figure out who was writing and distributing this timely publication. The main writer was someone named Jim Wallis, joined by others, apparently seminary students at Trinity Seminary, a strong evangelical institution in Chicago. I was encouraged. At least there were a few other people thinking the way I was.

It was a Friday afternoon. I took the copy of the *Post-American* into Hatfield's office as he was packing his briefcase to go home.

"This magazine arrived. I've read it over and it's really interesting. You might want to take a look at it over the weekend."

He put it into his briefcase.

When he came in Monday morning, I asked him what he thought about the magazine.

He looked at me and said, "Get these people on the phone. Today."

I phoned Jim Wallis and told him Senator Mark Hatfield wanted to speak with him. Hatfield thanked him for what he was doing, and said he was encouraged to know that other evangelicals were struggling in this way to know what our faith required of us in this time. And he invited him to visit him in D.C.

Over Christmas I went home to Chicago and looked up Jim Wallis and the "Post-American community." That began a friendship that would endure for decades. The response to their issue of the magazine had been impressive — more than they had imagined. So now they were trying to publish the *Post-American* regularly. They had moved to the Rogers Park neighborhood in Evanston, to be part of an urban environment, and were trying to live together in an intentional Christian community.

They looked like hippies — a coed group, guys with beards and some ponytails, everyone in jeans, eating granola and into simple living. But they shared a passion to live faithfully as a radical Christian community, and were trying to figure out what that might really look like.

Jim and some of the group did make a trip to D.C., and had an appointment to see Senator Hatfield. In my perpetual suit and tie, I met them earlier. They did have the look of a ragtag group that could have just flown in from Haight-Ashbury. I was so concerned that the meeting with Hatfield go well that I went in to brief him beforehand.

"Senator, they're not dressed like most people who come to see you. As Christians they really believe in simple living. You know, they even worry about how much razors cost."

My words were unnecessary. Jim Wallis — I think he had his big red beard then — Bob Sabath, Denis McDonald, and others came into Hatfield's ornate office, and a rich and memorable conversation followed. It was the kind of discussion Hatfield and I didn't often have because we didn't know who we could talk to in these ways. We knew the secular antiwar community. And we knew the evangelical community. Rarely did they overlap. Here, we could actually pray earnestly with other evangelicals who shared our convictions about Vietnam, and much more. Facial hair wasn't an issue.

Less encouraging incidents, however, still happened. Mark Hatfield frequently heard about Wheaton College but had never actually been on its campus.

"I'd like to pay a visit there," he told me. "Just something low-key. It might even be a school where one of my kids would go."

I told him I was sure something could be arranged. Pat Patterson, my childhood pastor from South Park Church, was now serving as college chaplain at Wheaton. I called him with the idea. Pat was thrilled. He would love to have the senator speak to the student body at Wheaton's required chapel service, and we agreed on a date.

A few days later Pat called me.

"Wes, I've never been so upset and distressed about something like this. I've even considered resigning. Here's what happened. President Armerding will not allow Senator Hatfield to speak at our chapel service."

I could hardly believe it myself.

Pat didn't know what to do. Some faculty had gotten wind of this, and they were up in arms about President Armerding's refusal. When pressed, Armerding said it was because of Hatfield's "political views," meaning, in particular, his opposition to the war.

Pat wondered if Hatfield would be open to a visit even without chapel in order to salvage something. I talked it over with the senator, who initially could hardly understand what had happened. His views about sending one of his kids to a college that wouldn't let their father speak in chapel were probably changing. But graciously, Hatfield was still ready to go, with or without chapel. That really hadn't been his point in the first place, he said. He just wanted to visit the college.

So Pat and other faculty negotiated with President Armerding permission for the senator to give a "talk" to students who voluntarily would come. It would be held in Pierce Auditorium.

Hatfield and I arrived at O'Hare. We were met by two Wheaton faculty members who immediately began extending their profound apologies for the way their president had treated the senator. It was obvious, as we listened, that this had become a campus-wide embarrassment and controversy.

Pat Patterson had made the arrangements on campus, and we arrived at the back door of Pierce Auditorium. Upon entering, we were stunned. Every seat in the auditorium was packed with students and faculty. And as Senator Hatfield walked up the stairs to the podium, the entire audience rose in a prolonged, standing ovation before he was even introduced or had opened his mouth.

Hatfield was overwhelmed.

"I don't know when I've received such a warm welcome," he said with a wry smile, and to the delight of the audience. And then he set aside his prepared remarks (the speech I had written), saying, "Let me simply answer your questions."

A rich dialogue ensued as Hatfield took questions as if in a town hall meeting. President Armerding was nowhere to be seen. Later, at the instruction of the board of trustees, Hudson Armerding came to D.C. to offer an apology. He had lunch with the senator in the Senate Dining Room in the Capitol.

These times were witnessing the beginning stirrings of modern evangelical conscience around questions of war, peace, and justice. The turmoil of American society and changes in the world began to impinge upon the evangelical world in ways that not all could ignore. The convenient isolation of faith to only a personal relationship with Jesus Christ didn't really account for the full biblical message of God's love for the world. Moreover, believing "in Jesus" couldn't be so easily separated from "believing Jesus" — meaning, actually embracing and following what he said.

The publication of John Howard Yoder's *Politics of Jesus* in 1972 added strong biblical arguments that the life and message of Jesus had a direct political and ethical relevance for his time, and should translate into a similar application in our time. Following Jesus took on a whole new meaning; he was not only our Savior, but also our way of life, which had clear consequences in the face of violence and war, nationalistic idolatry, and social inequities, both in his time and in ours.

By November 1973 such sentiments had resulted in a gathering in Chicago of like-minded evangelical leaders committed to publicly embracing the gospel's call to social action. About forty of us met at the YMCA Hotel; the constant noise from passing subway trains on the elevated tracks immediately behind the building accompanied our deliberations. The Chicago Declaration resulted, which received widespread attention as a watershed mark in evangelical history. Jim Wallis was one of the drafters, and leaders like Ron Sider, Rich Mouw, Paul Henry, Rufus Jones, Frank Gaebelein, John Perkins, and even Carl F. H. Henry were included. Mark Hatfield added his endorsement. Later, Dick Ostling, religion reporter for *Time* magazine, would say it was probably the first time forty evangelical leaders had spent a weekend discussing social action.

Evangelicals for Social Action was formed as a result, and the following year the Evangelical Women's Caucus was founded, working on the principles of biblical equality and mutual submission between men and women in the life of the church, rather than hierarchical male leadership. (It was actually this commitment in the Chicago Declaration that kept Billy Graham from signing it, according to a discussion he had with Hatfield.) The decades ahead would see continual attempts, from both the right and the left, to politically mobilize the evangelical community.

My own struggle was to integrate my growing understanding of the radical demands of the gospel with the political world, especially in the 1972 election year. At the same time, my link with Church of the Saviour and my hopes for a deeper interior life were still finding some space, though not enough.

Hatfield's reelection campaign to the Senate was focusing his efforts there, as well as some of mine in trips to Oregon to help in the campaign. The McGovern campaign for president was gaining momentum and moving toward the Democratic National Convention. By then, I was sharing a town house with John Holum, McGovern's chief policy aide, so I was connected informally, but enthusiastically, to their efforts. I also talked frequently to Gordon Weil, who was now acting as campaign manager.

Many years later, on New Year's Eve day of 2009, I saw Gordon again, for the first time in over three decades. We both were at the Renaissance Weekend in Charleston, South Carolina, an annual, off-the-record gathering of politicians, authors, media persons, business entrepreneurs, and a few religious leaders. Gordon, his wife Roberta, my son J. K., and I were having lunch, and talking about the 1972 McGovern campaign.

"You know," Gordon said. "Mark Hatfield really was on McGovern's short list for selection as vice president."

I had heard this before, but wanted to know the full story all these years later.

"In fact, Hatfield was actually my first choice. I proposed it to McGovern and pushed for it," Weil explained.

It would have been politically dramatic and unprecedented — a Democrat picking a Republican as a running mate. Weil reasoned that it would expand McGovern's appeal significantly. I have no idea whether Senator Hatfield would have been open to the idea. He would have had to leave his own Senate race, and leave his party.

McGovern's other advisers argued that his support among Democratic Party regulars was already weak; so much of his campaign was fueled by antiwar students and activists. That view prevailed, and McGovern selected Senator Thomas Eagleton. When it was revealed some days later that Eagleton had undergone shock therapy treatments at one point in his past for mental illness, McGovern had to dump him from the ticket. It was the first step in the unraveling of a presidential campaign that ended up in disaster, carrying only the state of Massachusetts.

At lunch in Charleston thirty-seven years later, Gordon was still angry at the way Eagleton had elaborately hid that event in his background and had gotten through the vetting of McGovern's staff. And I commented on the irony of Hatfield being on Nixon's short list in 1968 and on McGovern's in 1972.

In the summer and fall of 1972, I wanted to help McGovern's campaign as much as possible, and assist my friends John and Gordon. By that time Bob Shrum had also joined as a speechwriter, and I got to know and appreciate him. A fallen-away Catholic at the time, he loved talking about theology.

But there were more practical religious challenges. Gordon had come to understand, mostly through our conversations, the evangelical subculture. He was convinced that McGovern, as a strong Methodist from South Dakota whose father was a pastor, could appeal to evangelical voters. But how could he do that?

I explained that a strong center of affection in the evangelical world was Wheaton College. If McGovern could possibly speak there, it would get attention in the evangelical world. But arranging it would be a challenge.

Partly through help from Jim Wallis, we learned of a handful of students at Wheaton who were McGovern supporters. They could invite him to campus. The administration gave its approval on the condition that invitations be sent by student groups to both McGovern and President Nixon, not really believing that either would come.

But the invitation to McGovern, to the shock of many at the college, was accepted immediately. Gordon, now traveling on the plane with McGovern, called and asked if I could draft the speech. I did so, and with just a few changes, McGovern was pleased. It stressed the religious faith and social concern that were genuinely interwoven with McGovern's Methodist heritage, and the role of religious and moral values in addressing social issues of the day.

But the next day, as I remember, McGovern was taking a commercial flight to Michigan for an appearance. The pilot actually held up the plane to wait for the senator to board. And when he did, he went down the aisle personally apologizing to each passenger. One woman — a staunch Nixon supporter — would hear none of it, and continued loudly to complain so all could hear. McGovern walked up to her in exasperation and whispered in her ear, "Kiss my ass."

Well, the woman, of course, told the press. And the stories about this incident, which the press loved, quickly undid whatever interest McGovern's speech at Wheaton would have raised in the evangelical community.

Meanwhile, in Oregon Senator Hatfield's Democratic opponent was the former Oregon senator Wayne Morse. He also was a longtime dove on Vietnam, so the war was not an issue. Morse was older, and Hatfield had worked hard to reconnect with voters over the past year. He won with 53 percent of the vote.

Returning to Washington, D.C., I was exhausted from the politics of the election year, and still wondering about the politics of Jesus.

The Sounds of Silence

O N A HOT August Friday evening in 1972, I was having dinner with
Gordon and Mary Cosby. Gordon had become my spiritual mentor.
The intensity of the antiwar movement had subsided, and during the
year I had increased attention to my inward journey. Active in a Potter's
House mission group, I was working on the spiritual "disciplines," including keeping a journal of reflections, struggles, discoveries, and my dialogue with God.

Our dinner conversation was focused on my future vocational directions. If McGovern were elected president, my friends John and Gordon
would want me working in the White House with them. But Hatfield was
up for reelection in Oregon, and however the presidential election
turned out, I was wondering how long I should remain with him if he
were returned to the Senate. Perhaps there were other possibilities.
What did Gordon and Mary think?

Gordon replied with wisdom long remembered. He said I was extremely well suited, and had a special gift for the kind of relationship —
he called it a "pastor-prophet relationship" — that I had with Mark Hatfield. I should continue at present devoting my energies there. But then,
he felt certain that other significant opportunities for such service would
come my way. He had no doubt. The question, however, is whether I
would be "ready" for such a call.

Like others, Gordon could affirm the external gifts he saw me exercising as a young congressional aide to a unique senator. But he understood me far more deeply. What would determine my effectiveness, or lack thereof, in the long run, was attention to my inner self. He told me to read Thomas Merton's book on contemplative prayer, and especially the section on "dread." The Church of the Saviour was intent on directing its members to confront the hidden, hurting places of one's soul, and Gordon wanted my attention focused there, rather than dreaming about what it would be like to work in the White House.

Retreats focusing on silence, creating a space for deep prayer and reflection, were part of the Church of the Saviour's practice. The Dayspring Retreat Center, purchased as a farm near Germantown, Maryland, in the early days of the church's life, was a frequent destination for members. I had attended such retreats, initially finding long periods of silence to be threatening and almost bewildering. I lived in the world of words, constantly crafting how to say things. And my inherited language of prayer focused on talking to God about everything, rather than cultivating the art of listening for God.

Yet, something deep beckoned me in these directions. I remembered how in high school someone had given me a book, *The Cloud of Unknowing*. It was in my dresser drawer. I was fascinated to read from it, for its language and understanding of God seemed so different from the normal evangelical devotional material in our home.

Little did I know that the Church of the Saviour's approach to the spiritual journey was informed by practices of prayer, contemplation, and silence used for centuries in patterns of spiritual formation within the Catholic tradition. Gordon Cosby was raised as a Southern Baptist preacher. But he and the founding core of Church of the Saviour kept searching for ways to deepen the spiritual journey in order to strengthen the outward call to mission.

As the election year unfolded that fall, I kept my inner journey at least modestly alive. I knew what Gordon had told me was true. I also struggled with how to integrate the spiritual roots I was seeking and knew were necessary, with political actions seeking justice and peace, reflecting the values of the gospel.

The task was to build a movement that was at once spiritual and political. New political movements in our country achieve temporary influence and impact but then die as the political fashions of the day change. Even spiritual movements and groups — like Young Life, Inter-Varsity, Faith at Work, etc. — lack the concrete political reality to put into practice the love that is instilled in the human heart. We must form, I thought at the time, models of corporate, regenerate political living that flow out of the inner faith in Christ.

Of course, not all will follow us; some will argue that separation of church and state applies here. But where does God tell us that politics is a secular profession? Where does he indicate that the "political" must be separate from the "spiritual"? Those are not God's categories; they are human categories. Every Christian was political, in some sense; what we needed was a movement that was *at once* prophetic and pastoral, inward and outward, spiritual and political.

My relationship with Jim Wallis and the group in Chicago — they called themselves the People's Christian Coalition — was also growing. They too were searching for a fresh Christian spirituality in the midst of their activism and their attempts to live out a radical Christian community.

I offered to lead them in a retreat, patterned after what I was experiencing in Church of the Saviour. At the end of November, I flew to Chicago, joined by Basil Buchanan and Beth Burbank, friends from the church. I had arranged for the use of my grandparents' home in Williams Bay, on Lake Geneva. We arrived there on a cold weekend, turned on the water and the heat, and settled in for a contemplative retreat.

I only barely knew what I was doing. Jim and his friends had no idea. But I tried to explain the value of silence, centering prayer, journal writing, and contemplative practices. At one point Basil led them in an exercise of focused contemplation on an apple. I can still picture Jim, Bob Sabath, and others, whose passion was to turn the world upside down with radical Christian faith, trying to figure out why I had brought them to this cold house in Wisconsin to stare in silence at an apple for thirty minutes.

Thirty-five years later I encountered Bob Sabath at the Sojourner's Mobilization to End Poverty in Washington, D.C. He and his wife Jackie were living on a retreat farm in West Virginia, with friends formerly from the Sojourners community. Included there was a house for others to come for times of silent retreat and prayer. For years his Christian journey had been deeply shaped by contemplative spiritual practices. And he told me he had never forgotten his first exposure to such experiences at our retreat in 1972, including the now famous story of staring at an apple.

In December of 1972, exhausted from the year's electoral politics and searching for inward sustenance, I sat at my desk in the Senate office building. I was trying to plan a trip to get away, before Christmas, and couldn't decide what to do. First I had planned to go to the Virgin Islands. Then I had the idea of going to Montreal. Nothing seemed to feel right.

On my desk was a scrawled note with the phone number for Father Stephen, the guest master at Holy Cross Monastery in Berryville, Virginia. A friend from Church of the Saviour, Conrad Hoover, had told me about this Trappist monastery a few weeks before, suggesting that I might enjoy going on retreat there. Never having stepped inside a monastery, much less going there for a retreat, the idea frightened me. But at the same time, something drew me.

It was a Thursday afternoon when, instead of calling back a travel agent, I picked up the note and dialed the number. Father Stephen answered. Haltingly, I asked him about space for a retreat, starting right away; I was half hoping that there was no room. But he welcomed me. And even then, I remember the sense of peace that settled over me. It was very strange, and I proceeded to Berryville.

Holy Cross Monastery was like the Dayspring Retreat Center on steroids. The early chanting of psalms, beginning at 3:30 A.M., the singing of ancient hymns, the reading of Scripture, and the enveloping silence seemed to invite my soul into a comfortable solitude.

"O God, come to my assistance. O Lord, make haste to help me." Those sung invocations bathed the predawn darkness of the chapel with clarity and illumination. The monastic tradition waits in silence for the dawn to break, even as we wait for the kingdom to break into the world. The monks gather together for their first service, then individually wait and pray, convening again in the chapel and sharing the Eucharist — all as the sun begins to rise.

In the day they worked. Holy Cross baked bread — Monastery Bread — which I could buy at the Giant grocery store in D.C. Worship services punctuated the day, concluding with vespers. A converted farmhouse served as the Retreat House, where meals were shared with fellow retreatants, often joined by Father Stephen.

I found myself unexpectedly gravitating to the rhythm of these days, and drawn into the mysteries of grace revealed like mini-epiphanies in this welcoming silence. On the fourth day, I experienced a spiritual encounter with God that would stay with me, and shape me, for all the coming years of my life.

December 15, 1972

God reveals Himself to those who seek Him. He plants within them the response of love; one's love for God is there planted by God — by Christ; and God loves because He loves Christ — and through Him loves us.

In the morning, at the dayspring of the day, as I returned to the monastery chapel, an assurance suddenly flooded over me; I would and did know the reality of Christ's love — I would sense it, encounter it, as a real moving force; He would demonstrate Himself, and His love to me in ways that would be natural and genuine. And what is more, I believed and sensed within me the union with Christ and His love. Quietly from within, I felt a call, a stir, a beckoning, an affirmation; I was found as one in union with Christ; there my true self would dwell.

Merton called it the response that God plants within one — the response of love that is from God, and reaches out to him. In me it was a quiet sense of joy and peace, and a deeper openness. And after the communion service that followed, I felt a new kind of openness and warmth toward the other retreatants. And also, toward the people at church, at the office, and in my group — at every level a kind of warmth and love.

The experience was not at all dramatic; just a very quiet assurance and sensation, an intuitive apprehension. I would know, and did sense, in genuine ways, the presence of Christ's love — that this would be carried with me; and I was, at my core, united to him.

Sometimes for any of us, the truest wisdom and realities of God's search for us, and the response of our heart, are distilled into a few hours, or even moments, of pure and revelatory experience. It becomes a touch-stone for all of one's lifelong journey. That's what seemed to happen.

Following the afternoon service, I remained in the chapel. And as I prayed, I felt a spontaneous flowing of joyous adoration, and real love, for Christ. It was from within, from the heart, from the same root of experience — the same kind of apprehension; it was prompted from deep within me and was simply a sense of love and warmth for Christ. "Christ, I love you" — the Jesus prayer, which I had been repeating that morning — suddenly flowed out naturally. I simply let myself revel and dwell in this deep expression of praise; it was not just feeling or emotion. Rather, I intuited — I believed — that it was a response of my soul, of my *whole* self, toward Christ and his love.

As I pondered that love, and this experience, I thought of those closest to me — first, my family — Ron, Jan, Julie, Ronnie, Ralph, Marcia, Dad, and Mom. I felt as deep a love for them as I ever have — and I felt close to them — as close to them as I ever have; there was a special sense of intimacy and love for them.

And as I prayed for the members of my group, and for people in the office, I saw them for what they could be, saw them as being loved.

It was as though I was caught up in the force of the love of Christ; it was the inner response toward God — the response put there by God — the working of God's Spirit, bringing Christ alive, sharing in his life.

I knew I was in touch with that which was most real; and I thought of my death. Suddenly, in that context, I felt no fear, for in this love I was ready and willing to give all. To trust in the force, the power, the transcendent character of this love, Christ's love; I was ready and able, at that moment, to do so.

Those moments were life-defining. What I experienced and saw from within during those encounters was bright, radiant light. At prayer in the chapel, this sense of being overcome by this love was not just mental, or just emotional. The presence of light was tangible; it was real, and it was overwhelming me. I've found that sufficient for a lifetime. I have no doubt that God's presence and love is real. It touched me.

Father Stephen Usinowicz, the guest master, accompanied me through these days. Deeply experienced in years of contemplative life as a Trappist monk, he was also brilliant theologically, and most important, deeply intuitive in his approach to others, and to God. Father Stephen helped me to get beyond my thinking about God — and my preoccupations with my own inner dramas — and to focus on my experience of God during these days.

I had come on this retreat, in my typical fashion, with a list of things to address, which I summarized upon arrival: (1) my call, mission, and future direction in life; (2) my work with Senator Hatfield; (3) reflections on celibacy and marriage (this was simply a euphemism for trying to sort out my relationships with women); and (4) potential areas of growth in my life — specifically my empathy for others. It was all neatly organized and analytical. And by the end of my first day at Berryville, my agenda had been swept aside as basically irrelevant. Over years of many retreats since then, I've found this to be the common pattern.

My days at Berryville opened me to an inner, intuitive discovery of God's promptings and presence in my life. All this is deeply ironic in some ways. Raised as an evangelical, I had invited Jesus into my heart at age four. But the forms of piety that characterized the evangelical subculture as I grew up seemed superficial. Plus, so much energy was focused on rigid theology — thinking the right way — and on legalistic social norms — acting the right way — that the honest struggles and challenges of the spiritual journey were taken lightly. The "dark night of the soul" was not in the vocabulary of this piety.

The monastic tradition takes the transformation of one's inner self through the ongoing encounter with God's presence and love with utter seriousness. At least, that is what I was discovering, first at Church of the Saviour and now crystallized at Berryville. I was apprehending anew my experience of God.

Father Stephen wrote a paper — he actually dictated it into a tape recorder — summarizing the insights he shared regularly with those coming on retreat. The paper bore a heavy name: "The Personal and Social Image of the Trinity within Us and Intuitive Prayer." But the title suggests his insights. The relational nature of God, seen in the Trinity, invites us into its life, which is experienced through prayer that accesses our inner, intuitive life.

The other powerful, revelatory understanding of those days was the experience of God as love. It sounds so simplistic. But as I sensed being drawn into God's presence, this was a reality of overwhelming love. Experiencing this clarified so much.

The days that followed Berryville flowed rich in simple experiences of grace and love. Encounters with friends at church, and then over Christmas with my family, felt infused with a fresh presence and compassion. I found myself doing what today are called "random acts of kindness" — picking up hitchhikers, responding to simple needs, and showing generosity to strangers.

I met with Gordon Cosby and told him about my time, reading from my journal. He had officially become my "sponsor" as I was still in the process of moving toward full membership in Church of the Saviour. But as Gordon listened to me, he announced that my time of sponsorship was over. If I was willing and ready to commit, it was time to take my membership vows.

The last step was to write and share my spiritual autobiography with the Church Council, and be formally accepted. Then, at the Sunday service on March 11, 1973, I was called forward to make my membership commitment. Mark and Antoinette Hatfield came to the service to express their support. My small group gathered and laid hands on me as I knelt, and Gordon prayed that my life would be a clear channel for the love and grace of God.

This inward journey, so often interrupted by events in the world and distractions in my soul, had finally brought me to this place of commitment. Clearly, this wasn't what I had done. Rather, it seemed that I had finally relinquished sufficiently to the beckoning of God, and a new step in my journey now could be taken.

Afraid to Love

—————

I LEARNED THE important things about sex from Father Stephen, a Trappist monk. During those translucent days at Berryville, I asked him at one point about his views on celibacy. Immediately his face lit up, and he gave me the best discourse on and the most beautiful description of a love relationship that I have ever heard. It was a description of his relationship with a woman, which was totally celibate, that painted the most beautiful and Christlike picture.

Father Stephen referred to the spiritual, the sensual, and the sexual dimensions of each person. The key for him was to allow one's spiritual center to integrate the sensual and sexual parts of one's life and relationships. He explained that celibacy does not deny the sexual and sensual dimensions; in fact, "it was heresy to call these things bad, or evil, or undesirable," he said. Rather, celibacy simply rules out the genital expression of sexuality, and marriage.

Father Stephen described the relationship with his beloved friend, in which both felt the deepest sense of bonding and union with each another, rooted in Christ's presence and love. Sensual and sexual feelings were part of the relationship, integrated through their spiritual center. Celibacy was a clear gift and calling, which was never doubted. But the relationship he described seemed richer and more beautiful than those of most noncelibate people I know, or, for that matter, than my own relationships with women.

For Father Stephen, "loving your neighbor as yourself" meant being called to the work of inner integration. When one's spiritual center is shaping the sensual and sexual dimensions of one's life, then it is truly possible to love another as yourself, desiring the same wholeness for the other. Rather than seeking the fulfillment of one's needs, one desires the gift of mutuality and reciprocity, which grows from a relationship nourished in this spiritual center.

All this was startling, fresh, and a new vocabulary for me. First, I was trying to come to grips with the fact that a Trappist monk had more wisdom about sexuality, spirituality, and relationships than many others I knew. It was the last thing I had expected to discover at Berryville. But a simple truth was emerging: in some sense, for my life to be full of the love that I wanted, I had to open myself, in a deep way, to the reality of God's love and its ongoing expression in Christ.

In the months that followed Berryville, as my spiritual journey was focused and enlivened, and I was meeting regularly with Gordon Cosby, I began looking hard at my relationships with women. Father Stephen's words and vision kept challenging me. And I began to uncover deeper dynamics.

My inward journey was inexorably uncovering deeper levels of my psychological makeup even as it pushed me toward greater relinquishment to God's love. In college I was notorious for dating one girl after another, never having a steady relationship, and that pattern was continuing. Now I was beginning to understand that commitment terrified me. I started to grasp the psychological reasons why.

March 31, 1973

What is the source of this threat, this sense of being sought after?

Psychologically, I would guess that it is rooted somehow in my relationship to my mother. For often I have felt, through my life, that she has tried to shelter me, possess me, keep me protected, or enslaved. And in sensing this, I have often felt distant from her — wanting to avoid her, fending off her encroachments on me. So I suppose, maybe, that the more I can feel real love for Mom — love purely for her sake, love that forgives, and that is

rooted in the certainty of my own freedom and independence —
the more I can experience such a love, the more certain I will be of
my own inner ability to love, freely, rather than to withdraw from
the threat of being possessed.

In the year ahead I would come to know how deeply this was true.
My journey was revealing a primal reality: I was afraid to love. Moreover,
it was unlocking the spiritual pathways that would overcome that fear
with God's love. Even though inner transformation is an ongoing journey, I found it to be true that "perfect love casts out fear." Further, in the
years to come, my relationship with my mother would be profoundly
changed.

Father Stephen's words about one's spiritual center integrating one's
sensuality and sexuality also opened new insights. Like so many evangelicals of that time, I was obsessed with being a technical virgin. (Years
later, when the lurid details of Bill Clinton's relationship with Monica
Lewinsky became public, revealing that he hadn't had actual sexual in-
tercourse with her, my friend and colleague Bruce Laverman said to me,
"Now we know for sure that Clinton is an evangelical.") But all this was
largely hypocritical.

Maintaining such a distinction did nothing to integrate my sexuality
in a healthy way with my whole self. Sex was a source of guilt and fear.
Because of those feelings, it was as much a way to distance myself from a
relationship as it was to draw me toward it. But since Berryville, I had a
framework for integrating in a more healthy way my attitudes about sex,
my relationships with women, and my journey with God. It was making
sense to me.

And it goes back to the vision of love I sensed at Berryville; simply be
ready to love all others, with Christ's love — relating to them with his
love — being grounded in that love and letting it flow out to the other.
Letting it move wherever it would, and being open to discovering what it
gives in return.

My soul still yearned for solitude. In August I embarked on a pilgrimage — to Norway. I got on an SAS plane for Bergen and wrote in my journal, "My pilgrimage begins . . . with an inward spirit that is beckoning me
away from the normalcy of my life, and toward a far more vivid and life-

sustaining exploration of the soul. . . . I do not flee anything . . . rather I feel I am running toward something, Perhaps, I believe, towards myself."

With me were a journal, a Bible, and three books: Thomas Merton's *Asian Journey,* which Gordon Cosby had given me the day before I left; Henri Nouwen's *Pray to Live,* a book about Merton; and John Howard Yoder's *Politics of Jesus.* My plan was to travel through the fjord country and then take a coastal steamer all the way to the North Cape. I would spend some days there, near the top of the world, in Kjollefjord, a village I had found on the map.

I wrote volumes in my journal, including a long treatise critiquing, from the perspective of radical Christian faith, political, economic, and social realities of the day, as well as thoughts about my vocation and re-flections on whether I was called to celibacy or marriage.

This journey upward in the land of the midnight sun was a pilgrim-age within. Toward the end I found myself in the village of Hellesylt, at one end of the Gieranger fjord. I walked out on a pier at the end of the fjord. It was late — about 10:30 or 11:00 P.M. The sky was clear and bright with stars; the moon nearly full. The mountains outlining the fjord made a vivid image against the sky in the light of the evening.

I prayed. My inner self cried out, extended out to God. To love him with all my heart, all my soul, and all my mind — my whole being reso-nated with that desire. To do anything, to give up anything, to achieve that life. To discover my hidden self — my real self — myself in Christ — and to do whatever he desired in order to reach that completeness. My whole being reached out for that oneness with him, for that knowledge, the realization, of his life in me.

I marveled in the wonder, in the glory of that time. And nothing in the world seemed as important. It was grace — a deep vital moment given to me. His Spirit was there, beckoning my own.

At the end of the trip I went to Copenhagen. Sitting by a group of trees in Deer Park, I was graced with some clear reflections summarizing my relationships with women. It struck me that my need cannot be at the root of relating to women. At wedding ceremonies we hear that God knew Adam was alone and gave him a helpmate. The two became one. That is good. It is wonderful.

But if the love of a man for his wife is to be patterned after Christ's love for his church, then the man cannot enter into such a relationship because he needs it! The pattern of Christ's relationship to the church is that of utter selflessness — the giving up of prerogatives for the sake of the other, because of love for the other.

The inner void is filled only by Christ.

I cannot build love for women out of my need.

"Perfect love casts out fear." My emotionally haphazard history of relationships with women was driven by my fear of love and commitment. It would require a more integrated and transforming experience of love — specifically of God's love — to overcome the dynamics that kept my relationships with women locked in self-defeating cycles of emotional need and neurotic fright.

Mission to Japan

———————

THREE WEEKS after I returned from my solitary pilgrimage to Norway, a letter appeared on my desk in Senator Hatfield's office from Karin Granberg, who was teaching in Japan. Karin and I had met when Bill Starr took me to visit Hope College some years earlier; her dad, Lars, was the psychology professor so admired by Bill. Our paths crossed again in 1967, the summer I graduated from Hope, when she was a counselor at Camp Geneva, a Reformed Church in America camp near Holland, Michigan.

We discovered a deep, intuitive, and romantic connection with each other. But I was at Princeton Seminary while she was at Hope, having transferred there after a year at St. Olaf. We worked on a long-distance relationship. When she graduated from Hope, she moved out east to teach in Paterson, New Jersey, while I was in D.C. We struggled with an on-again, off-again, on-again relationship, with our families hoping, and expecting, that we would announce our engagement. But my fear of commitment — which I really didn't understand at the time — paralyzed me. For Karin, my hesitant, conditional responses were hurtful, confusing, and increasingly hard to tolerate.

Finally, in November 1971, over dinner at the Ginger Mill Restaurant in New York, across from Lincoln Center, we ended our relationship. It was difficult for both of us, but the uncertainty was causing each of us too much pain. Karin asked that we agree to never see or talk to each other again. I was in such turmoil I flew home to Chicago to give the news to my parents in person; they were crushed. Karin applied for a short-term mission position through the Reformed Church in America (RCA) to teach English in Japan, eventually ending up at Miyagi Gakuin women's school in Sendai, about a two-hour train trip north of Tokyo.

Two years later, provoked by seeing an actor in a movie who resembled me, she wrote me a letter. She debated whether to write, but said, "With the Pacific Ocean between us, it seems harmless enough." She shared news of what had happened in her life in the past two years and said she had decided to become a pastoral counselor. She went on, "I'd like to tell you that what I most remember when I think of you is the quality of our spiritual relationship," and added why this was significant for her future.

The letter floored me. I was surprised and joyful — and deeply moved in ways I would never have expected. We exchanged letters, but feelings were stirring within me, even as I continued to deepen my contemplative quest. After talking with Gordon, Betty O (Elizabeth O'Connor), and other trusted friends, all of whom affirmed my reawakened feelings, I decided to take a retreat to sort all this out. I went to Hilton Head Island, in South Carolina, so I could walk on a beach.

With me were my journals, letters from Karin saved from past years, letters from me to her that she returned when we broke up, and even tape recordings I had made at the time. It was an intense time of inner work. I saw so clearly my previous inability — my fear — to love in the way that was required for a healthy relationship. And more important, I discovered and acknowledged the depth of my love for her — my affirmation of her deepest self and my desire to share this love.

Wanting to communicate all this, I proceeded to write what became a twenty-four-page letter, declaring my love for her and sharing my journey over the past year, beginning with the transformative days at Berryville the previous December. I was open to exploring what all this meant, and where it could go. I mailed it, waited, and prayed.

Her response centered on her own journey. In December she had gone to Hokkaido, the northern island of Japan, to join RCA missionaries and sing in a Christmas concert and outreach. During those days she'd had a deep and renewing charismatic experience of God's Spirit, and was still reflecting on its meaning. Both of us, in different ways, were undergoing dramatic experiences in our spiritual journeys, and it was not easy to discern where all this was leading.

I wrote again and proposed that I come to Japan to explore together our relationship. She said no; she'd rather wait until her return in the summer. It was clear that Karin was hesitant, for good reason, to reopen an encounter that had been filled with years of uncertainty and pain. Conferring regularly with Gordon, I was in a quandary about what to do.

Gordon affirmed my response to Karin. He grasped fully how this was connected to the spiritual journey that had intensified since Berryville, resulting in deep inner movements addressing issues I previously had neither understood nor confronted. But he said Karin had to be able to trust that response; it would take being together to do so, but she might not be ready. He suggested that I call her on the telephone and simply ask once more if I could visit, being clear about my desire, but also accepting of her response.

This was, of course, well before the Internet, and international telephone calls were rare. People wrote letters. But I called her parents to get her number, and placed a call through the international operator.

Karin was shocked to hear my voice. "Why are you calling?" she asked.

"To tell you I love you."

"Did you get my last letter, and do you still feel that way?"

"Yes. I'd like to come see you if possible."

"You're nuts."

"I don't think so. And I don't want any long, drawn-out exploration of our relationship."

"That's good news."

"We could work this out quickly. By next summer we can know what's in store for us."

"You really think so?"

"Yes."

We agreed that I would come for about ten days during her vacation beginning in late March.

I planned this trip like the mission of a lifetime. So many psychological, emotional, and spiritual currents were swirling within me as feelings for Karin, whom I had not seen for two years, were focusing more clearly. At a dinner with my friend Basil Buchanan one evening, I told him I would either marry Karin or make a commitment to celibacy.

I made my reservation on a Northwest Orient flight that would begin in D.C. and, after a couple of stops, end in Tokyo. Yoshi Ogawa was a fellow graduate of Hope College and a friend who worked on legislative issues for Northwest in the nation's capital. When I called and told her my plans, she was thrilled, and said she would try to arrange an upgrade for me to first class. Today that would probably violate some rule regulating favors from lobbyists, but at the time I was more than pleased.

When the flight made its first stop, I got off to call Yoshi and thank her for the first-class seat, in the upper level of this new 747 jumbo jet. And then I asked a question that flashed through my mind:

"I don't need a visa to go to Japan, right? It's just like going to Europe, isn't it?"

Yoshi was stunned.

"You don't have a visa? You have to get off that plane immediately!"

It turns out that the airline is responsible for seeing that its passengers have the proper visas or required documents for entering the country where they land, and the airline can face penalties if they fail to do so. Apparently the ticket agent at check-in failed to check my passport thoroughly while he was upgrading me to first class.

I told Yoshi there was no way I was getting off the flight. Karin would be waiting for me, and it was impossible for me get in touch with her. Finally, Yoshi said she'd contact Northwest operations in Tokyo to alert them to the problem.

When the plane landed in Tokyo, a high-ranking Northwest official and two Japanese customs and immigration officials came on board to meet me. I was apologetic, but they were not happy. I explained that Karin was waiting to meet me. So the officials accompanied me to where she was. She imagined it was just some kind of protocol since I was working for Senator Hatfield. But in the first moments of this long-awaited encounter, I explained that I had no visa, and was in trouble.

The officials allowed her to accompany me to a small office. I was actually in detention. The alternative they were discussing was to deport me to Hong Kong, where I could then apply for a visa from the Japanese consulate — a process that could take at least two or three days and would be costly. That was a gracious response, since in reality I was guilty of attempting to enter the country illegally.

I asked if I could make one telephone call, and they consented. Yukio Satoh had served as a high official in the Japanese embassy in Washington, D.C., and made a point of relating to senators and their foreign policy aides. I'd been at embassy functions with him and also at dinners at his home. When he was transferred back to Tokyo, he gave me his card, including his home number, and urged me to be in touch if I ever visited. I had the card with me.

It was a Sunday evening, and my call found him at home. Apologetically, I explained the whole embarrassing situation, including the story of coming to be reunited with Karin. He told me he would come to the airport. About an hour and a half later, Yukio entered the office, dressed in his formal business suit. He greeted me and Karin, and then launched into a stern lecture to the immigration officials who were holding me in custody. I had no idea what he was saying, of course. But when it ended, the officials, who understandably had been harsh and unsympathetic until then, began bowing and apologizing to me.

Yukio then explained that I was being released into his custody, would spend the night at the airport Hilton, and would return Monday morning and receive my visa. Perplexed and enormously grateful, I left the airport with Karin and Yukio, and the three of us went to dinner. So my long-awaited time of reunion and conversation with Karin came in the company of Yukio Satoh from the Foreign Ministry of Japan.

At dinner I asked Yukio what he had said to the officials. The previous year the Okinawa Reversion Treaty had passed the U.S. Senate. This was a measure restoring Japanese sovereignty to the island of Okinawa, a step intensely desired by the Japanese since the end of World War II. Hatfield had been in favor, and I never needed to give the matter much attention.

Yukio smiled in response to my question and then said, "I told them that the Okinawa Reversion Treaty never would have been approved by the U.S. Senate without you."

The next morning friendly immigration officials handed me my passport and visa, with apologies. Karin and I boarded the *shinkensen* — the "Bullet Train" — for her home in Sendai.

The following days were filled with wonder and joy. In Karin's small, Japanese-style home in Sendai, we sat for hours at her *kotatsu* — a low table over a recessed floor with a heater underneath — covered by a thick blanket to stay warm without central heating, and sipped tea while we talked about our lives over the past two years and about the future. We enjoyed meals with friends in Sendai's missionary community, most of whom were from the United Church of Christ.

Then we traveled to Sakunami, a famous hot springs site, to Matsushima, Kamakura, and eventually back to Tokyo. The entire time one question was on my mind — and hers. Were we called to be married?

Karin loves hot springs as well as the Japanese public bathhouses, called *sento*. Historically, these establishments have been widely used by Japanese as common places to wash and bathe, as most homes had been without bathtubs or showers. A partition separates the men's area from the women's. One first washes his or her body with soap and water from a faucet, rinses off completely, and then sits in a large communal tub of very hot water.

I suggested we go to a *sento* in Tokyo. I washed and sat in the hot common pool as the only non-Japanese man. Then I called to Karin over the partition.

"Can you hear me?"

"Yes."

"Will you marry me?"

"Yes."

It was, like most everything else in our journey together, unique. We met as we left the *sento*, joyful, startled, and wondering what was next. I was leaving Japan in forty-eight hours, and we now had the rest of our lives before us.

Monastic Psychotherapy

O N THE FLIGHT HOME from Tokyo, still upgraded to first class, I
wrote almost continuously for hours in my journal. The flight at-
tendants couldn't believe it. I was trying to capture, summarize, and process all that had happened during these life-changing days in Japan with
Karin.

Feelings of excitement, anxiety, joy, doubt, and longing swirled, as
my head strove to understand my heart. Returning to D.C., I talked first
with Gordon and then with other close friends about my trip. I called
Karin after sharing our news with the congregation at Church of the Saviour. She and I were trusting and embracing the love we had discovered,
and the promises we had made, during those ten days.

I was living in an apartment complex called McLean Gardens, not
far from the National Cathedral, bordered by a wooded area. I'd often listen to the music that Karin and I loved in our past: albums like *Wild-
flowers* and *In My Life* by Judy Collins, and the Brahms *German Requiem,*
particularly sections like "How Lovely Is Thy Dwelling Place." To be sure,
it was a strange combination, but it worked. And I would walk down into
the woods to a special holly tree, and remain there praying for Karin.

I also had more feelings of anxiety than usual. Gordon, trying to help
me understand my anxiety and perplexity, asked me a question I've
never forgotten. "Is it the kind of anxiety that causes you to question
your basic call?" The answer was clearly no. Then, Gordon explained, it

was anxiety rooted in other fears and wounds. In time, the causes might become clearer, and the anxiety would diminish. The important thing was to stay focused on my sense of call.

Months before my trip to Japan, Father Stephen had told me that Holy Cross Monastery would be experimenting with a program called "Retreatants in Community." Those attending would spend at least a month living in the community with the monks. This was much more than a week's retreat at the guest house; it was an opportunity to experience more fully the monastic community's worship, work, and life together.

Deeply intrigued by the possibility when Father Stephen first mentioned it, I asked Senator Hatfield for time off to do it in the spring. He had graciously said yes, and we arranged for a five-week stay from late April to the end of May. Now this was coming just a month or so after I returned from Japan.

On Tuesday, April 23, 1974, I left my apartment for Berryville, Virginia, driving my 1968 Saab, which looked like an elongated VW Beetle. On a Virginia divided highway, while I was going about 65 miles per hour in a strong crosswind, the car's left tires slipped off the pavement onto the shoulder. Perhaps I was just inattentive. But at that place, the shoulder was eroded, and when I turned the wheel to get back on the road, it caught the side of the pavement, putting the car into a skid, and it then flipped and rolled over three or four times on the highway and onto the grass of the median.

The car landed upright when it stopped. I smelled gas, got out of the car, laid down on the grass, and found myself thinking immediately of my love for Karin. That focus remained with me in the ambulance. The doctor in the emergency room found I was unhurt, except for a shoulder bruise from the seat belt that — along with the Saab's safety design — saved my life. I was still in some shock when Senator Hatfield appeared in the ER. He had been notified because of the Senate ID in my wallet, and now was taking me to his home to rest and recover.

The accident provided a confirming revelation. While lying on the grass and later in the emergency room, I knew at the deepest level, with unshakable certainty, that the love between Karin and me had an eternal foundation; a bedrock, forever solid and strong, was discovered. It was just something I knew; it was simply there. In the shadow of death, it was revealed and discovered.

My car didn't fare so well — it was totaled. The spiritual director in my mission group, David Dorsey, drove me to Berryville a couple of days later. My room was in the quarters with the monks, and now I was entering into their life not as an interested observer, but as a full participant. My alarm went off at 3:00 A.M. There was time for a cup of instant, Hills Brothers coffee, and a piece of monastery toast before vigils, which began at 3:30. I had a "stall" in the chapel where I joined with the monks in chanting psalms and listening to readings.

During the two hours after vigils — if I could remain awake — I would pray, read, or write in my journal, waiting for the dawn to break. By 6:00 we'd gather in the chapel again for lauds, followed by the Eucharist. Then I was assigned work in the morning, sometimes helping the abbot, Father William, in the garden, or cleaning, or helping at the bakery, which produced Monastery Bread.

A shorter worship service at noon preceded our main meal, eaten in silence while listening to readings, in the Benedictine tradition. My afternoons were free, and I'd read, walk, write, or listen to tapes of Thomas Merton giving talks to novices that I discovered in the library. On Wednesdays and Sundays at 5:00 P.M. I'd meet with Father Stephen, usually taking walks with him through the fields. Vespers then came before a light supper, and compline ushered in the "Great Silence" at about 8:00 P.M.

This was the framework in which some of the most intense inner work ever in my life took place, psychologically and spiritually, over these five weeks.

The monastic environment intensifies time and consciousness. It's like a crucible, where silence and detachment serve like a refiner's fire, burning away layers of psychic protection and distilling the core realities of one's inner self.

As I began writing to Karin, I realized that my letters to her were like my journal, and so I made carbon copies. They filled a whole notebook. With other entries, these chronicled my inner pilgrimage during these weeks. Dreams became vivid, intense, and pregnant with meaning. Phrases from chanted psalms and other scriptures penetrated my soul.

Christ's body and blood provided daily sustenance and strength as recesses of my psyche were opened to the gift of insight and to the touch of God's radical grace.

A monastery was preparing me for marriage.

In the first few days, as Father Stephen listened to my unfolding story of commitment to Karin, he observed how our relationship — and our lifelong covenant — rested on faith, hope, and love. Its foundation was in faith, and in times of spiritual or emotional uncertainty, this faith provided the enduring bedrock of the relationship. As trust was built between us in countless ways, we had the grounds for hope in the richness of our bond together. But as Paul writes in 1 Corinthians 13, the greatest of these is love, which overflows as God's gift.

All this requires an absolute dependence on grace, for in the end, these qualities of faith, hope, and love are not of our own doing, but come from God's work in our lives. Further, the physical and intellectual dimensions of the relationship are integrated through our spiritual union. That rests at the heart of it all.

This all made theological sense out of my experience and provided a compelling framework for understanding what I was discovering. What I was not prepared for, however, was the experience of inner "annihilation." The monastic environment was allowing my inner life to be taken apart, piece by piece. Merton wrote about this in *New Seeds of Contemplation,* a book I devoured during those days. His descriptions felt revelatory, and I tried to describe what was happening to Karin:

May 2, 1974

I picked up New Seeds and read chapters 29, 30, and 31. So suddenly I was struck by the utter futility of so much of my mind's pre-occupations . . . my heart suddenly ached over all the needless and idiotic worries and thoughts and speculations that have possessed me. . . . It was the pain of it all that I felt, the scar that burns, the sore wound that aches, from knowing that His Life has been touched . . . and that is all in the world that matters.

I sobbed and swore for during the past few days I have given so little room, so little attention, to even trying to open myself, and yearn simply for his presence. The pain cut so sharp and deep that all else seemed so insignificant — so unworthy of even a trifle of concern, much less the laborious hours of continual pre-occupation. . . .

In just a few moments, one can catch a glimpse of the futility of hours, of days, of months, of years.

Those themes and feelings continually gripped me during those days. I was learning the meaning of radical detachment and then critiquing the models of "self-actualization" and fulfillment so widely accepted in society with the gospel's call to abandon oneself to God. Was Jesus of Nazareth, hanging on the cross between two criminals at the age of thirty-three, a model of an integrated, self-realized personality?

One morning I was captivated by one central truth that kept driving itself into me — namely, that I am *nothing* apart from Christ's love. A lot of my unconscious pride, pretension, and self-righteousness — or, more basically, the belief in my own invincibility — was being destroyed. I had a deep sense of the utter futility of all that I did that was centered around the self, and was prompted by its demands. I was encountering my own emptiness, my nothingness, in the truest spiritual sense. I was experiencing inner "annihilation."

I felt a general sense of meaningless and dread from time to time as far as me and my life were concerned, apart from being united to Christ's love. This is not something established once, in a dramatic conversion, or even periodically, on special retreats, etc., but something that must be done daily, even hourly. To open one's life to the presence of this love in all that one does seems impossible. But how futile and worthless all else is.

And of course, the final irony is that being in that presence is purely a gift. We can do nothing to make it so. We can only empty ourselves, open ourselves, and wait. And be fully content waiting, and hoping, in that emptiness.

Raised as an evangelical, I was told that the problem with Catholics was that they believed in salvation through works — by trying to be good, going to Mass, and saying prayers. We believed in salvation by grace alone, through faith. Further, I embraced the Reformed tradition, which begins with a declaration of our "total depravity" and, in the Reformers' reaction to the ("Catholic") church of their time, insists upon our utter dependence on the initiative of God's grace.

But here's the truth of my journey. I learned more about the depth of my sin, and I experienced more fully what it means to rely only on the gift of God's grace, from the monastic tradition of the Catholic Church than I ever did from reading the Heidelberg Catechism. Further, the Catholic contemplatives and mystics I've read seem to understand and live the truths of utter depravity and radical grace more persuasively than most other Christian pilgrims I've encountered.

This journey into the "dark night of the soul" that I touched upon during those weeks at Berryville could never be described as simply "spiritual." It reaches the whole of one's self — psychological, emotional, and intellectual as well. At least for me, this happened in unexpected ways.

I began reading the writings of William of St. Thierry, a twelfth-century monk and mystic. He was a friend of Bernard of Clairvaux, a better-known leader and reformer of the monastic tradition in that time. William's mystical theology stresses how spiritual reality reintegrates the physical and rational dimensions of life, and that the deepest way of knowing is a "loving knowledge." He also was fascinated with the Song of Songs, as was Bernard of Clairvaux and many other mystics.

These mystics regard physical love as the best and clearest analogy to describe the union of one's soul with Christ. In the Song of Songs the bride is an individual's soul or heart. The Bridegroom is Christ. So they take the most sensual story in the Scriptures to portray the vision of one's love and quest for union with God.

Fascinated by all this, I read some of William's reflections, and then began to read through the Song of Songs, which I hadn't done for years. I naturally identified the Bridegroom's description of the bride's physical beauty with Karin. It was a deep, flowing affirmation of her physical beauty, which I tried to convey to her: "I felt compelled to go up to the chapel and pray. And as I did, I found myself just thanking God for your simple pure beauty."

I went to sleep that evening with a sense of delight and euphoria. Then I had a bizarre and jarring dream, which included troubling images of my mother. So much of my childhood had been shaped by the desire to please and be the good Christian boy, receiving the praise and meeting expectations of my parents, and especially my mother, whose love felt more conditional than my dad's. Patterns of outward submission resulted in inward emotions that were frozen. In reaction, as I grew older, I developed a strong sense of self-sufficiency. Psychological defenses operating mostly on the subconscious level would protect space for my own ego, or sense of self, and resist any attempt to be possessed again by a woman.

That's why commitment to a woman was so threatening. Further, because any sexual activity became so easily associated with guilt, this also became a means for preserving my emotional insularity from women. But now the inner psychic roots of these fears were becoming more transparent, illuminated by spiritual clarity of the love I had discovered for Karin.

During these intense days, I picked up a book in the monastery library by Karen Horney, titled *Self-Analysis*. She seemed to put her finger on what was going on with me. She describes ten "neurotic trends" that, while often fairly normal, can create conflict and difficulty when they are especially pronounced. One of them hit home with me immediately: the need for "self-sufficiency and independence." In psychological language, Horney was describing the neurotic tendency that had become so clear to me during my monastic sojourn. Her description, which could have come right out of my journal, read like this: "Necessity never to need anybody, or to yield to any influence, or to be tied down to anything, any closeness involving the danger of enslavement. Distance and separateness as the only source of security. Dread of needing others, of ties, of closeness, of love."

These insights were providing concrete psychological content to my spiritual experiences of "annihilation." My weakness and brokenness were being revealed in more and more transparent depths. I was also understanding my lack of empathy and my fear of strong emotional feelings. All this was defining, far more comprehensively than ever before, the scope of sin in my life.

May 12, 1974

For me, a major thrust of sin has been the drive to keep me independent from love, under the myth that I am everything I need to be within myself. This is what has been so profoundly revealed to me as the root of so much of my sin. And it is in this way that I have been experiencing real annihilation.

In this inward journey, my love for God and my love for Karin intersected at the point of my woundedness. Confronted with all my narrow and petty self-absorption, I was dependent only on God's grace to receive the gift and joy of dwelling in God's love. And confronted with my defensive self-sufficiency, I was dependent only on God's grace to dwell in that liberating love, received from Karin, and offered to her. In the end, it all depends only on that grace.

Dayspring

M Y WEEKS at Holy Cross Monastery allowed me to access my emotional life at new levels. Not only was I coming to understand the reasons why many feelings and emotions had often been so easily blocked; my emotional life was also breaking forth in surprising ways within this monastic environment.

One theological way of understanding this centered on the working of the Holy Spirit. At the time, Thomas Harris's book *I'm O.K., You're O.K.* was popular, employing what he called "transactional analysis." In this version of popularized psychology each person has a "Parent," "Child," and "Adult" within him or her, including the various "tapes" from our past that each part of our self carries. Psychological health consisted of a healthy integration of these three dimensions.

Father Stephen was familiar with this approach and adopted it as an analogy for understanding the work of the Trinity and our participation in its life. God the Father functioned like the Parent, who endeavors to give shape and form to behavior. The Holy Spirit was the Child, who is full of spontaneity, feeling, and fervor. The Adult was Jesus Christ, who integrates the qualities of the Parent and Child into a whole and loving personality.

Obviously there are some theological gaps in this analogy, but it did provide me a window for understanding how I dealt with the emotional dimensions of my life. My "Child" was repressed by my childhood, and certainly wasn't yet liberated. I was far more comfortable giving and receiving information, which is more the "Adult" role, than dealing with the world of feelings and emotions.

But ever since my first retreat to Berryville in 1972, my spiritual experiences were shaped by uncovering and discovering levels of deep feeling, centering on the presence of God's love. In fact, after my initial encounter at Berryville, Gordon Cosby advised me to alter the "Jesus Prayer." Instead of praying, "Lord Jesus Christ, Son of God, have mercy on me, a sinner," he suggested praying, "Lord Jesus Christ, Son of God, I love you." He sensed my need to open and access those deeper feelings of love, and of course this later became a key in my relationship to Karin.

All this became connected to my understanding of the Holy Spirit. My spiritual life was always comfortable with ideas, but now it was deepening my experience of God. Those qualities of spontaneity, joy, inspiration, and fervor seemed to be the result of unlocking the work of the Holy Spirit in my life.

Now of course, I know that any mature theology of the Holy Spirit is never limited to personal experience. The Spirit moved over the water at creation; the Spirit breathes life into every living thing; the Spirit forms God's people as the church; the Spirit goes ahead of us, sending us into mission. But the Holy Spirit also brings the power of God, which resurrected Jesus from the dead, into the center of our lives, transforming our whole being and imparting spiritual gifts to every follower of Jesus.

During my weeks living within the monastic community, I discovered that a couple of the monks had experienced a classic charismatic renewal. They spoke in tongues and often had prayer services with a few Pentecostal friends who would visit. They invited me to join them. I was intrigued and also comfortable worshiping and praying with them, although this was a completely new experience. The irony was not lost; my first experience of a Pentecostal prayer service took place at a Trappist monastery.

Without hesitation I can describe the intense spiritual encounter with the presence of God's love that I experienced in my initial retreat at Berryville as a "baptism of the Holy Spirit." I did not experience some of the classic signs of such a "baptism," such as speaking in tongues. And I also know the theological reservations some of my Reformed friends may have in using that language. But for me, my encounters with contemplative spirituality opened my inner, emotional life to the transforming power of God's love through the active work of the Holy Spirit. I would not know how else to name this.

With this growing accessibility to my world of inner feelings, more dreams came alive. None, perhaps, were as dramatic as those involving my mother, but images of airplanes struggling to take off and of my nervousness prior to conducting an orchestra performing the Brahms *Requiem* conveyed the anxious anticipation of my soul.

After I completed my stay at the monastery, the intermingled feelings of anxiety and experiences of grace accompanied me as I tried to reengage my work with Senator Hatfield. I also had something else on my mind — a wedding.

After our two and a half weeks together in Japan, Karin and I were separated again — she still in Japan and I in D.C. — as we planned an August wedding. She couldn't return until the beginning of July. But distance didn't deter the ongoing, inner work in my life. Maybe it enhanced it.

While dealing with all the complexity of our feelings, we also tried to address the practical realities of not only a wedding, but also whether we would stay in D.C. Letters and then tapes chronicled our hopes and our anxieties. We both were facing our fears while embracing the love that beckoned us each so deeply.

I was struggling to integrate the contemplative practices that had been a natural rhythm of life at the monastery with the familiar, hurried, and incessantly demanding pace of work on Capitol Hill. My apartment had become like a retreat. I returned there one Friday evening and decided to go outside for a walk. First, down to the grassy field I went, and after walking and praying I sat there, looking into the trees. Here is what I wrote in my journal:

> [I] was absorbed in the sense of presence with God's Spirit and love. I believe I was praying the Jesus Prayer, but then just let my inner self be carried in the flow of this presence, dwelling there without words, simply aware of Love. It was the first time in a while since the fullness of Spirit in this way had so captivated my inner, truest self. . . .

Out of the poverty of spirit, the gift of God's grace can grant moments when the veil over Truth is just partially lifted. It is only out of one's humiliation and nothingness that God can act at all. Then His Spirit may give a measure of grace where one simply discovers . . . the truth that his life is totally dependent upon God, given and sustained by God, existing only for God's glory, and ultimately rooted in God's being. . . .

I walked on down to the holly tree, where I remained for some time. The love simply swept from my heart to hers and then back to God's with overpowering force. . . . In prayer for her I reached out from my soul, in abandonment, communion. It was as if my life was just poured into hers; this was the yearning during those moments. . . .

Within me was the deepest peace — that which passes all understanding. Joy filled my heart as I sang and let my spirit dwell in praise of Christ's love. There was no need to analyze, or ask anything. All was given and revealed beyond all the answers given by the mind. . . .

I returned to the apartment to make a tape to Karin.

Karin returned from Japan on July 1. I flew to Kennedy International Airport to meet her. While at the airport I went to Our Lady of the Skies Chapel to pray. As I fixed my attention on the cross behind the altar, in front of a depiction of the Lord and his disciples at the Last Supper etched into the marble backdrop, these words came to me with forceful clarity: "We are His Body."

When I met Karin, we were overcome by wonder, joy, happiness, and radiant love. There was the free-rushing overflow of feelings — of warmth, intimacy, attraction, beauty, wonder, love. We were oblivious to all else.

During my days at the monastery, I had come to love the dawn. Waiting for the sun to rise, and God's light to break open upon the world, came to symbolize so much. So I couldn't image a better time for a wedding. Karin agreed. But while I had assumed inviting "all my friends," Karin wanted a more intimate gathering. The result was a wedding with about one hundred invited family and friends, held at 6:00 A.M. at the

Church of the Saviour's Dayspring Retreat Farm, outside of Washington, D.C.

My parents and family — and probably Karin's too — were so relieved that the dramatic revival of our relationship was resulting in marriage that they didn't dare question the strange time of day. Nothing else about our story seemed very normal. My uncle Ken simply said, "You two deserve each other." And my brother and sister couldn't believe they were paying to stay at a Sheraton, but would have to get up at 4:30 A.M. with only about four hours of sleep.

The service mirrored our discovery of love, and sense of God's call. It included Bach's "Jesu, Joy of Man's Desiring," "Morning Has Broken," Elizabeth O'Connor and Easter Dorsey reading from *New Seeds of Contemplation,* my uncle Ralph reading Psalm 139, and Karin's close friend Priscilla reading John 15.

Gordon's sermon lifted up two words — "grace" and "pain" — and described the interplay of these, and the ultimate gift of God's grace, in the story of God's people, and then within our relationship, and in any healthy marriage. It was unlike any sermon I have heard at a wedding even to this day.

Then we shared with those gathered in celebrating communion, led by Rudy Kuyten, an RCA missionary who had been close to Karin in Japan. We included the music "How Lovely Is Thy Dwelling Place," and "Death, Where Is Thy Sting" from Brahms's *German Requiem.* At the conclusion, we turned and sang "Amazing Grace" to and with the congregation. It all seemed to flow together.

A dawn wedding also allowed us to fly that day to Norway. The pilot on the SAS flight announced our status as newlyweds (we were wed just hours previously) and gave us a bottle of champagne. We landed in Bergen, flew on to Alesund, and took a bus to Hellesylt, my favorite place in the fjord country, which I had discovered a year earlier. I wanted us to spend our wedding night there, at the Grand Hotel. The truth is, we were utterly exhausted from being up for the previous thirty hours, and slept for the next fourteen hours.

The Reformed tradition, with most historic Protestant churches, believes in two sacraments, baptism and the Lord's Supper, as opposed to Catholic and Orthodox churches, which include other rites and practices as sacraments. A sacrament is generally defined as "an outward and visible sign of an inward and invisible grace." It should come as no surprise, then, that I would quickly agree with those who add marriage as a sacrament. Our worship folder for the ceremony read "The Sacrament of Marriage." Certainly in our experience, marriage became the physical means through which God's grace touched our wounded selves with redeeming power.

Downward Mobility

ⸯ

Jᴵᴹ Wᴀʟʟɪꜱ, Karin, I, and a couple of Jim's friends sat together in our D.C. apartment in McLean Gardens. Jim had traveled there from Chicago with a few others to explore moving to Washington, D.C. The *Post-American* had struck a nerve in the Christian community with its call to radical discipleship, its commitment to alternative Christian community, and its message to "de-Americanize" the gospel, freeing it from the cultural captivity of the age.

Jim's small community was still living in the Rogers Park area of Chicago, close to Evanston. But forming Christian community had not been easy. Further, while the *Post-American* had made a strong initial impact, we weren't sure about its name and felt its style would be difficult to sustain for the long term. Jim's vision was for a strong monthly magazine that would carry a consistent voice in the Christian world, and for a community of witness and advocacy that would be seen and heard in the heart of the nation's political world.

Most of us, including Jim, were convinced the name had to be changed. This would be part of the strategy to launch the new monthly publication. Several ideas were being tested. At one point I suggested *Solomon's Portico,* from Acts — a name, in retrospect, so bizarre that it alone could have easily sunk the new venture. One other suggestion was put forth by Karin. It was *Sojourners.* She was convinced it conveyed what we were looking for. It captured the sense of community, had an intriguing biblical connection (Hebrews 11), suggested a journey, and was poetic and evocative — all things that could not be said about *Post-American.*

That evening a consensus began to emerge around *Sojourners.* But much more had to be decided, including whether the nascent community in Chicago would move to D.C., and if so where it would locate and who would be a part of it, in addition to how to start a new magazine.

Even then, in 1974, Jim sensed that the prophetic message of the magazine needed to be heard not simply by receptive voices mostly on the margins of the church, but also by those in the corridors of power. Further, he felt that the presence of Church of the Saviour in D.C. could provide helpful counsel to the group's attempt to form a sustainable Christian community. Jim also yearned for Karin and me to be a part of what he hoped could be born in Washington, D.C.

I was restless. My work with Mark Hatfield still held meaning, but with the focus no longer on Vietnam, directions were shifting. Hatfield had felt that perhaps world hunger might be a new point of advocacy, and I had accompanied him to the World Food Conference in Rome in October 1974 — my first trip away since marrying Karin. ("The one left at home is always lonelier," Hatfield told me.)

But Senator Hatfield was also becoming consumed working for projects in Oregon. His new position on the Senate Appropriations Committee gave him power and influence that he was using for the good of his home state. Nothing was changing his courageous and prophetic instincts, but I was wondering how they'd get expressed and, more to the point, whether my long-term future would be played out as a Senate staffer.

Beneath all this was the tug I felt toward a more radical, countercultural way of living out the gospel. Yoder's *Politics of Jesus,* along with William Stringfellow, Jacques Ellul, and others, had opened a whole new vista for understanding what it meant to be a follower of Jesus within the culture of our time. This, of course, was the same chord being struck by Jim Wallis and the *Post-American.* Moreover, Jim's vision was that the *Agenda for Biblical People* (his first book) had to get lived out from the base of a countercultural Christian community, in solidarity with the poor. This resonated deeply with me.

Church of the Saviour had been the birthplace for the spiritual revitalization of my faith, and its fervent missional focus engaged all its members in outward expressions of hospitality, compassion, and justice. But I yearned for something more — a Christian community where we lived, worked, and worshiped together, in a neighborhood with the poor. That's what Jim also envisioned.

Karin, however, was at a different place. Before our engagement, she was tentatively planning on enrolling in Fuller Seminary's School of Psychology. But we decided to start our married life in D.C., in part because Church of the Saviour was there. Karin had used Elizabeth O'Connor's book *Our Many Selves* in a small group with fellow missionaries in Sendai, and "Betty O" had come to Japan at Karin's invitation to speak at a conference for missionaries. Karin was looking forward to being nurtured in the life of Church of the Saviour, with Gordon, "Betty O," and others.

Our differences had ironic expressions. Troubled by the excessive land and fertilizer required to produce beef, compared to that needed for other forms of nutrition, I self-righteously announced I was giving up meat. Karin's response was that she had been living on a diet with hardly any beef for two years, and what she most looked forward to now was a good steak.

In the first couple of weeks after our honeymoon, Karin realized that cooking breakfast for me in the morning before I left for Capitol Hill, and then waiting for my return, was not going to be a fulfilling existence. She talked with Gordon, who suggested she explore Wesley Theological Seminary, located a few blocks from where we were living. It offered a masters in theological studies, and Karin could focus on pastoral theology. She enrolled.

Karin's passion centered on counseling and healing. She wanted to accompany others on their inner journeys toward wholeness, and she focused on the church's role in such pastoral ministry. Karin desired to find her own place in this calling.

Meanwhile, I was struggling with how to exercise a prophetic role, working for and trying to live out the gospel's call to justice and radical discipleship. My dilemma was how to relate my continuing inner call to the contemplative journey with the desire for outward, activist engagement in prophetic witness around burning issues of the day.

My hope to be part of the intentional Christian community that Jim and his friends would establish in D.C. was strong, even intense. But Karin felt little response. She sensed a "missionary zeal" in it that would include rigidity and legalism. Further, she was comfortable with the nurture she was experiencing in Church of the Saviour. This became one of the first major tests of our new marriage.

On a July day almost a year after we were married, we talked with Father Stephen at Berryville. He stressed that, ultimately, the point was not what we did, but rather, out of what did our actions come forth? He wanted to know if our desires or wishes were rooted in our internal spiritual centers. It was one of those helpful reminders.

We realized that whatever else might happen, we were called to being in community and mission together. If that mutuality wasn't present, then we could not embrace that call. Moreover, the intensity of change and challenge for Karin, transitioning from Japan into our new life together, in a new place, with new friends, was taking an emotional toll. We didn't have clarity, and this was no time to join a new experiment in Christian community. We welcomed the group when they arrived from Chicago in September 1975, but we remained in our apartment and the Church of the Saviour's mission group for the next year.

My vocational journey, however, continued to seek new directions. That year I was working on Senator Hatfield's forthcoming book, *Between a Rock and a Hard Place.* This was a summation of Hatfield's views, and his experiences of how his faith related to the political issues and challenges he faced. I had been doing the writing for the book, sitting with the senator to discuss ideas and then producing a draft. In many ways, it felt like the last major contribution I could make, working with him to produce something that could be genuinely helpful to a growing number of Christians struggling to connect their faith in Christ to political, economic, and social issues. Hatfield was serving as a role model for many, especially younger evangelicals.

Yet, I yearned to write in my own voice. Jim wanted me to be part of the new magazine, and Karin knew such a move was important for my future. But *Sojourners* was just a start-up idea, with very little money. Moreover, their salary structure would be based on alternative, simple lifestyles. This was downward mobility.

I agreed with Hatfield's office to work half time with him and half time with *Sojourners,* as a beginning experiment. But this was not to be understood as a step toward joining the community. I was relinquishing that agenda.

My position was associate editor. Russ Reid, whose advertising agency rapidly multiplied the constituency of World Vision, advised us on how to build our circulation. (His mother had been a friend of my mom's at South Park Church.) We were learning how to develop a sustainable magazine. But more than that, the magazine was growing as the voice of a movement.

Influenced by the theology of Yoder, Ellul, and others, while still clinging to the insights from my contemplative journey, I struggled to articulate how I saw my call to Sojourners. I wanted to balance words of judgment and prophetic critique, which seemed to be our strength, with the message of God's love. I wrote in my journal on February 3, 1976:

> Am I willing to take on the future of Sojourners? To give myself to it?
>
> How does the truth of God's judgment and God's love come together in one whole? They must be integrated together. In community they are. That is the context — love for one another — out of which mission and prophetic witness must emerge. . . .
>
> So it is that Christ calls us forth into a new community. He calls forth a new people, who together are set free from the old.
>
> And thus, he calls those structures, those values, those ways into judgment which dominate our present order so that his love can more fully reign over all.
>
> We must be Sojourners for the sake of love; we love the world in the same way as Christ did. . . .
>
> What, then, is God's word to institutions? To governments? To structures? It is that they are part of a world loved by God, but a world fallen, in bondage. They must be called to truer manifestations of God's justice and love. They always will be; ours is not the task to justify them in their paradoxical, compromised situation, but to call them, and their people, to repentance.
>
> Does that mean reform?

Yes and No.

"Yes" in the sense that the agenda is never completed. There must always be greater change.

But "No" in the sense that the point is in the proclamation of the Kingdom of God. This Kingdom draws all else to it like a magnet — and then it undermines all that is. It is a subversive force, in the best sense. It speaks from a framework, from a vision, beyond the parameters of the present institutions, and it always does. . . . Its effort, in the end, it is catalytically revolutionary.

Out of this vision, I can give myself; I can place myself into the full thrust of the magazine. . . . I believe God is beckoning me to it.

Being fully a part of the magazine's ministry was clear. But being fully a part of the Sojourners community was not.

We began worshiping and relating to the community. However, Karin's discomfort was deep and abiding. The community was forming itself around strong concepts of mutual submission, one to another, and to the whole. They belonged to one another, and all major decisions, vocational aspirations, gifts, skills, and money were submitted to the authority of the community and its leadership. Committed to simple living, the community would place financial resources in a common pot, as in Acts. The new community, intending to live as Christ's body, would take this shape, and serve as a defining center of existence, over against the cultural and social pressures of society.

Karin's journey was moving in the opposite direction. She was seeking to define for herself those directions and paths that were truest for her, rather than relying on external authoritarian voices — either in her past or in her present — to make those decisions for her. She understood this as moving from an "infantile" relationship with God to an "adult" relationship.

Sojourners community didn't feel like a safe and nurturing place for her, despite her affection for many of its members. Those at Church of the Saviour were older in years and wiser in experience. They appreciated the complexity, and often the shattering turmoil, that could accompany one's inward spiritual journey, and trusted the Spirit's work within an individual's process.

Our conflict about being part of Sojourners continued and was often painful. Karin understood my call to the Sojourners community even though she was not called. And I knew my primary call was to Karin. But working through the depths of these feelings was difficult, resulting in countless conversations, counseling, probing self-examination, and intense prayer. Karin found it hard to trust the community's confrontational and sometimes self-righteous outlook on those who did not understand the gospel's mandate in the same way. This meant that my attachment to the community was continually challenged.

Part of the conflict was that for me, this was no mere choice between preferring different church groups and seeking a reasonable compromise. I had come to understand my faithfulness to the gospel as living with an intentionally committed Christian community like Sojourners. In retrospect, that seems so theologically and ideologically exaggerated, and so harmful. But the whole climate around Sojourners in its early days — both the magazine and the community — was imbued with the call to follow biblical imperatives. And I was convinced this was right.

Any emerging, renewal community is founded necessarily on that kind of theological and spiritual certitude. Nuanced convictions never start a movement or establish an intentional Christian community. Yet, I also knew that a radically committed group, seeking to live faithfully as Christ's body, was not the only source of truth and guidance.

I returned to Berryville for retreat, and an intense time of reflection, journaling, and prayer helped clarify how to discern call.

I understood marriage as a sacrament: a special means of grace calling for nurture and a unique type of givenness to each other. It is a calling of God.

But we are also called to Christ's body. How do I discern the two calls?

God's will for my life — which is the only true "freedom" — will be discerned through being deeply open to hear his voice in solitude, in marriage, and in community — in each of these contexts to be listening together, mutually, for God's word — and moreover, to be fully living in my love for Christ, for his body, and for Karin.

The depth and roots of our love, which first became unlocked for me through my contemplative journey at Berryville, provided the only certain foundation to which I could return. The recovery of God's love invading my life and the rediscovery of my love for Karin were inextricably linked. That provided an unshakable trust and faith in our relationship, even in the midst of perplexing and painful conflict. What drew us together kept us together.

We lived in this ambiguity toward the community while my work with the magazine thrived. In 1976, an article by Jim and me entitled "Plan to Save America" exposed the right-wing political involvement of some evangelical leaders long before the "Religious Right" emerged. The piece helped Sojourners gain greater visibility. We interviewed Dorothy Day and Dom Helder Camara. Billy Graham talked to us about his opposition to the nuclear arms race. Henri Nouwen began contributing. We were becoming a major, recognized voice in the Christian world and beyond on issues of justice, peace, and the call to follow the radically biblical message of the gospel.

In September of 1977, Karin and I went camping in the mountains for a time of discernment over a possible move. The community had relocated to the neighborhood just off the "Fourteenth Street corridor," the area that had been devastated by riots after the assassination of Martin Luther King Jr. They were living in three different homes within a block of one another. Another nearby home was for sale on Thirteenth Street, and we were considering buying it.

For Karin, Sojourners community still felt like "a glove that didn't fit." But we decided to purchase the home to be in the neighborhood, and then test once and for all whether life with them would work or not. We weren't pooling our money with the others, and the home would be ours. But we would worship together and be in a "household" group. We decided to move ahead.

Except for some occasional consulting, my work with Senator Hatfield was now over, and I took the bus every morning down Fourteenth Street to the magazine's offices on Vermont Avenue. Once a week Karin would cook lunch for the staff — we all took turns — and I'd carry a large soup pot full of a dish from the *More with Less Cookbook*, hoping it wouldn't spill.

Karin says the most "downward mobility" we ever achieved was learning to eat lentils and chickpeas. But bus rides through D.C.'s inner city carrying a soup pot felt like a long way from the halls of the U.S. Senate.

Our relationships with Church of the Saviour friends remained. At a dinner in her apartment, Elizabeth O'Connor introduced Karin and me to Dr. Janelle Goetcheus. She and her husband Alan had planned on being medical missionaries to Pakistan, but visa arrangements couldn't be made. So now she was wondering how to use her medical skills in mission in D.C.

Karin had finished her degree at Wesley Seminary, writing her thesis on Lutheran pastor Granger Westberg and his pioneering work in establishing holistic health centers in churches. She and Janelle began dreaming about a holistic health center, combining medical care and counseling, in the Adams Morgan neighborhood of D.C., where the Church of the Saviour's Potter's House and other ministries were located.

Dreams became reality as Columbia Road Health Services was founded. It became another of several remarkable ministries spawned by the Church of the Saviour, and Karin had a place to offer her gifts and passion. Today it serves five thousand patients a year with medical staff, social service workers, and mental health counselors.

It seemed that we were finally arriving at a comfortable place together for our life and ministry. But now I began to experience misgivings, centered on my relationship with Jim. He had become my closest friend, and we worked hard together on the magazine. But in the end, it was his vision, and ultimately he gave the direction. Our relationship, of course, was complicated by the struggle Karin and I had been experiencing with the community. But more than that, I began to feel that I would be in his shadow as the magazine grew in size and influence.

My journal was full of worries about whether I just wanted attention, recognition, and a powerful position. Couldn't I be freer from my ego's need for public affirmation? Shouldn't I simply serve the mission of the magazine and not worry about whether Jim became its sole public face, and simply support him and his extraordinary gifts?

I had left Senator Hatfield, in part, because I wanted to be my own person and seek ways to express my own voice and leadership. But at times I felt like I was moving back to a similar place. Jim was enormously gifted with creative vision, charismatic influence, and brilliant expression. I admired him deeply, but I also began to doubt that our work on the magazine would be the kind of true partnership we had imagined.

But there was more rooted in my own needs and frailties. On August 26, 1979, I wrote:

> The quest for "being somebody" must not be followed. Rather, the quest to discover my hidden self — my true self which is bound up, and intertwined, with Christ — this is the quest which beckons me to follow. Where it will lead I do not know. But this is work of spiritual clarification and I believe this is the source of much of my dis-ease, depression, and estrangement. . . .
>
> I do not feel deeply nurtured and supported in my search for my true identity, hidden in Christ. . . . What I sense when I come here (Berryville) — the call to abandonment before Christ, defining my fidelity to Him — seems not be to nurtured in the depth or way I yearn for within the community. The focus there seems more on how we relate to the community, and to each other, almost exclusively. I feel the difference when I am here, and miss deeply this inner calling.

Further, despite all my genuine efforts at relinquishment and my commitments to live in relationships of mutual submission, whether in my marriage or in my work with Jim and others, I was coming to see my brokenness more clearly.

> November 1, 1979
> I have a will, quiet, which can yet be like steel.
> And I defend myself as righteous.
> I have a need to be seen as faultless, as the good one. Like my shit doesn't smell.
> It is a contrite heart, and a broken spirit, which God now wants to give me. The wax must be soft.

When speaking invitations came, we'd meet as a staff and divide them. When an invitation came from a student ministry retreat and a church in Montana, I volunteered. I'd never been there. The retreat was in the mountains; what I most remember is that the campus minister, Gayle Sandholm, took me to a stream, and I caught a trout. This all was a long way from Thirteenth Street in the District of Columbia.

We then went to Missoula where I was to speak on the book of Revelation to the folks at Community Covenant Church. The congregation was part of the Evangelical Covenant Church. But some years before it had undergone a charismatic renewal and reached out to students at the University of Montana and others in Missoula's thriving counterculture. Dramatic conversions had occurred, and the congregation itself was radically changed.

They had numerous ministries in the community, a strong worship life, and groups — they called them "Acts groups" — based on strong accountability and sharing. Deeply influenced by the message of *Sojourners,* they were part of an informal network of church communities seeking new ways of radical discipleship.

But they also seemed full of grace and joy. I went to the home of Pastor Dan Simmons and his wife Leola, which was on the side of a hill overlooking the Missoula Valley. Their hospitality was overwhelming. We sat on the deck with hors d'oeuvres as dusk came and the valley began to sparkle with the lights of Missoula. I asked to use the phone, and called Karin. "You won't believe this," I reported. "You've got to come here."

The next summer, in 1979, I returned with Karin for a vacation, and then to participate in a pastors retreat. When we arrived, they lent us a car packed with food and sent us alone to a cabin by a lake in the Seeley-Swan Valley. We drove from there to Glacier National Park, listening to a tape of Rachmaninoff's Second Symphony. We fell in love with the place, and with the people extending their hospitality.

Karin and I were also struggling with whether or not to have children, and if so, when. We seemed to trade convictions, never both agreeing at the same time to start a family. What we didn't want to admit was our deep hesitation about starting a family, and raising kids, in the inner city where we lived. That seemed like a betrayal of our idealistic commitments. But it was true.

All this converged. That fall Jim and I tried to work through our relationship, both of us with the best intentions and love for each other, and both of us with wounds that got in the way. We had process, prayer, and difficult conversations with those in the community. In November Karin and I flew to Missoula to explore moving there. We drove down to Sleeping Child Hot Springs in the Bitterroot Valley. The hot water of the outdoor pool amidst snow-dusted ponderosa pines, reminiscent of hot springs in Japan, helped finalize our decision to move to Missoula.

I wanted to think of this as a sabbatical. By that time I had spent twelve intense years in D.C., and I was getting burned out. I knew beyond any doubt I was spiritually depleted; the well was running dry. So we'd rest, regroup, and see what God had in store. Maybe we'd be there for a year and then come back. The folks at Community Covenant were ready to welcome us.

But Jim and others felt more like this was a desertion. He earnestly believed we were called to lead this emerging magazine and ministry together. Our experience and gifts complemented each other. I was an essential part, and now I was walking away, betraying the vision and relationship we had shared. He couldn't understand why.

Yet I knew this was the right step — right for me, for Karin, and for our marriage. But the pain was terrible. Jim had been my best friend, but now the relationship was ruptured, seemingly beyond repair, and he felt the same way.

We sold our home on Thirteenth Street to the community, shipped our possessions, and began driving in December of 1979 to Missoula in a 1969 Ford, with a blue trailer and the words "Missoula or Bust" painted on the back. We had enough money to live on for three months.

I had left the Senate office four years earlier for an unknown magazine. Now, as the magazine was succeeding, I was leaving for a nearly unknown town, with no job. My old Capitol Hill associates were mystified. Our Church of the Saviour friends were understanding, but sad. Our Sojourners friends were regretful and perplexed, and some were angry. But Karin and I, beneath the pain of departure, were content, expectant, and even happy.

Missoula or Bust

I BOUGHT A Woolrich red wool coat with a black stripe, like a Hudson's Bay blanket; Tony Lama cowboy boots; and a brown Resistol cowboy hat. People said I looked like the Marlboro Man. I was loving Montana.

Somehow, though we were without jobs, our realtor, Sandi Tarr, had gotten us a mortgage on a tiny green and white house, with a white picket fence, near the railroad yard. We wanted a dog, and Sandi had one waiting for us when we arrived.

Like many houses in Missoula, it had a wood stove for heat as well as a furnace. Karin and I would sit by the stove, periodically adding a log, and read. I had decided to tackle Karl Barth's commentary on Romans. We were seeking "shelter" — a safe and secure place of rest. So that's what we named our dog.

The Good Food Store was a small storefront in downtown Missoula selling organic and bulk foods. It was owned and operated by Community Covenant Church, which had welcomed us to Missoula, promising to give us shelter. How the church came to own the store was instructive. The store was started by Marcia Herrin, with the help of her sister, Carol King. It fit right in with the university crowd and with Missoula's countercultural environment in the 1970s.

However, Marcia and Carol were among those touched by the ministry of Community Covenant Church at that time. They became Christians and were part of the church's revival and search to be an authentic,

New Testament–like, Christian community. Reading in Acts about the believers giving all their possessions to the apostles, they essentially gave the Good Food Store to Community Covenant Church.

So the store became one of the church's ministries, along with Emmaus Road Restaurant, a group home for mentally disabled young adult men, and other creative outreach efforts. The Good Food Store often employed those in Community Covenant Church who needed work. I qualified and was hired.

It was humbling. My dad called one day and said, "So are you still selling bread?" He liked telling others about my work with a U.S. senator. Now he didn't know what to say. But it was good work, shared with others from the church. Further, our friends at Community Covenant were doing all they could to extend hospitality, make us feel welcomed, and provide shelter.

Karin's work with holistic health care and healing ministries yielded new connections that remained with us in Missoula. When we were still in D.C., she had been contacted by Herb Muenstermann, who worked with the U.S. support board for the Christian Medical College and Hospital (CMC&H) in Vellore, India. This institution, begun by a Reformed Church in America (RCA) missionary, Dr. Ida S. Scudder, had become a leading medical center in India, with an intentional, Christian identity and character.

The hospital's leadership and staff believed strongly in "holistic" models that sought to integrate the healing ministry of the church with modern medical practice. Herb Muenstermann got its chaplain, Rev. A. C. Oomen, in touch with Karin, and that began a nearly ten-year relationship between us and this amazing center in Vellore, India.

Shortly after we arrived in Missoula, we were on a plane for Calcutta and then Madras to attend an international conference on the church's healing ministry, hosted by Vellore CMC&H. Karin became deeply impressed by Vellore's model of an integrated healing ministry, and I took a particular interest in their work in rural development and community health. A consulting relationship with the U.S. board, including more trips to India, continued for several years from that time on.

In Missoula we were patching sources of income together while resting in our new life and church community. Its worship life was rich; services blended "renewal" music from sources like Betty Pulkingham and the Community of Celebration with communion, or the Eucharist, each Sunday, followed by prayer for healing. Our "Acts group" was a wellspring of personal sharing and mutual support.

We had no communication with Jim Wallis or the Sojourners community, and the wound was festering. One day, at the end of a worship service, still gripped with the pain of those broken relationships, we asked for prayers for healing. Our closest friends, Tom King and Sharon Murfin, urged us to go back to D.C. to seek reconciliation. We did so. Meeting with Jim, and Bob and Jackie Sabath, in the basement apartment of the home on Thirteenth Street that we had previously owned, we each confessed those feelings and actions that had broken our relationships, with both Jim and the wider community. Forgiveness and reconciliation flowed naturally. It was a breakthrough of grace and healing.

Today, Jim and I remain the closest of friends. I served as his board chair for a decade, and we've worked very closely on numerous political and religious initiatives. But it would have been difficult for Karin and me to find the next steps in our ministry without the healing of those past wounds, and I expect Jim would say much the same. In my experience, deep wounds and unreconciled relationships have a paralyzing effect not only on those directly involved, but also on the wider church or Christian community in which they occur. There is sound reason why Jesus instructed his followers to be reconciled with one another before they worshiped God.

Missoula and Community Covenant Church were serving as a place of healing, renewal, and regeneration for us. Our marriage, begun out of such a dramatic and resonate discovery of love and spiritual reality, had faced difficult stresses and tests in our years in D.C. The foundation was secure, but now we could grow together in a place and a Christian community we each loved.

Community Covenant was inspired by the same vision of intentional Christian community that was motivating Sojourners and other similar groups. But there were differences. First, Community Covenant was an existing congregation that was renewing itself; it was not an entirely new group. Second, a spirit of hospitality and grace seemed to reside in its DNA. And third, it was situated in the Missoula Valley of western

Montana rather than at Thirteenth and Euclid in Washington, D.C. It feels apologetic to say that this location made such a difference for us, but it would be foolish to pretend that it didn't.

Upon moving to Missoula, we decided to hyphenate our last name to Granberg-Michaelson. In 1975, Karin and I were involved in the national conference of the Evangelical Women's Caucus (EWC), which was born from the Chicago Declaration on Evangelical Social Concerns two years earlier. We both became committed to "Christian feminism" as we explored the understanding of several biblical passages on marriage as well as male-female roles and relationships. Karin's ongoing involvement with the EWC continued that dialogue with others on the same journey.

Our conviction was, and is, that the overarching biblical model of marriage is that of mutual submission, one to the other, rather than various understandings of "headship" present in many conservative evangelical churches. When biblical passages equate the marriage relationship with Christ and the church, the conclusion is that a totally sacrificial outpouring of love, one for the other, is required.

But what should that mean for our name? Some of our friends, out of their convictions that a wife's last name should not simply be replaced by the husband's, had kept their original last names after being married. However, we felt our last name should reflect our union. Karin didn't want to just go back to being Karin Granberg. So we decided that both of us should go by a last name that reflected two of us linked together equally as one, and hyphenating our two last names together did so. Moving to a brand-new place was the time to do this.

I can't begin to recount the hassles this has caused for airlines and credit card companies, and for us when we've made reservations or purchases over the phone. On one occasion an airline reservation agent was having a terrible time printing out my ticket. He finally said to me, "I'm getting a message saying 'too many people.'" Another time, a perplexed United Airlines ticket agent in Newark asked me why my name was hyphenated. When I explained to her the truth, she said she had never heard of that, and liked it so much that she upgraded me to first class. In the long run, we've been comfortable with this cumbersome last name, for it's been a small way of stating what we believe.

Far more was happening between us in Missoula than a newly hyphenated last name, however. Our love was thriving, and now we felt ready to make a decision about children. We prayed about it, and I shall never forget Karin's prayer. It was a pure prayer of the heart. She prayed that God's love would be the source of our love, that it would be what enabled us to love each other and to love our child.

I felt deeply that our life together was a life to be shared, to be given, to be extended, and to be passed on. There is a special sense of wonder about this — the passing on of our life together.

Our son was born in Missoula Community Hospital in September 1981. We named him Jon Krister. We had in mind the Fourth Gospel, plus a favorite theologian, Krister Stendahl. But with our decision to hyphenate, he ended up with enough names to start his own law firm. Today, he goes by "J.K." He became our focus for much of the new life that was beginning to break forth for us in Missoula.

For a dozen years I had thought about and worked with how the gospel related to the issues of war and peace, nationalism, world hunger, and other issues of justice. I had barely thought about the environment. The modern environmental movement, as an organized grassroots effort, began with Earth Day in April 1970, spearheaded by Senator Gaylord Nelson. Totally absorbed by the antiwar efforts at the time, I took little notice. Further, Earth Day and the movement it catalyzed had no visible presence to or involvement from the church.

A decade later, environmental concerns were prominent in Missoula. The University of Montana had a strong environmental studies program, and stories about local environmental issues would make the front page of the city's daily paper, the *Missoulian*. For some, care for the earth and alternative, ecologically sensitive lifestyles were like a religion. I started to pay attention.

Perhaps providentially, I was invited to a conference hosted by Cal DeWitt and the AuSable Trails Environmental Institute in Michigan. Cal was like a prophet crying in an evangelical wilderness. The AuSable Institute, directed by Cal, was committed to doing environmental education from a Christian perspective. The conference gathered various professors of the natural sciences from mostly evangelical colleges who shared deep concerns about threats to the environment.

I was stunned. For four days I listened to assessments of ecological threats that were far graver and more serious than I had ever imagined. Moreover, apart from lonely voices like those at the conference, the Christian community seemed deaf and dumb when it came to threats to the environment. Furthermore, there seemed to be a vacuum of theological reflection and biblical study around these concerns. It was as if God's gift of the creation had been dropped from theological consideration in favor of a focus on God's mighty acts in history, and the liberating pathways this suggested.

Back in Missoula, I learned that most environmental activists and writers directly blamed Christianity for the environmental crisis and wanton destruction of the earth. The biblical instruction to "subdue the earth" reinforced a cultural mind-set that led to ecological destruction. A famous article by Lynn White Jr., "The Historical Roots of Our Ecological Crisis," which made this argument, had become gospel for many environmentalists, and the environmental movement at that time, unlike the civil rights movement or the antiwar movement, seemed entirely secular.

Those experiences started me on a new path reflecting, reading, and writing about how Christian faith regards the earth, and what biblical passages actually do teach about God's creation and humanity's relationship to it. A whole new world of theological exploration and practical activism around ecological concerns opened up to me. In many ways, this was simply a result of moving from Thirteenth Street in D.C. to the Missoula Valley in Montana. We used to say at Sojourners that your theology is shaped by what you see when you wake up in the morning, meaning that living in a poor neighborhood rather than a more wealthy community affects one's theology. This principle was proving true for me in a whole different setting.

Vocationally, I wondered now where all this was leading. Politics was still in my blood. I began to wonder if I should run for the Montana House of Representatives. A new friend, Dan Kemmis, had served as speaker of that body, and he told me what it was like to live in Helena, the state capital, when the state legislature was in session, and commute back to Missoula on weekends.

But something deeper was at stake. Was God calling me to work directly in political structures, as I had done in D.C.? Or was I being called to give my life more fully to the church? Ever since Church of the Saviour and Sojourners, I had a feeling of wanting to have a pastoral role in helping to shape and guide a Christian community. Should I work for the changes I wanted to see in society through politics, or through the life of the church? Both were valid paths. But where was I called?

The Christhaven Retreat Center was a converted motel not far from Anaconda, Montana, about two hours from Missoula; it was directed by a Catholic priest. It had become a periodic destination. When I had gone there in February 1981, Karin was pregnant. Thoughts of fatherhood, vocation, politics, and pastoring were swirling within, and needed some inner clarity.

Several priorities seemed to come clear during long morning walks across the fields, importantly about politics and pastoring. It seemed right to me to put my primary energy on the theological and reflective aspects of a theology of creation, rather than on the political side. First, I was not confident that I was free from my ego regarding the political, and second, focusing on the biblical side, the theological, seemed the place to begin any venture. I wanted to read, reflect, and write on several topics, including the land, farming, Wendell Berry, Joseph Sittler, Jeremy Rifkin's ideas, Eastern Orthodoxy, etc.

Those directions continued to be affirmed in the following months. I was moving away from politics and toward the theological work that was now captivating me. And thus I wanted to invest myself vocationally in the life and witness of the church. The call to writing focused on trying to do a book. Western Theological Seminary in Holland, Michigan, one of two seminaries of the RCA, had a "scholar in residence" program, and Karin's parents lived in Holland. With our young son, Jon Krister, we went there for six months so I could study and write. Roy Carlisle from Harper and Row, a friend and editor for Jim Wallis, gave me a contract for the book. *A Worldly Spirituality: The Call to Take Care of the Earth* was published in 1984.

While at Western Seminary, however, I confronted another major life decision. If in fact I was being beckoned to work with and through the church, didn't that mean I should seek ordination? That seemed a natural destination of my journey.

I sat down with Dr. Robert Coughenour, dean of the seminary, and he worked out what course work would be required, taking into account my one year at Princeton and subsequent work and writing. He was generous. Then I met with the Holland Classis — a local group of pastors and elders in the RCA's polity responsible for ordination — and came under their "care," meaning I was on the path toward ordination.

The process was compressed. Back in Missoula, our second child was born, our daughter Karis. Her name is the Greek word for grace, and in countless ways she lives according to that truth. Our family returned to Holland in the spring of 1984, when I finished required courses. The examinations by the classis, the local ruling body of the church, which normally were spread over three years, had to be taken in one day.

Tim Brown, current president of Western Seminary, was one of my examiners. The RCA at that time had three confessions — the Belgic Confession, the Canons of Dort, and the Heidelberg Catechism — that are foundational for us. Each minister of Word and sacrament has to ascribe to the truthfulness of these confessions.

So Tim said, "Wes, do you have any reservations about any points in our three confessions?"

"Well, I don't believe in drowning Anabaptists," I replied, tongue in cheek. Our confessions don't actually say that, of course, but the Belgic Confession, written in 1561, is pretty hard on Anabaptists. It "detests" their error in allowing rebaptism (a later translation in 1988 softened that language to "regret") and "denounces" them, right alongside the "anarchists," for rejecting civil authorities and "introducing the common ownership of goods."

In truth, the history of Reformed and Lutheran actions toward the Anabaptists is grim. The Anabaptists were persecuted and, at times, even drowned because they wanted another baptism besides infant baptism. These actions were so terrible that in 2010, more than four centuries later, the Lutheran World Federation formally issued an apology for their sins to the Mennonite World Conference. The Reformed community should follow suit.

My problem was that, from my days at Sojourners, I knew modern-day Anabaptists and neither detested them nor felt like denouncing them. In fact, theologian John Howard Yoder influenced me profoundly, and I admired the sacrificial service around the world of groups like the

Mennonite Central Committee. So my response to Tim was more than jest, and I explained my reservations. On the central issue of covenant and the baptism of children, however, I had become thoroughly Reformed.

The classis approved me with affirmation that I remember to this day. On June 10, 1984, at Third Reformed Church in Holland, Michigan, I was ordained as a minister of Word and sacrament in the Reformed Church in America, called to a "specialized ministry" in Missoula, Montana.

Karin's work was also blossoming. Her first book, *In the Land of the Living: Health Care and the Church* (Zondervan), was published in the same year. Missoula was proving to be a fruitful home, as we now had started our family and were finding new and clarifying directions in our ministries.

Wanting to put roots down more deeply, and sensing an abiding call to work further within the Christian community on the biblical call to care for the creation, we dreamed of beginning an institute that would be the center for this work, as well as providing an expression for the church's healing ministry.

The next year, the New Creation Institute (NCI) was born and organized as a 501(c)3 nonprofit. This provided a base for my ongoing speaking, writing, and organizing around environmental issues within the Christian community. Further, we sponsored a counseling center where Karin and other colleagues carried out this local ministry. We dreamed of a retreat center in the Bitterroot Valley south of Missoula, and commissioned architectural drawings of facilities utilizing alternative energy that would be a place of healing and renewal.

Those dreams, connecting the wonder and gift of creation to the contemplative journey of prayer, healing, and renewal, didn't just begin in Missoula but had their roots in my personal spiritual renewal. The images of past moments of oneness with God's love are linked to my memories of places in creation — the holly tree behind my D.C. apartment, the trees and sky there, the brook at Berryville, the pond with the ducks, the river and the mist at Berryville, the fields at Dayspring, the log across the Thomas Merton pond. These are holy places to me.

Our relationship with Community Covenant also deepened. Its senior pastor, Dan Simmons, who was so instrumental in welcoming and accompanying us, decided to move to Oregon. Karin and I were invited into a new pastoral team, led by our close friend Tom King, and including two others (Sharon Murfin and Andy Elsen). Tom was the full-time, paid lead pastor, but the rest of us participated in preaching, worship leadership, and pastoral care.

For a while it seemed like life and ministry had converged in fruitful and fulfilling ways. We loved the church, and NCI held promise as I worked hard to raise funds and continued my speaking and writing. Our work with the Vellore Board continued, providing connections in the global church for expanding NCI's ministry, including a consultation on "Earthkeeping" in India. I edited a book, *Tending the Garden,* that grew out of another conference held at the AuSable Institute, and then worked on a third, *Ecology and Life.* But the pressure of building a sustainable financial base for NCI was continual, and difficult.

But, by 1987, serious fissures and divisions had began to develop within Community Covenant Church. Explanations of what happens when a church community enters a conflict are always shaped by the views and biases of the one doing the explaining. For me, and for Karin, it seemed clear that a group in the church were moving toward a conservative fundamentalism. They had fears of and objections to "feminist" views that they ascribed to Karin and to Sharon Murfin, the other woman on the pastoral team. Further, the connections to other intentional Christian communities in a network that had originated from Sojourners were deeply suspect for assumed political and theological views.

As always, deeper dynamics were involved. For almost twenty years, Dan Simmons had been the pastor and charismatic leader. Many in the church had been converted through the ministry he had facilitated. His presence, in some ways, was like that of a parent. Differences in the community were manageable because everyone respected and trusted Dan, and his pastoral presence held the community together. When he left, inherent tensions began to surface.

We convened a group, the Council of Reconciliation and Mission, seeking to engage the community in honest dialogue. But the fissures were deep, and some of the most conservative members began leaving.

By 1987 Community Covenant, which had become for Karin and me such a treasured place, was beginning to feel threatened and fragile.

In the fall of that year a letter arrived from Preman Niles, director of the Justice, Peace, and Integrity of Creation program at the World Council of Churches (WCC) in Geneva, Switzerland. He was inviting me to an international consultation entitled "Integrity of Creation" in Granvolen, Norway, in February 1988.

About a year earlier on a trip to Vellore, India, Karin and I stopped in Geneva to visit the WCC. Jean Stromberg, the executive assistant to Emilio Castro, the WCC general secretary, was a Wheaton College grad and had some family connections to South Park Church, where I grew up. We met with her and a few other WCC staff. It seemed like a visionary and almost magical place, trying to draw the churches of the world into fellowship and unity and to address critical global issues.

But now, unexpectedly, this invitation had arrived to take part in this WCC consultation. I suppose it felt as if I had been playing ball faithfully in the minor leagues for a few years out in Missoula. But now, I got a call to try out in the big leagues. I wondered what it meant, and how I would do.

An Ecumenical Ski Jump

$\mathbf{A}$RRIVING IN Granvolen, about an hour north of Oslo, I was full of nervous anticipation. The sports metaphor in my mind was the ski jump at the Olympics, where the Norwegians were famous competitors. The Granvolen event in many ways was the climax of my move to Missoula eight years earlier, and my commitment to the issues of a theology of creation. I thought about soaring like Erik Johnsen, the Norwegian ski jumper.

About fifty people from around the world had been called to this consultation. The World Council of Churches (WCC), at its Vancouver Assembly in 1983, had adopted a commitment to a "conciliar process on justice, peace, and the integrity of creation." While the WCC had done extensive work on the issues of peace and justice, the integrity of creation was new. People weren't even sure what it meant. So the consultation in Norway had the goal of producing a report that would focus the ecumenical understanding of the "integrity of creation."

The prime minister of Norway, Gro Brundtland, was on hand for the opening worship service. The service was dry — the liturgy seemed to have no life — and the prime minister's speech was good, but the questions afterward were better. The informality of it all was striking — here was the prime minister of Norway traveling to an isolated village for a church event.

The most moving part of the proceedings was the presentation by

Aruna Gnanadason of India and Anna Karin Hammar from the WCC women's desk. Never have I heard a more compelling presentation of women's perspectives as they influence the integrity of creation issues. Likewise, their style was participatory and drew from shared experience and insight, rather than from proposition.

I was learning the method of WCC consultations. Representatives of different constituencies or program areas gave presentations, such as youth, faith and order, indigenous peoples, women, church and society, and the Orthodox. Then a consensus document on the integrity of creation was framed whose wording all could agree to.

A persistent tension developed between those doing theology from the "bottom up," rooted in experience and struggle, and those doing theology from the "top down," starting with the history of the church's theological reflection, the creeds, and biblical theology. The issue is central. The intense conflict between the feminists and the Orthodox is an example of the difference in theological method.

Even though we had met only briefly once before, Preman Niles asked me to help organize the framework for the report, including how to deal with these two different theological approaches, and wanted Aruna and me to draft the final report.

We worked easily together through the afternoon. And then I drafted language, in about forty-five minutes, to bridge the two approaches. I remembered the ski jumper. And when the drafting committee reconvened, Stanley Harakas, on behalf of the Orthodox, pronounced that it was "fair." Aruna thought it was wonderful.

With the final report adopted by the consultation, we went to our closing worship, and Preman said to me, "You really came through for me, man, and did just what I wanted." It was stunning, because coming to the consultation, I wasn't aware of any expectations he had for me.

That evening Aruna and Anna Karin sought me out and strongly encouraged me to apply to be director of Church and Society at the WCC, whose work would focus on issues relating to the integrity of creation. They even referred to the WCC's "structural bias against North American white males" and thought it could be overcome. But as good feminists, they also wondered what Karin could do in Geneva, and tried to imagine possibilities.

Flying home, I was awestruck by how the experience in Norway had far exceeded any of my expectations. I felt completely at home within this ecumenical environment, listening and summarizing different points of view, identifying key questions, helping to discover common ground, and expressing this in writing. And now a completely new possible option had emerged — an opening for a senior staff position in my area of interest at the WCC.

Karin and I had already been thinking about options for the future, and they centered on the Reformed Church in America (RCA), and Western Seminary in Holland, Michigan, in particular. Western's president, Marv Hoff, had proposed moving the New Creation Institute's work there in a partnership with Western, and my serving as an adjunct faculty member in ethics. Marv was enthusiastic, and in the spring he invited us out for discussions and to meet with the faculty. But in May, Marv called apologetically to say the whole proposal had fallen through, apparently because of opposition from some faculty members.

Gene Heideman, the executive in charge of programs for the RCA, had also been in touch with me. Their staff position for social witness was open, and Gene wanted me to take it. I asked where the office would be. Gene said South Holland, Illinois. The RCA had a building there that looked like an old shoebox stuck next to the expressway south of Chicago.

South Holland's churches, at that time, were among the most conservative in the denomination. They were more influenced by Moody Bible Institute's radio station, WMBI — a station I had been weaned on as a kid listening to *Aunt Theresa's Story Time for Boys and Girls* — than by their membership in the RCA. Trying to give this a chance, Karin and I drove through the community of South Holland during a trip to Chicago. We couldn't imagine ourselves fitting comfortably into the community or its churches, and told Gene.

Heideman then opened the option of working out of the RCA's New York office, which would mean probably living in New Jersey. If we had to leave Missoula, our first choice was to locate in Michigan because Karin's family was there and my family was only three hours away in Chicago. But Heideman said there was no space in the RCA's office in Grand Rapids, so that option was not on the table. We remained in conversation, but this whole exploration didn't seem to be working well.

Then I received a call asking me to come to Geneva and be interviewed as one of three final candidates for the Church and Society position. On a beautiful June morning, I was sipping coffee and eating a fresh croissant at the Hotel Suisse, right across from the train station in Geneva, and pondering my forthcoming interview that day. Up early because of jet lag, I had centered myself deeply in prayer.

Two convictions registered with me. First, it was likely that one or both of the other candidates were from the global south, and it did seem like a matter of fairness for them to be given preference. The longtime director of Church and Society had been an American, Paul Albrecht, and he was followed briefly by David Gosling from England. Second, this couldn't just be my decision in any event; it had to be Karin's as well; we also had to consider our two young children, J.K. and Karis, who were six and four.

The archbishop of York from the Church of England, Rev. John Habgood, chaired the interviewing committee and also headed the board overseeing Church and Society's work. The conversation flowed freely, and toward the end I mentioned my understanding about the need for those from non-American and non-European backgrounds to have leadership in this work. The committee then told me the other two candidates were Europeans. Moreover, Archbishop Habgood announced that all the candidates and the committee would have lunch together shortly — one of the more bizarre features of this interviewing process.

Leaving Geneva, I was told that the committee would make its recommendation to the general secretary, Emilio Castro, who would finalize the choice in the next couple of weeks. But our family had a long-planned vacation to Yellowstone Park at that time. They told me simply to phone Geneva.

Our rustic cabin in Yellowstone, of course, had no phone. So I went to a pay phone near the viewing area for Old Faithful and placed a call to the WCC's personnel office in Geneva. A secretary answered and cheerily said, "Oh, yes, Emilio has selected you."

At first, Karin and I were exhilarated. But then we were anxious, and even bewildered. What would this mean for Karin? And for the kids? How should we proceed? Perhaps providentially, I had been invited to Geneva for a World Alliance of Reformed Churches consultation on justice, peace, and the integrity of creation that summer, so Karin and I decided to go together to explore what life would be like for us there.

For Karin the picture seemed grim. Swiss law made it extremely difficult for spouses of those on the WCC staff to do any kind of work for pay. Work permits were tightly regulated. Everyone was congratulating me, but Karin and I were wondering whether moving to Geneva was viable or right.

Back in Missoula we were in a quandary. Taking a couple days at Christhaven, I read through all my past journals, struggling to find some inner clarity. Gordon Cosby's words to me sixteen years earlier, in 1972, jumped off the page. "You'll have opportunities. The question is, will you be ready?" I relived the call to our marriage, wanting to center myself in the depth of that love, while wondering what this might mean for the choice we now faced.

The past year I had gone into therapy, deciding that I wanted to work on issues around my relationship to my mother as a child, and how that was still affecting me. What I discovered was my need to receive love from Karin and accept her nurture, free from fears that such nurturing love would cripple my own sense of self-identity, as had seemed to happen to me as a child. So I was also striving to relate these insights to our present predicament.

Karin feared a repeat of our struggle over Sojourners. I had a clear calling, and a compelling desire to respond. But she couldn't embrace it as her own. In the possible future we now faced, I'd be completely captivated by my work, traveling around the world, and she'd be left in this strange new town across the ocean with nothing, and no opportunity to exercise her own gifts. Further, she was still angry over things not working out in Michigan.

We worked intensively, separately and together, to find some clear and completely shared discernment. I struggled deeply with detachment — from my ego, my agenda, and my sense of self wrapped up in achievements rather than grace. Further, we each knew in our souls that we were to "journey together," wherever we ended up.

After Karin and I had a long counseling session with the campus minister, Gayle Sandholm, who had originally invited me to Montana a decade earlier, we got in our car and I said, "Karin, you come first." She knew that I meant it. I didn't want to hold on, or hold out any longer. Karin replied, "That's music to my ears."

We began talking about the option of working with the RCA, and living in New Jersey. It was the only other concrete possibility, and we tried to imagine our way into it. I called Herb Muenstermann, who said housing prices in a suburb like Oakland were affordable. Karin and I also agreed that no decision was "right" versus "wrong" in either direction and we would simply look for God's grace, and could expect to find it there.

The next day we decided to meet for a picnic lunch in Missoula's Greenough Park, following Karin's counseling appointment. We sat down at the picnic table. Karin looked at me and said, "Let's go to Geneva." She was clear, and already planning the move. I was surprised to my core. At dinner we told our kids.

It seems as though mutual relinquishment had finally worked — even in the midst of strong clarity about the call by me, and strong resistance by Karin. Only when I said and felt that Karin "came first," and that I was genuinely open, could Karin discover the freedom she needed.

The week before our family boarded the Swissair plane for Geneva, I had a vivid dream — almost like a vision. My grandfather, "Big Daddy," who had died from leukemia two decades earlier in 1968, was sitting right behind me. He wore a blue sweater, and said to me with real warmth and affirmation, "I just want you to know how proud I am of what you are doing." In the dream, my immediate impulse was to go and tell Grandmother of this amazing happening. And when I awoke, I was startled to have felt so much like being in his presence; it seemed very real.

We were headed into a new and uncertain future, filled with hopes and fears. The kids would begin their elementary schooling in the local, French-speaking grade schools, never having heard a word of French. Karin and I had drafted a "covenant" outlining promises to evaluate our experience, maintain connections to the RCA in the United States, seek avenues for her vocational expression, and return home after a period if this wasn't working for us all. I was enthralled with the WCC but anxious about the psychological and cultural adjustment now consuming us.

The complexities of the human psyche are well known. But I found comfort in the thought that perhaps, somehow, Big Daddy, though long dead, was supporting me in the ecumenical pathway now lying ahead. Maybe it wasn't only the price that persuaded him to sell that parcel of the farm.

The Gospel of Community

From 1536 to 1564, John Calvin preached from the pulpit of the Cathedral St. Pierre in Geneva, which became a center of Protestantism. A walk down the cobblestone street from the cathedral leads to the Place du Bourg-de-Four, a picturesque and famous center in Geneva's old city. At one end of that center sits a former aristocratic residence behind a beautiful iron gate. Today this houses the Evangelical Lutheran Church of Geneva.

Reformation history tells us that at the end of the seventeenth century, under ongoing persecution, Lutherans petitioned authorities in Geneva for a place to worship. Their permission was given, but apparently Geneva's Calvinists didn't want the Lutherans to erect a competing church building, so instead a residence on the Place du Bourg-de-Four was purchased for this purpose. For three hundred years Lutherans have worshiped there, in the shadow of the cathedral made famous by John Calvin.

Karin, I, and our kids also worshiped there. A handful of English-speaking congregations function in Geneva, and we found the Lutheran church at Place du Bourg-de-Four to be engaging and warmly hospitable. Probably half of its members were non-Lutheran, like us. The late Marlin van Elderen, from Calvin College and the Christian Reformed Church, who served on the communications staff of the WCC, was president of the congregation when we began worshiping there. Many other

143

ecumenical colleagues and their families made this their church home in Geneva.

This was the first "normal" congregation Karin and I belonged to in our married life. We believed that the gospel must take root in community, and our experience in the first fifteen years of marriage had been in alternative, "intentional" Christian communities — Church of the Saviour and Sojourners community in Washington, D.C., and Community Covenant in Missoula, Montana.

All three of these Christian communities understood themselves as models for the renewal of the church. All were built on small groups — "mission groups" or "households" or "Acts groups" — which provided a context for deep sharing and high accountability to one another. Leadership was seen as arising from among the community and being empowered according to an understanding of gifts. Witness in society as a "countercultural" presence and voice was seen as integral to their identity. Today all these could be cited as models of missional ecclesiology.

Community Covenant Church in Missoula was perhaps the most "conventional" of the three. It actually was part of a denomination — the Evangelical Covenant Church in America. Unlike Church of the Saviour and the Sojourners community, its pastoral leadership was ordained by a denomination it belonged to. Yet, the Missoula congregation had thoroughly reformed itself around the model of being a "renewal community."

All this reflected, in some sense, broader cultural movements of the 1970s. The authority of all institutions was under siege by those questioning and rejecting the dominant values of the social order. The Vietnam War and Watergate provided iconic proof for questioning the legitimacy of those who held power and led institutions in society. In that light, it should not be surprising that the authority of denominations and religious institutions was also under serious question.

Such ferment nourished a proliferation of experiments in how to be the church, how to form radical Christian community, and how to foster creative and prophetic witness in society. In an interesting way, the charismatic movement at that time also contributed to the search for authentic Christian community. While much of that movement was centered on individual renewal through experiencing more fully the gifts of the Spirit, many also stressed that the Holy Spirit created the church, and continues to call disciples today into expressions of highly intentional forms of Christian community like those found in the book of Acts.

Thus, the 1970s saw the birth of numerous experiments in forming intentional or radical Christian community. That also led to the rediscovery in these circles of the Anabaptist tradition, and its long and varied history of living in forms of well-structured Christian community. During that time, it felt like various streams were beginning to flow together — radical Christian witness like the Catholic Worker communities, parts of the charismatic renewal, experiences of the Anabaptist tradition, and voices of biblical and countercultural prophetic critique like Stringfellow, Ellul, and Yoder — to shape new expressions of the church as a sharply defined, highly committed, and deeply engaged Christian community.

Some of these emerging groups were linked together in a loose circle of fellowship that was called "the Community of Communities." These included the Community of Celebration, which grew out of the ministry of Episcopalian charismatic leader Graham Pulkingham at Church of the Redeemer in Houston, Texas; New Jerusalem Community founded by Richard Rohr in Cincinnati, Ohio; Reba Place Fellowship in Evanston, Illinois; Christ's Community led by Gene Beerens, from the Christian Reformed Church, in Grand Rapids, Michigan; Community Covenant Church in Missoula; and several others. The Sojourners community and Jim Wallis played a facilitating role for this network.

Reflecting back, I find it striking how many of these Christian communities no longer exist. Previously I described the conflict at Community Covenant before we left for Geneva. About a year later, on a trip back to the United States, I attended the worship service celebrating its past life and marking its formal dissolution. Christ's Community in Grand Rapids also disbanded. Graham Pulkingham, highly influential as a charismatic leader around the world, admitted to serious sexual misconduct with other men, was suspended as a priest, and died of a heart attack after he and his wife witnessed a robbery at a supermarket. Prior to this, the Community of Celebration in Colorado encountered serious problems. Eventually it relocated to Aliquippa, Pennsylvania, and became a religious order in the Episcopal Church.

The Sojourners community also came to an end. When Karin and I were with them, and the magazine was just beginning, the community played a central role in all we did. Rich and inspired worship (including music from Betty Pulkingham, Graham's wife, and the Fisher Folk), household groups, a daycare center, a food pantry, and other ministries in the neighborhood characterized the life of the Sojourners community. But over time, that expression of intentional community couldn't be sustained.

However, the core ministry of Sojourners — its magazine, its growing electronic constituency, and its advocacy on issues of justice — has flourished. The organization has a budget of about $4.5 million and a staff of fifty, and Jim Wallis has emerged as one of the nation's most respected voices on issues of social justice and peace.

In a similar fashion, the Good Food Store in Montana, once a ministry of Community Covenant Church, now functions as a highly successful nonprofit, employing 185 people, supporting local food production, doing several million dollars of business a year, and giving thousands of dollars in grants and support to the local community. Likewise, the music of Fisher Folk, rooted originally in the Community of Celebration, has influenced tens of thousands of congregations around the world.

So some of the ministries spawned and nurtured in these intentional Christian communities have outlived the failures and even the life of these experimental expressions of the church. But it's worth reflecting on why some of these communities failed, and why others endure. Fresh experiments in radical Christian community are emerging again these days, seen in movements like the "new monasticism" among younger evangelicals and many attempts of Christian social activists to live in community and minister among the poor. Perhaps lessons can be learned from similar attempts launched three to four decades ago.

First, enduring models of intentional, highly committed Christian communities have to integrate children into their shared life and transfer the vision between generations. One reason why monastic communities have been sustained for centuries as the most successful model of intentional Christian community that the church has ever known is that their members are single and celibate. Children are never a consideration, and the vision is passed to younger novices on the basis of their call rather than their family.

The models of intentional Christian community Karin and I participated in, and also visited, all involved families. Frequently, commitment
to the vision of the community as a biblical and radical expression of the
gospel was embraced by a couple, but the arrival of children would raise
a whole new set of questions. It's one thing for adults to make a con-
scious decision to embrace a simple lifestyle, live amongst the poor, and
seek mutual submission in a group around major life decisions. But what
happens when an infant is introduced into this equation? Or a nine-
year-old?

Communities that have survived and thrived, in my view, have
learned how to be flexible with the particular and legitimate needs children place on any parents. Ideological rigidity has to give way, joyfully,
to the goal of cherishing children and embracing the demands they
bring. Otherwise these experimental Christian communities become
simply an adventure for idealistic and courageous young people who
will move on to something more conventional once they are married
and start a family.

Second, models of leadership and decision making become huge issues in all such communities. The communities I have been a part of all
had strong, charismatic leaders — Gordon Cosby, Jim Wallis, Dan
Simmons. It was the same for other communities in our wider fellowship
— Graham Pulkingham, Gene Beerens, Richard Rohr, and many more.
Without the vision and particular gifts of these leaders, none of these
communities, and the incredible and creative gifts of their ministries,
would have emerged. That's a simple fact to acknowledge and celebrate.

But the journey of these communities and their leaders is similar to
the dynamic I see in new church starts, as well as in emerging social
movements. It takes an individual with particular gifts and personality
characteristics to start a new church. Denominations invest considerable resources today into testing and evaluating those desiring to start a
new congregation to see if they have the personal traits that are predictive of success.

You can guess in general terms what these traits are: an entrepreneurial spirit, the willingness to take risks, the capacity for vision and
imagination, a winsome, persuasive personality, a near dangerously high
sense of self-confidence, and the ability to inspire others. These are the

qualities that equip one to start a new church — or an intentional Christian community.

But once the church is launched and begins to grow, a crisis is likely to occur in about three to five years. Now the vision and mission of the new church have to be more and more internalized by its members. Their sense of ownership has to grow. The church can't remain dependent upon the personal charisma and gifts of its founder. Further, the leadership style of the pastor has to change. The task is to see that the vision is truly appropriated by others, and that they are empowered to offer their gifts. Otherwise, the founding pastor should move on to start another church, which often is a good solution.

These dynamics were intensified in the life of the intentional Christian communities emerging and multiplying in the 1970s and 1980s. Further, the bias of the counterculture tended to reject leadership of any kind, and assert that all decision making should be done in egalitarian, participatory ways. That made the journey of these communities all the more difficult.

Some of these communities weathered the storm as leaders and their members negotiated the ongoing transition from "strong leadership" to growing participation and empowerment. Other communities got caught in unhealthy patterns where members began dismissing and rejecting any recognition of leadership, and where leaders clung to the same patterns of inspiring and controlling leadership that were necessary to found the community, but wouldn't sustain it for the long term.

The third lesson I observed is the critical importance of inward spiritual formation that is supported and nurtured by the culture of the intentional Christian community. The Church of the Saviour, whose vision and "DNA" is now carried forth by a diverse group of small Christian communities and ministries, has been marked by its commitment to nurture the interior spiritual life of each of its members. That continued, though perhaps not as consistently as in its earlier days, before the church intentionally divided into a network of smaller, diverse expressions. But focused, consistent attention to the "inward journey" is the main reason, in my view, that the legacy of the Church of the Saviour has survived and continues to find expression in a variety of ways.

In some of those experimental versions of the church, it felt at times that the community was the gospel. The reasoning was, and is, that God's life took on flesh in Jesus, and through the Spirit takes on flesh in the gathered community. So as the "body of Christ," the community lives out the sacrificial love, the values, and the way of life demonstrated by its Lord. This new community becomes the focus and center for one's whole life. Relationships within the body become of primary importance for they are to demonstrate the mutual submission and love that are the gift of God's Spirit. So the gospel is expressed through such a community, and the gospel almost seems to depend on the authentic life of the community. It can easily become a gospel of community.

To this was added a harsh critique of American individualism. All the emphasis on one's personal right to be free and experience happiness was actually opposed to the understanding that one existed "for the community," and his or her personal ambitions were submitted to the community. Inviolate personal prerogatives were part of the mythology of Western culture that was resisted and overcome in the life of the Christian community.

Such an emphasis devalued the personal, internal spiritual journey. Time spent in private retreat, or preoccupations with individual, isolated spiritual practices, went against the grain of life lived intensely in relationship with others and sacrificially serving the whole. It's not that such communities ever prohibited such things. Rather, the culture of these communities was shaped by the conviction that our spiritual fulfillment and nurture came through giving ourselves fully to the life of the community. It's notable, for example, that my four years of participation in the Sojourners community are almost completely devoid of any entries in my personal journal.

Models of monastic communities remind us again that alternative Christian communities that have endured take seriously the task of inward spiritual formation. This, perhaps, is the most important lesson to be learned from the creative experimentation with alternative expressions of the church as intentional community, and the continuing search for such models today.

My heart, and my ecclesiology, is still drawn strongly to the models of church that Karin and I experienced in the first fifteen years of our marriage. We still find it hard to imagine "doing church" without some small group where we share our lives. Church for us should be centered on transforming experiences of *koinonia* that equip and sustain us for mission in the world.

Starting with the Evangelical Lutheran church in Geneva's old town, for the last two decades our church life has been centered in well-established congregations, linked to tradition and related denominationally to the wider body of Christ. We've loved these three congregations — in Geneva; Oakland, New Jersey; and Grand Rapids. Yet, I remain convinced that the creativity of the Holy Spirit continues to work on the fringes of established church life, and in fresh initiatives by those disillusioned by safe congregations that are too well adjusted to society. Therein lies my hope.

Discovering the Global Church

E MILIO CASTRO, general secretary of the World Council of Churches (WCC), invited me to his office when I arrived in Geneva to begin my work as the WCC's director of Church and Society. A pastor from Uruguay who had previously headed the WCC's Commission on Mission and Evangelism, he had been chosen by the narrowest of margins over Arie Brouwer, formerly general secretary of the Reformed Church in America, to head the WCC. Emilio was warmhearted, collegial, and hospitable. The door to his office was nearly always open, inviting conversation.

"So, I understand you come from a strong evangelical background," Emilio said. Not knowing where this was going, I acknowledged my gratitude for my evangelical upbringing but went on to talk about my various ecumenical experiences, which at that time were actually fairly modest. But I wanted Emilio to be certain of my commitment to ecumenism.

"That's good, that's fine," Emilio replied. "But here, I want you to be an evangelical."

Emilio went on to explain and lament the gulf that existed between the WCC and the global evangelical community. He had a deep concern for developing links with evangelicals, in part because his own journey blended an unapologetic commitment to the gospel with a passion for human rights and justice. The WCC had a staff task force on relationships with evangelicals, which apparently had become dormant, and

Emilio said he was appointing me immediately as moderator, much to my surprise.

I was hired, however, to direct the WCC's work on church and society, which had a legacy of outstanding studies relating scientific and technological developments to the ethical concerns of the churches. In many respects, I was unprepared and probably unqualified for that task. It was hoped, however, that its future work would focus on the issues of "integrity of creation," which was why I had been selected.

One task I inherited was to arrange a consultation on the ethical issues and safety concerns over nuclear energy. A member of the Church and Society board was a physicist from Kinshasa, Zaire (now the Democratic Republic of the Congo), and he strongly proposed that the Kimbanguist Church, to which he belonged, host this meeting. I wondered why experts on the ethics of nuclear energy would assemble in a country that had no nuclear reactors; in fact, only two existed on the entire continent, both in South Africa. But I was learning how the WCC functioned. Representation regularly trumped content.

We went to Kinshasa. The discovery of that consultation, at least for me, had nothing to do with the ethics of nuclear energy, nor the book produced as a result. Rather, it was the history and life of the Church of Jesus Christ on Earth by His Special Envoy Simon Kimbangu, the full name of the Kimbanguist Church. The twenty-five or so participants in the consultation were welcomed by thousands in the huge compound of the church in Kinshasa. Worship and music, including their brass band, went on for hours. I sat at a privileged place on the platform, stunned.

The church was founded by the "prophet" Simon Kimbangu during the colonial period of the Belgian Congo. In 1921 he began a preaching and healing ministry that quickly spread. Regarded as an insurrectionist by Belgian authorities, Kimbangu was arrested and spent much of his life in prison. But the church grew as an indigenous expression of Christianity, rather than as part of European colonial rule.

The Kimbanguist Church is one of hundreds of African Instituted Churches that have sprouted within African culture, independent from, and often in opposition to, the legacy of Western colonialism and its associated mission work. The Organization of African Instituted Churches, headquartered in Nairobi, claims 60 million members in its churches.

The Kimbanguist Church is one of the very few that have joined the World Council of Churches, and that was not without controversy. A theological team from the WCC had to first examine whether its founder, Simon Kimbangu, was regarded as a supernatural prophet almost akin to the Trinity.

The church functions as a strict hierarchy, and the head of the church is called, in French, the *Chef Spirituel.* Few of his followers doubt his supernatural powers. When in Kinshasa, I reached Karin on a poor phone connection. She told me that J.K. had taken a bad fall, hitting his head on concrete, and had been taken to the doctor. I couldn't understand anything more.

That evening, a meeting had been arranged between me and the *Chef Spirituel,* who was S. E. Diangienga at that time. He asked in our conversation about my family, and whether there was anything he could pray for. Since I was deeply worried about my son, I shared the news I had received earlier from Karin, and he prayed.

A day or so later I finally got another call through to Karin. It turned out that J.K. was fine. He had gone to the doctor, but there was no concussion or injury more than a bad bruise. That evening, one of the *Chef Spirituel*'s aides asked me how my son was doing. When I told him J.K. was fine, his face lit into a broad smile. "Of course. I knew he would be," he declared. "Our *Chef Spirituel* prayed for him."

This was my first trip to this continent, and I was discovering the explosive power of Christianity throughout most all of sub-Saharan Africa. The Kimbanguist Church is estimated to have about 5 million members. Its development is an example of how Christianity in Africa has grown from only a few million in 1900 to over 360 million a century later; it is one of the most dramatic stories of modern Christian history.

But I also discovered that the African Instituted churches and groups representing much of the vitality, spiritual power, and electric growth within African Christianity were largely absent from the WCC. The Kimbanguist Church was one of only a handful of exceptions. Further, I began realizing that the culture of the WCC, with its bureaucratic, document-driven, quasi-parliamentary style, would be a difficult fit for churches accustomed to enthusiastic, Spirit-filled, vision-driven ministry.

When I joined, the WCC divided its work into about sixteen "subunits." Church and Society was one, along with Faith and Order, the Programme to Combat Racism, the Churches' Commission on International Affairs, Inter-faith Dialogue, and so on. Each one had a director, a governing board, a budget, and a few staff. The WCC was a classic example of an organization functioning with separate "silos." Over this was the 150-member Central Committee that was supposed to approve key staff appointments and the overall budgets, programs, and priorities. It was a recipe for organizational dysfunction.

Contributions and revenue were shrinking, so the costs of maintaining this kind of structure were becoming unsustainable, to say nothing of the lack of coordination that seemed like standard operating procedure. So Emilio, with backing from his executive committee, launched a restructuring effort. I was enlisted to serve on the staff group, and jumped in enthusiastically. I had never met a structure I didn't want to reform.

Countless hours were spent in meetings and consultations and in drafting proposals, stretching more than a year. These silos had deep foundations and strong defenses. Finally, a plan emerged that Emilio decided to bring to the Central Committee at its meeting in Moscow. On an Aeroflot charter plane from Geneva to Moscow, filled with staff and some governing board members, I was seated ahead of my colleague Ninan Koshy, director of the Churches Commission on International Affairs (CCIA). Ninan was seated next to one of the WCC presidents and key governing board members. I overheard Ninan speaking to him, taking apart the restructuring plan piece by piece; what a staff group had worked on for eighteen months was dismantled in the eyes of the president by the time we landed in Moscow.

As its director, Ninan wanted to protect the autonomy of his work, the CCIA. I could understand that desire. But what surprised and disillusioned me was the pattern of senior staff lobbying directly influential members of the governing board against the decisions and position of the general secretary. I began to see this constantly. Of course, that meant that Emilio's role as general secretary and chief of staff was constantly being undermined by his own colleagues.

The Central Committee, influenced by a few voices that had been swayed by a few staff voices, postponed the restructuring plan. It took a couple of more years until a partial restructuring plan was finally adopted. In the process, I learned that the problems and frequent dysfunction of the World Council of Churches were far deeper than matters of structure. In fact, it's a frequent mistake to think that needed organizational change should begin with restructuring. I made that mistake as a WCC staff member.

The WCC's problems during this time had far more to do with clarifying its vision, examining its culture, and recovering a sense of its spiritual vocation. One unintended consequence of the prolonged restructuring process was a proposal from Metropolitan Mar Gregorios, another WCC president, to reexamine the WCC's guiding vision and understanding of its unique role. That launched a process that came to be known as the Common Understanding and Vision (CUV) of the WCC.

Stretching on for several years, this effort sought to clarify and answer the most basic issues of the WCC's identity and unique calling. The CUV process reminded the WCC that at its heart, it is the relationship of churches one to another that forms and informs its life. This counters the image of the WCC as a bureaucratic organization distinct from the churches carrying out programs on their behalf.

Recentering the WCC around the relationship of its churches one to another, and the cooperative efforts in mission, witness, and advocacy for justice that they can undertake, is a continuing challenge to this day. It requires a fundamental paradigm shift. This also mirrors the same changes required in the self-understanding of denominations and other ecumenical organizations.

The CUV process directed the WCC both to deepen the relationships between its member churches and to widen relationships with the many churches outside of the WCC. In fact, at the 1998 WCC Assembly in Harare, where I was a delegate, I quoted from a chorus I had sung as a child: "Deep and wide, deep and wide, there's a fountain flowing deep and wide." The challenge facing the council then, and now, is to carry out both of these tasks, simultaneously.

The task of deepening relationships within the council became centered on the place and voice of the Orthodox churches. For most American Protestants, their understanding of the Orthodox is probably limited to noticing a Greek Orthodox church and imaging their services as centered around lengthy and obscure liturgies. My knowledge of the Orthodox upon arriving in Geneva centered primarily on some of their theologians who wrote perceptively about the theology of creation. But I had little knowledge of their life as churches, and the dominant role the Orthodox Church plays in Russia, several eastern European countries, Greece, and elsewhere, as well as the enduring life and witness of Orthodox churches as small minorities in countries of the Middle East.

Therefore, being in the WCC allowed me to discover the life and witness of the Orthodox churches. This came at a time when the relationship of Orthodox churches to the WCC was fragile and tenuous. In part, this was due to the fall of communism. The ecumenical relationships of Orthodox churches in those countries were under the watchful eye of communist authorities in ways that often compromised church leaders. When those regimes fell, Orthodox leaders were held accountable for their past collusion with state authorities — whether real or perceived — and newly empowered conservative forces in those Orthodox churches severely questioned participation in groups like the WCC.

But more was involved. The Orthodox made up at least 25 percent of the membership of the WCC. Yet, their voice felt like a much smaller minority. Their representation on staff was low. Their concerns often felt marginalized. Moreover, the style of the WCC, with its parliamentary rules of order and decision making, felt alien to them. How could a 51 percent majority be equated with God's will? Creative ecumenical worship seemed theologically confusing to them, and at times was outright offensive to their sensibilities. And the WCC's agenda addressing social and political issues seemed too often influenced by trends in the secularized West.

By the time of the Harare Assembly in 1998, these relationships were reaching a crisis point. Because Orthodox churches were threatening to leave the WCC or distance themselves from its activities, a Special Commission on Relationships with the Orthodox was formed, made up equally of Orthodox and non-Orthodox members. I was asked to serve on this body.

Our meetings over the next few years were held largely in Orthodox settings. So much, I learned, depended on understanding the contexts in which these churches lived and seeing their life and witness firsthand. We were committed to this kind of encounter, along with an open and honest sharing of our perceptions, questions, and convictions. This whole style was atypical for the culture of the WCC.

Previously, an off-the-record, informal conversation had been convened by the moderator of the Central Committee, His Holiness Aram I, at the administrative headquarters of the Armenian Orthodox Church in Antelias, outside of Beirut, Lebanon. About fifteen of us gathered, including Konrad Raiser, then the general secretary of the WCC; Mary Tanner from the Church of England; Leonid Kishkovsky from the Orthodox Church in America; and key Orthodox and non-Orthodox members of the Central Committee.

Over fresh hummus and pita bread, *fattoush, tabbouleh,* grilled lamb, fresh fruit, and wine, we talked honestly about Orthodox fears and concerns about the WCC, and whether its "culture" could adapt to be genuinely hospitable toward them. At the same time, Protestants expressed hesitations and frustrations with the Orthodox. Some of these involved fundamental ecclesiological differences. For instance, at one point I simply asked, "When will you as Orthodox ever be able to recognize the Reformed Church in America as a church?"

That private encounter helped establish the trust necessary to embark on the process of the Special Commission. Its work addressed issues of decision making and resulted in the groundbreaking proposal that the WCC adopt a consensus model of group process and deliberation at its Central Committee and other governing board meetings. Likewise, agreements were reached on how to conduct worship and prayer at WCC meetings. While necessary, these tended to erode much of the creativity in ecumenical worship that had been positively received by many of the churches.

In the end, the Special Commission was a powerful example of what it means to take relationships between member churches in the WCC with the seriousness that its claim of being "a fellowship of churches" requires. If the Orthodox churches had left, which some of my colleagues at times wished would have happened, the WCC's tenuous claim to seek the unity of the world's churches would have been shattered.

With the Catholic Church only as an observer, participating selectively in certain programs, and most evangelical and Pentecostal churches living in a different religious world, the WCC is comprised primarily of historic Protestant and Orthodox churches, representing only about one-quarter of world Christianity. Without the Orthodox, the WCC would become a coalition of Protestant churches engaged primarily in causes of international advocacy and social justice — activities worthy in themselves, but far from being a "privileged instrument" for the unity of the churches.

THE WORK THAT CALLED ME to the WCC originally, dealing with the integrity of creation, took root and began to grow. Early on we made a decision to address the issue of climate change. In 1989, this was barely on the world's radar, much less the church's. Yet, it seemed that this was a key example of how misguided human activity could threaten the "integrity" of God's created order.

We put together a study guide, made a video, and sent representatives to the second meeting of the Intergovernmental Panel on Climate Change, the UN body that gathered scientists from throughout the world to evaluate the causes and threats of climate change. Our presence surprised people but was welcomed. Religious voices at that time were largely silent on the threat of climate change.

Several of my WCC staff colleagues were skeptical. The issues of global economic injustice had long been in the forefront of the WCC's advocacy work, and some contended that environmental issues were primarily an agenda from the north. "Why worry about the oceans rising a few inches decades from now when thousands die daily from hunger, poverty, and disease?" Yet, research was showing that those who would likely suffer most from climate change were the poor and marginalized, unable to cope with spreading deserts, crop failures, and increased hurricanes and flooding.

In 1990 the WCC held its long-anticipated Convocation on Justice, Peace, and the Integrity of Creation (JPIC) in Seoul, Korea. The goal was to allow churches to make "covenants" to act together in the face of threats to justice, peace, and the integrity of creation. My responsibility was to work with others on the integrity of creation portion, and by the end, the convocation directed one of the four covenants it adopted to address the threats of climate change.

Once every seven years a General Assembly of the WCC is held, and in 1991 this global gathering, the Seventh Assembly, was conducted in Canberra and attended by about four thousand representatives from all the member churches in the world. Its theme was "Come Holy Spirit — Renew the Whole Creation." One of four subthemes was "Giver of Life — Sustain Your Creation," and I had the staff responsibility for that part of the assembly's work. The group of delegates addressing these concerns affirmed a range of initiatives including the WCC's work addressing climate change, and the whole JPIC process was strongly embraced by the assembly for future WCC work.

The next year, the United Nations held the "Earth Summit" at Rio de Janeiro, Brazil, the most prestigious global gathering ever convened to address environmental threats, with most heads of state joining at the conclusion of the summit to ratify its agreements. Fourteen hundred nongovernmental organizations were officially represented, and 9,200 journalists covered the event.

We decided to hold an ecumenical event at the Earth Summit, gathering 176 delegates from 54 countries and 70 churches. It served both to give voice to the aspirations of the churches at this global event and to deepen the commitment of the churches to preserving the integrity of creation. A "Letter to the Churches" was written, along with other resolutions and actions.

What I remember most, however, was the final evening, on the eve of Pentecost. The participants were invited to join hundreds of others at the cathedral of Duque de Caxias, where we held an all-night vigil. Songs, prayers, and experiences were shared. Then with torches and candles, joined by hundreds more, we marched through town for a sunrise service of thousands in the town square. We offered praise and prayer for the earth, and the work of the summit. Emilio Castro preached an inspiring sermon, and Eszter Karsay, a Reformed Church pastor from Hungary, "blessed bread" that was then distributed to all.

It's difficult to know what really is effective in changing attitudes, commitments, and actions of Christians, and their churches, toward biblical imperatives such as preserving the integrity of God's creation, or any number of other issues taken up by the World Council of Churches. Its dominant method has been to listen to various voices from the churches, work to produce a consensus report, have it ratified by a governing body, publicize it in ecumenical channels, and distribute it to its member denominations. More recently, of course, its Web site plays a key role in communication.

However, when I look back on all the reports and documents I've had a hand in producing at the WCC, I question whether they've made significant differences or motivated substantial change. Lasting change requires far more than getting the right words onto paper. It takes a transformational process that reaches deep into one's being with spiritual power and is supported by relationships of mutual caring, love, and accountability. I'm skeptical of how much words, however inspiring, produced by a WCC meeting or adopted by its assembly, or for that matter, resolutions adopted by a general synod, or a conference of bishops, can produce the change they intend. They must be accompanied by a process of genuine discernment and infused with spiritual commitments to transformational actions, to have any chance at making a lasting difference.

The World Council of Churches does have the ability to at least put certain challenges or issues on the agenda of the churches. Maybe that's enough. The commitment to "justice, peace, and the integrity of creation" is an example. Take away all the consultations, papers, resolutions, and reports, and the challenge contained in that simple phrase remains, reminding the churches that these three dimensions of what God intends and desires for the world are inextricably linked. Google that phrase and you'll see it associated with countless Christian groups, including Catholic ones, even though the Vatican refused to cosponsor the JPIC world convocation.

Even just the three words in the provocative phrase "integrity of creation" captured the interest and imagination of many Christians, motivating them to recover the resonant biblical themes emphasizing the gift of God's creation, and humanity's divinely appointed task to tend and keep the earth. The WCC's work on climate change, inspired by that phrase, has quietly persisted for two decades, all the way to the Copenhagen summit, carried forth by faithful servants like Elias Ambramides and David Hallman.

Yet, I'm dubious that the WCC's dominant methodology of consultations, conferences, and reports will produce their desired results. But

I do recognize the value of the global church discerning together key challenges and callings that can be embraced by denominations, congregations, and Christian communities as part of their life and faithful witness.

The most serious challenge facing the World Council of Churches is the contraction of its constituency in light of trends that are redrawing the map of world Christianity. General Secretary Konrad Raiser, who succeeded Emilio Castro, wisely described the four "families" of global Christianity: Catholic, Orthodox, historic Protestant, and evangelical/Pentecostal. The chasm between the WCC and evangelical and Pentecostal constituencies seems to grow deeper as those parts of Christ's body expand with explosive power, especially throughout the global south.

The prospect of bridging this chasm is formidable, as I experienced on the task force Emilio appointed me to head when I began my work on staff. Perhaps that was best illustrated by the relationship at the time between the WCC and World Vision. In our efforts to address climate change, we formed a working group with various partners, including World Vision of Great Britain, which had a keen interest in addressing this challenge.

Michael Taylor at that time was the director of Christian Aid in Great Britain and coordinator for all the European church-related agencies for international development that contributed significant funds to the WCC. He wrote a furious letter to Emilio demanding that we stop any cooperation with World Vision. He saw them as a competitor, and working with them was a betrayal of ecumenical discipline. Emilio was in a quandary of how to respond.

Eventually I had the chance to meet with Michael and talk directly with him. In our tense discussion, I asked him if he would have any objection to adding a Buddhist organization to our working group, for we had been thinking about interfaith cooperation. "No, that would be fine," Michael answered.

"So you're happy for the WCC to cooperate with Buddhists, but don't want us to cooperate with World Vision," I responded.

Eventually, with Emilio's blessing, we decided to have a consultation — or perhaps it was better named a conversation — between World Vision and the WCC. The truth I discovered was that these two were barely on speaking terms. Some WCC colleagues regarded World Vision nearly as the evil empire, seeing it as a pawn of U.S. foreign policy, with a narrow focus on charity that encouraged paternalism and avoided matters of justice.

I was not unfamiliar with those critiques. When working for Senator Hatfield, he had been appointed to World Vision's board, and I was the staff liaison between the senator and the organization. During that time, I witnessed World Vision "de-Americanize" its governing structure. Unsubstantiated charges of collusion between World Vision personnel and the CIA in places like Cambodia were met not only with a clear statement of policy, but with Senator Hatfield introducing legislation banning the CIA from using any missionary personnel as agents, and that became law.

World Vision rewrote its basic values to focus its work not only on compassionate care for children, but also on community development as well as advocating for issues of global economic and social justice. To be sure, one still heard horror stories of World Vision personnel throwing money around and acting with total disregard toward other church-related aid agencies. But the organization was changing, and didn't fit the convenient stereotype held by some of my WCC colleagues.

The conversation took place in Geneva, and included representatives of WCC churches and of World Vision in the global south. Some of the mutual stereotypes began to crumble. But what was most revealing was to see the conflict between the WCC and World Vision from the perspective of those on the ground in places like Africa and Asia.

At one point, an African church leader said to the group, "We have a saying in Africa. 'When two elephants fight, the grass gets trampled.'"

From the perspective of those like him, the ecumenical-evangelical tension was a product of the churches in the north that was then exported into his region. They learned how to relate to both groups, speaking their different ecumenical and evangelical languages, but the conflict and lack of cooperation served only to damage grassroots efforts to liberate the poor and marginalized.

It proved difficult to build meaningful bridges between the WCC and evangelical constituencies. A few evangelical leaders, and fewer Pentecostals, would come to the WCC assemblies every seven years, and to other major gatherings; usually they would form their own caucus and issue a statement outlining the various reservations and criticisms they had of the WCC. Even after I spent time with the editors of *Christianity Today*, I felt they were more inclined to cling to evangelical critiques of the WCC from the past than to look carefully at opportunities for evangelical participation in the present.

By the time we approached the Harare Assembly in 1998, it was clear to WCC General Secretary Konrad Raiser and many others that a neutral, safe "ecumenical space" would have to be created for any hope of establishing genuine fellowship among all four major families of the global Christian community. That couldn't be initiated under the WCC umbrella.

But it could happen, and desperately needed to be explored. That led to the proposal at Harare to establish a global forum that would offer the opportunity of bringing churches and leaders from the historic Protestant family, the Orthodox family, the evangelical and Pentecostal families, and the Catholic family into a common place of exchange and fellowship with one another. That was the genesis of the Global Christian Forum, which has emerged over the past decade as a place to fulfill that vision.

The lasting impact of my time with the WCC had less to do with programs, and more to do with relationships that opened doors to amazing and humbling discoveries of the global church. Worshiping at midnight at an Orthodox cathedral in Romania on the eve of Easter, and watching thousands uplifted by the joy of the resurrection; receiving the hospitality of Christians worshiping and working faithfully in Kuala Lumpur, Malaysia, a country that is 98 percent Muslim; accompanying an inspiring Catholic bishop in his work among the poor in Rio de Janeiro; exchanging crosses with other Christian leaders to the drumbeat of an African chorus under a worship tent in Harare — these are the experiences that have enlivened my Christian pilgrimage and forever changed my life.

Claimed by a Call

MY DAD HAD bypass surgery shortly after he retired from Reed's Candy Company. I came back from D.C. and went to the hospital in Evanston with him and Mom to look at his angiogram. The blockages were serious, but the procedure would correct them. The operation basically went well, though one of the intended bypasses couldn't be completed, leaving a vulnerability. The doctor told him to watch his diet and not to "work up a sweat," which, I think, was music to his ears.

About fifteen years later, on November 9, 1991, Dad had chest pains and went to Central DuPage County Hospital, near their home. He and Mom had been wallpapering the kitchen that day; I don't know if he worked up a sweat, but I doubt it. The angiogram showed blockages once again, requiring another bypass surgery. It was scheduled for November 12. I boarded a plane in Geneva to fly home to Chicago.

At 5:00 A.M. Dad had a massive heart attack. He was rushed into surgery, and his life was saved. But he remained in critical condition. For the next three weeks, he was on an unpredictable journey, vacillating between steps toward life and moving toward death.

My father was a source of unconditional love in my life. He'd come into my bedroom when I was a child, kiss me, and always say, "Good night, pal." Certainly he had his moments of anger and disappointment toward me, but for whatever psychological reason, those never seemed to register. I was his pal.

At the same time, I wondered as I grew up if he had strength and assertiveness. Mom seemed more deliberate, and when she was disappointed with me, I knew it.

But now, with Dad hovering between life and death, Mom was devastated. She found it hard — almost impossible — to spend long periods with him in the hospital. So I took on that role, beginning to keep vigil with my dad. He was my pal.

My brother Ron, sister Marcia, and brother-in-law Ralph were also there faithfully, and with Mom we had constant discussions with doctors about Dad's prognosis and potential courses of action, or inaction. In the evenings, however, I'd often remain there, reading Scripture, holding his hand, and being with him. Often he was alert and could respond, except for the tubes in his mouth. But we communicated.

During those days, as my father was facing death and wondering if he could live, I began to see qualities in him I have never forgotten. He displayed such courage and clarity. When we decided, at his urging, to take the tube out of his mouth, the doctor thought he might die. Dad understood. After the procedure he was fine, and lifted his hands up as if to say, "What now?" He seemed decisive as he understood the gravity of his condition. And he was strong in the face of death.

Two weeks after surgery, we took the kids out of school and Karin flew to Chicago with them to join me. We wanted them to see "Pop" one last time. At times he was alert and interacting. We even watched a Bears game. He hung on, but his prognosis was grim, and death seemed only a matter of time.

But by December 5, my family and I were out of time. I'd been away from my work for almost a month, and the kids were missing nearly two weeks of school. Feeling we couldn't just keep on waiting more days for his death, we decided to return to Geneva. The day after we returned, Dad went into a downward spiral and died. My mom, who had decided to come to the hospital, was at his side.

I made a decision not to get on a plane and fly back to Chicago for the funeral. I told my mom this might happen, and had left a tape to be played at the service. But it's a choice I regret deeply to this day. Instead, our pastor, Steve Larson, led a memorial service for my father at the Lutheran church in Geneva, and many of my ecumenical colleagues attended. They shared the pain of living with geographical separation from parents in times of crisis.

Nevertheless, the time that mattered with my dad was those three weeks when I was often by his side. The qualities I saw in him during those days seemed to change me. I found deeper reserves of clarity, strength, and courage. Perhaps, in some complex, inner way, I had been waiting all my life to see these things in my father because I wanted to find them in myself.

I would need those qualities in the coming two years in ways I could not imagine. By the beginning of 1993, the WCC was lurching forward through a restructuring. The same pattern kept happening. Revenues were dropping, no one seemed able to determine priorities, more work was being done by fewer staff, and the internal organization was being rearranged in an attempt to cope with these dilemmas.

Work of several former "subunits," including Church and Society, was now consolidated, and a new "unit" was established on justice, peace, and creation, flowing out of the imprint of the JPIC process. It needed a permanent director. Several of my colleagues strongly encouraged me to apply. They trusted me and felt I'd be ideally suited.

I did so, and presented clear ideas to the search committee and General Secretary Konrad Raiser on how the work of this unit could be carried out. It seemed like the next step forward. But staff appointments in the WCC are invariably complicated by regional, confessional, and political issues. Moreover, I think Konrad had a different long-term plan, which was his prerogative as general secretary.

Sam Kobia, a Methodist pastor from Kenya, who previously served on the WCC staff and now was working as general secretary of the National Council of Churches of Kenya, was selected by Konrad to head the unit. I later learned that Konrad had sent a colleague to Kenya to encourage him to apply. And at one level, it made sense for the WCC's work on justice, peace, and creation to be headed by an African rather than a white North American male.

The news came just as I was on my way to a climate change meeting in Toronto, and my reaction was one of deep anger, frustration, and dismay.

Back in Geneva, knowing I had to come to terms with my feelings, I took a retreat day, on a boat. Lac Leman (called Lake Geneva by tourists) is one of Europe's most beautiful places, stretching for miles from Geneva to Lausanne and to Montreux. Mont Blanc, to the south, is in the distance, and steep hillsides with ancient vineyards rise from its northern shores. Classic passenger boats run scheduled trips between the cities, and I liked nothing more than to be on the water.

Surrounded by beauty and in isolated serenity, I thought, prayed, and wrote:

May 25, 1993

All my life I have been rewarded for being the "good person." Everything I've wanted I've generally achieved. Each position has come about. . . .

Now, at the WCC, I've been the "good person." I've done everything right, produced good work, received recognition, etc. Except that now, I've not been rewarded as a result. Instead, I've been marginalized institutionally.

So how do I respond?

Why have I been the "good person" — to achieve reward? Am I caught in the same cycle from my youth? Or have I been responding with more inner freedom during these past 4 1/2 years? . . .

I have been deeply upset and depressed since not being appointed as Unit III Director. . . . I feel such anger at being marginalized, and I must discover the roots of this anger.

I had taken my journals with me, as was my practice, and as the boat cruised the lake I pored over reflections and insights from previous pivotal times in my journey. The theme I kept rediscovering was not rooting my identity in the things that I did, but rather in the reality of being claimed by God's love.

I came to understand that, first, I had not been functioning out of a spiritual center in my work at the WCC. I felt spiritually disoriented. Second, too much of my ego and identity was tied up in the position of director, and my position in the council. And third, I knew I was a leader — that I wanted to lead, giving vision, inspiration, and administration. This is part of who I am — the issue was how it was to be expressed.

The impulses about leadership were connected to the feelings I had at the time of Dad's death. I worked to recenter myself, and looked at those areas in the WCC's life where I could make a vital contribution, not dependent on holding the position of a unit director. They were clear: the Task Force on Relationships with Evangelicals, the working group for the next WCC assembly, and the Common Understanding and Vision process. In addition, my work on integrity of creation continued. In all this, I had the desire to work with others to see a renewal in the spiritual depth of the council's work and life.

Earlier that spring, on a trip back to a conference in the United States, Ed Mulder, general secretary of the Reformed Church in America, asked to have lunch with me. Ed was a member of the WCC Central Committee, and we'd spend time together when it met, discussing the business and issues facing the council. But this lunch, I discovered, had a different purpose.

"Have you ever thought about being a candidate to succeed me as RCA general secretary?" he asked. I was genuinely surprised. No, I never had.

As we talked, I began listing all the reasons why I hadn't ever thought of that as a possibility.

"I wasn't raised in the RCA. In fact, I had never heard of the RCA until I went to Hope College. And the church communities that have impacted me most are experimental models of renewal, like the Church of the Saviour. After my ordination, I didn't pastor a typical RCA congregation. Karin and I were in Missoula, with Community Covenant Church, starting the New Creation Institute. And then, for the past five years I've been in Geneva, totally out of the loop, with the World Council of Churches. Plus, I'm not even Dutch."

Ed listened, like the good pastor that he is. Then he replied.

"The experiences and influences you name in your journey would bring to the RCA things we'd need, and would enrich us. Those are the reasons why I hope you would give consideration to being a candidate."

I didn't know what to think. It was an unexpected and startling idea. Meanwhile, I had been invited to speak at the "ecumenical breakfast" at the RCA's General Synod in June 1993 in Vancouver. Further, prior to the synod, RCA staff person John Paarlberg had arranged a seminar on "earth-keeping," held on Galiano Island and facilitated by Loren

Wilkinson, a friend teaching at Regent College who had written an out-standing book on that theme. John invited me to take part.

At General Synod I watched the RCA function and connected with friends. John Jacobson, the president of Hope College, was there. The college was searching for a dean of the chapel. A job description had been sent to me in Geneva, and John and I talked about that position during the Vancouver synod. But in truth, it didn't excite me, and nothing came alive within me to take the conversation forward. Subsequently, John named Ben Patterson to the position.

I questioned Al Poppen in Vancouver about Ed's prompting that I consider being a candidate for general secretary. Al was the wise and long-serving director of ministry and personnel for the RCA. Years earlier, he had interviewed Karin and approved her service as an RCA short-term missionary in Japan.

Al and I took a long walk. The June evening was cold, with a brisk wind. But the conversation sparked lively interest within me. I also told Al that I had not been selected for a position I wanted in the WCC, and I was asking the question I had learned from Henri Nouwen: "What is the meaning of what seems to be?"

Karin's response surprised and amazed me. Even though she had finally secured a job in Geneva as communications director of the World YWCA, she was deeply supportive of this exploration and was suddenly envisioning the prospect of living in New Jersey. We were beginning to sense that, whether for the RCA or something not yet on the horizon, we would be returning to the USA the following summer, a year from then.

So as I tried to focus my reflections and prayers, I saw the year ahead as a time to deepen my life spiritually, as well as making time with Karin and the kids a high priority. If there was any realistic prospect of eventually serving as the RCA's general secretary — and this was still very speculative — I knew the transition would require deep inner resources.

In the ensuing months I followed the search process and explored this prospect. Arie Brouwer, who had served as general secretary prior to Ed, was in Glen Rock, New Jersey, suffering from terminal cancer. We had a long and helpful telephone conversation. In his methodical way, Arie outlined the main issues he saw facing the RCA, the way he would organize work in the new internal structure that had just been approved, and how he had divided his time when he served as general secretary. He encouraged me to be a candidate.

The search committee, consisting of twenty-one members, was organized in the fall. I submitted an application, wondering what would happen. Around the first of the year I received a call from Harry DeBruyn, chair of the committee, saying I was one of the final candidates and asking Karin and me to come to Chicago for an interview with the search committee in February.

Suddenly this prospect had become very real. It was no longer an interesting, but hypothetical, option. And I needed to know where my heart really was in all this; more important, I yearned to know, as far as was possible, where God was in all this.

In mid-January I set off by train for a day retreat at Grandchamp, near Neuchatel. This had become my frequent retreat destination; usually I didn't just board a boat on Lac Leman, and this was winter. Grandchamp had a convent of Protestant sisters who were affiliated with the Taize Community in France. Their worship was quiet and pure, and on occasion I had talked with Sister Albertine for spiritual direction.

I had coffee and croissants during the hour train ride on one of Switzerland's fabulous trains to Neuchatel, and then took the tram to where I could walk to Grandchamp. The community is located near Lake Neuchatel, and by a river that flowed into it.

Reflecting first on words from past journals, I was struck once again by Gordon Cosby's probing question years ago. I'd be given many opportunities, he predicted. The question was, would I be ready, in terms of my inner journey, and my spiritual and psychological integration, to discern what was God's call and to freely embrace and fulfill it?

As always, I took a long walk. It was frosty but not frigid, with swans floating against a January wind, and even some forsythia blooming in the sun against the side of a house.

January 16, 1994

Coming back, I see a perfectly round, beautiful table standing in a field, not far from a barn. What was it doing there? It speaks to me immediately of communion and community. A table prepared . . .

The morning after Harry DeBruyn's call, I awoke with the hymn "The Church's One Foundation is Jesus Christ her Lord" going through my mind. . . .

My own inner spiritual journey is directly related to the kind of leadership which I yearn to offer, and discover more fully. . . .

Perhaps the key question — *how do I get nurture?* And the word that such nurture should not come from my vocational accomplishments or positions in themselves — from Unit III Director, from RCA G.S. It must come from my own inner pilgrimage and faithfulness, which then gets lived out and expressed.

The day went on like this, rich in insights, but I was seeking clarity and guidance. I went out again down to the lake.

After a walk to the lake, it now seems clear that I have received what I came for. At the lake by the closed-up restaurant, I faced the cold hard wind, with driving bits of snow, and asked if this was a call which beckoned me. Yes it is. . . .

It all was just that clear. I am called to seek this position. And it does come from the abiding call to serve the church. . . . And the waters crashing against the shore again remind me of the oceans of God's love and grace. . . . Since Berryville, the connection between the flow of water, and the currents of God's love, have been present . . . always related to the power of God's love in the world.

On the train back to Geneva that evening, I kept writing. The Swiss trains run so smoothly that you can write legibly as they glide through the countryside at 90 miles per hour.

There is something about the RCA job — that I didn't seek it; it seemed to seek me. That it isn't my dream; that I haven't planned it; all this seems healthy. So do I "need" to do this? No. Am I called to? Yes. And the challenge will be to preserve an inner detachment from using the job for psychological security and reward. That nurture of the self must come from within, and from God.

The search committee was meeting at the Ramada O'Hare, about a mile from the house where I grew up in Park Ridge and where my grandfather sold part of the farm to the Catholic church. Karin and I flew there a day early, and on Sunday we attended the Church of the Good News, a small RCA urban church start on the near north side of Chicago. The committee had sent ten potential questions. I had studied hard in Geneva, poring over RCA papers and statistics, and compiled notes and points in a blue, three-ringed binder.

The first question asked by the committee was about the qualities of spiritual leadership needed in this position. It was stunning how that matched so much of my reflection over the last six months. From there the dialogue flowed freely, even though dealing with a search committee of twenty-one members felt unusual. The committee had insisted that Karin and I both be present throughout this time, and that was a strong confirmation of how we had sensed together this call and potential direction.

At one point the committee directed a question specifically to Karin: "How would you feel about you and the family living in the New York area?"

"The only thing that could cause us to move to New York would be an act of God," she replied with her usual candor. And she meant it. That was exactly how both of us were understanding this whole process.

We were told that the committee would inform us of their decision the next morning. Harry DeBruyn, the chair, with Jack Elliott, Nancy Miller, and Gregg Mast came to our hotel room.

"It was a difficult decision," Harry began. "We had two highly qualified candidates. We discussed things thoroughly. But in the end, like in a basketball game, the winning basket went in for you."

Karin and I were awestruck. This really had happened.

We began to digest what all that this would mean. The decision wasn't final — it had to be brought to the meeting of the General Synod Council (GSC) in April, and then to General Synod in June for confirmation. But with twenty-one members from every corner of the church, and a process of discernment that, I later learned, resulted in a surprising unanimous consensus, the path was set.

The other candidate was Ken Bradsell. He was serving on staff, head-

ing up the denomination's work in resources for Christian education and
discipleship, and by all accounts doing an outstanding job. I barely knew
him, but Karin had been at Hope College with him. I called him, thinking
of the profound disappointment he and his wife Marcia were feeling. It
was akin to my own experience at the WCC. He'd given years of faithful
and committed service, and an outsider had been chosen instead of him
for a position he desired. I asked that Ken not make any immediate decisions about his future, and at some point I wanted to have a face-to-face
conversation with him. Ken graciously agreed.

Karin and I returned to Geneva and began planning our transition,
knowing my selection still needed confirmation. In March I went to
Grandchamp for a final day of retreat there. I focused on what I should
do to see that my inner life would be nurtured in this new responsibility
in the midst of external demands that I could only begin to image.

Further, I decided that in my remarks to the General Synod Council,
I needed to give a clear account of how this sense of call had emerged
from deep within me and then found confirmation from the search committee. Further, I wanted to ask to be held accountable not only for my
job performance, but also for practices and disciplines that would help
sustain my spiritual journey and my life as a husband and a father.

Karin and I went to New Jersey to find a place to live — we chose the
third house we saw — and then to Chicago for the GSC meeting. It
proved to be a smooth and confirming process. Rev. Moody Yap, a Chi-
nese American RCA pastor from the San Francisco area, asked if I had a
vision for the future of the RCA. The issue of discovering clarity in the
RCA's mission and vision had been a strong and persistent theme of my
time with the search committee. I told Moody, and the GSC, that while I
had ideas, I saw my task as working with the governing bodies and leadership of the RCA to discern that vision.

General Synod was held on the campus of Central College in Pella,
Iowa. My remarks focused on "calling, commitment, community, and
covenant." My brother and sister were there with their spouses, and my
mom was there with Bob Smith. Bob was a kind, gentle man living in the
same retirement complex as my mom, and he had lost his wife. He and
my mom had discovered a love for one another, and they were engaged
to be married in September.

My Young Life club leader and mentor, Bill Starr, came from Arizona, and longtime friend Jim Wallis traveled from D.C. Both participated in the installation service. Karin was by my side, expectant of the new future for both of us.

The person I missed was my dad. I so wished he could have shared in the joy of that moment. But I also knew that the days I spent at his bedside had imparted not just memories, but qualities that I now would draw upon in following God's call.

Making Space for Vision

E D MULDER and I sat in the general secretary's office on the eigh-
teenth floor of 475 Riverside Drive on New York's upper west side. It
has a spectacular view of the Hudson River, going up to the George
Washington Bridge; directly opposite the north-facing window were the
spires of Riverside Church, with Grant's Tomb nearby. I was spending my
first week as general secretary with Ed, posing countless questions and
listening to his wisdom and counsel.

In addition to the annual General Synod, the governing body representing each "classis" (forty-six assemblies of pastors and elders in a local
region), the RCA had a General Synod Council (GSC) of about sixty-seven
members that met three times a year. General Synod did its business with
a sizable and detailed "workbook." But additional workbooks were then
prepared for each meeting of the GSC.

I asked Ed, "When you finish the fall meeting of the General Synod
Council, then what do you do?"

"Well, staff then start preparing the workbook for the January meeting. And after that, the spring meeting, and then General Synod," he explained, almost apologetically. I wondered aloud when staff had time to
do anything else, and Ed understood my question.

Reformed and Presbyterian bodies are known for doing the business
of the church "decently and in good order." I respected that, and had seen
plenty of examples at the WCC of business done indecently. But my

sense was that more than just the normal business of the church needed to be addressed if we were to face the deepest challenges before us. And it seemed as though there wasn't much space to do so.

Moreover, I sensed the yearning for a more fundamental renewal in the RCA's sense of mission, and a hunger for a vision to guide its future, as had been strongly commended to me by the search committee. This felt linked to the calling I had sensed to bring spiritual as well as administrative leadership to my service as general secretary. But how to go about this was a mystery.

At my first meeting with the General Synod Council, I proposed that we spend the next meeting, in January, on a retreat. We'd have no workbook or normal business; that could easily wait until the spring meeting. Instead, our sole assignment would be for each of us to read the book of Acts. Since I was brand-new, they agreed, willing to try something different.

We gathered at a Franciscan retreat center near Phoenix. In worship, small groups, and sharing together, we reflected on what we read in Acts and how that could relate to the Reformed Church in America today. Time was focused on what we heard both for our personal renewal and for corporate renewal. The themes of community, healing, empowerment by the Spirit, and inspired preaching emerged along with creative ideas for how to enrich our life together in congregations, classes (plural of "classis"), and the other gatherings of the denomination.

This retreat experiment had opened up a place for this large governing board to focus its energies on the call to renewal and the challenge of clarifying our basic sense of purpose. We began seeking the potential directions that God's Spirit could be prompting the denomination to follow. But the lesson I and others learned was that this could happen only by intentionally creating the necessary space in the board's life and work.

Simply doing the business of the church doesn't lead to the mission of the church. In the RCA, the default position of our assemblies — consistory, classis, regional synod, general synod — is to focus carefully on transacting a well-ordered business agenda. Those tasks are necessary. But there's a difference between transactional business and transformational experience. I was beginning to learn how to navigate between these, and was seeing a crucial part of my leadership as opening up space in our life together to discover God's future.

But to do so, I also needed to open space in my personal life for listening to the promptings of God's Spirit and for centering myself in my call. The Carmel Retreat Center in Mahwah, New Jersey, was a few miles from our home in Oakland. Formerly a lavish summer home for a member of the New York Stock Exchange, it rests in the Ramapo Valley against a small mountain. It was given to the Carmelite Order and made into a retreat house.

When I made my way there, I met Father Eugene. The space was physically comfortable and spiritually hospitable. It seemed like a place provided. Father Eugene agreed to serve as my spiritual director. My commitment, which I had shared as well with the General Synod Council, was to spend one day a month there in personal retreat. I had shared this with others because I wanted folks to hold me accountable to this practice.

When Father Eugene was reassigned after a couple of years, he was replaced by Father Ivan Marsh. For several years Father Ivan served as a skilled spiritual director, wise counselor, and friend. The day set aside in a given month for retreat always seemed at the outset like a meddlesome intrusion into a schedule with so many demands. But when I got there, invariably I found rest, peace, and perspective. My inner life found replenishment. So I tried to establish this rhythm, sometimes missing scheduled days but usually keeping this promise, and growing more and more to depend on what such a day would provide and reveal.

During this first year of service, in probing discussions throughout the church with committees, staff, pastors, lay leaders, and ecumenical friends, some common themes began to emerge. First, it was becoming clear that the denomination's role as a "regulatory agency" in the life of its churches would never build unity, inspire mission, or motivate congregational renewal. Certainly a set of agreed practices and procedures is necessary. But if the primary face of the denomination, in the eyes of the local congregation, was one of regulatory enforcement, the opportunity of a denominational fellowship to provide a unifying sense of encouragement, vision, and inspiration to its congregations would be lost.

Second, folks were resonating to the theme that "mission is one." The legacy of the RCA's global mission program is rich and inspiring. For a denomination of our relatively small size, our missional reach around the world has been incredible. But now we were coming to realize that mission is everywhere — across the street as well as across the ocean. Congregations could no longer be comfortable with sending their dollars to support a missionary in Bahrain while ignoring the changing faces and needs in their communities. A fresh conversation was under way about what it meant to participate in God's mission.

The first General Synod under my service as general secretary, in 1995, was an opportunity to imprint some of these ideas, and also refashion how the synod would function. It was to be in New Jersey, but I changed the location, and then we introduced a theme — "Evangelism in a Changing World." I called my friend John Perkins, who agreed to come and address the synod. John is a widely known black church leader in the evangelical world, and an inspiring voice for justice, community development, and racial reconciliation. A simple but powerful point of emphasis began to emerge — we need to extend our life outside of ourselves, our congregations, and our comfortable structures. That would require a radical attentiveness to our changing culture.

On my fiftieth birthday, during synod, Karin asked how long she thought I would be serving as general secretary. I said maybe seven or eight years. And she challenged me, saying she thought this call should endure at least a decade, and maybe longer. That struck me deeply. And I determined to give myself fully, without reservation, and with an open-ended commitment into the future.

That long-term certainty of commitment would be needed as the RCA was confronted by a divisive theological controversy. Rev. Dick Rhem had pastored in the RCA since his graduation from Western Theological Seminary. A gifted theological student, he had been so conservative in seminary that he challenged the orthodoxy of his New Testament professor. But over time, his views moved from one end of the theological spectrum to the other.

In the early 1980s, Dick and I were part of the editorial board of *Perspectives* magazine, a newly formed journal of Reformed theological dialogue. The board would meet at the Alma Matthews House in Greenwich Village, New York, and we'd have stimulating theological discussions about the kinds of authors and subjects to feature. But then we'd adjourn to the White Horse Tavern nearby and continue in spirited, theological explorations of any number of subjects. What got Dick into trouble, in a way, was that he didn't draw a line between what he shared privately at the White Horse Tavern and what he said publicly from the pulpit and put into writing.

He loved to raise questions, and a key one was whether Jesus was the "only way" to salvation. He'd use the analogy that God's light would shine through windows of other religions just as the sun illuminated the different stained glass windows of a cathedral. While there are plentiful theological perspectives for understanding the particular uniqueness of God's incarnation and work of salvation in Jesus Christ, while being open to the presence of God's grace in other religious traditions, Dick pushed the edges of even a generous orthodoxy.

In the Reformed Church in America, the classis acts like a corporate bishop and is responsible for the faithful teaching and practice of its ministers of Word and sacrament. Dick Rhem pastored a large and thriving congregation of one thousand members in Muskegon, Michigan, but most of the other ministers in the Muskegon Classis were conservative in their theological views and became increasingly alarmed at Rhem's pronouncements, which many saw as falling outside the boundaries of orthodox faith.

Attempts at dialogue proved unsatisfactory, and the conflict moved toward a formal action of the classis to suspend Dick Rhem as a minister in the RCA. As general secretary, I had no direct authority within our polity over the actions of any classis. My influence can only be pastoral. But I did have a responsibility to seek and preserve the unity of the denomination. And the conflict with Rhem was spilling over into other parts of the church. Some saw it as a test of the RCA's orthodoxy. Others, not as conservative as the Muskegon Classis, were deeply alarmed that any classis would be taking this kind of action against a minister with as long and distinguished a career as Dick Rhem's. Moreover, the incident was drawing national attention; later it would even appear on the front page of the *New York Times*.

Changing plans, I decided to attend the decisive meeting of the Muskegon Classis. The evening before, I went to the home of my pastor, Norm Kolenbrander, sharing my troubled heart and asking for prayer. In talking to Norm, it became clear that I could not go to the classis meeting intent upon "fixing everything," controlling the outcome, being the savior, and so forth. I wanted to be pastorally present and to stay centered, and not to act or speak out of anger. I needed to remain rooted in presence, not centered on myself.

At the classis meeting Rhem spoke of his twenty-five years of ministry, in which he preached forty-seven Sundays a year from the biblical text. He asked why there couldn't be room for one like himself, realizing he was a gadfly, but wanting to stimulate healthy discussion. He wouldn't pull back from the views and statements that had gotten him in trouble, but asked for a place within the family that had nurtured his Christian journey.

The classis leadership wouldn't pull back either. I spoke about our call to unity and asked whether the classis was holding Dick to a higher or different standard. I fully understood the theological difficulties with his views, but my concern for the wider church was whether we would go down a path of heresy hunting. Nevertheless, the classis moved forward.

I was distraught — the Muskegon Classis voted to end their relationship with Dick Rhem — and wondered whether I did enough, said enough, on Dick's behalf. In retrospect, I don't think any additional words from me would have altered things, but I still felt defeated.

I turned my attention to the pastoral leadership that I needed to exercise at this point in the wider church. When I had begun as general secretary, Jack Elliott, an RCA pastor and member of the Search Committee, gave me a copy of Edwin Friedman's book *Generation to Generations*. This masterful book applies family systems theory to religious organizations. Friedman coined the term "a nonanxious presence"; he writes about the challenge of being a self-differentiated leader who is not caught in the emotional reactivity of conflictive, unhealthy systems but offers instead a clear, courageous, steady presence that can help heal and redirect an organization's energies. Those were the qualities I now needed to discover and put into practice.

The General Synod Council, meeting just four weeks after the Muskegon Classis decision, provided the test. Anxiety was high. Members wondered where all this would lead in the RCA. While very few would agree, at least publicly, with Rhem's theological positions, many were alarmed by the precedent of pushing him out of the RCA. Nothing like this had happened in years. Others were convinced that lines had to be drawn to protect the theological integrity of the RCA.

Giving my report, I spoke from my heart about the deep spiritual value of the ties that bind us together, and the vows we had taken to uphold that unity. A community has to define and then uphold its boundaries, I said, causing at times deeply painful decisions, but the weight of biblical instruction lies with "making every effort to uphold the unity of the Spirit in the bond of peace" (Eph. 4:3).

Then I told the story of my uncle Ralph. Big Daddy and Grandmother had six children. All went to Wheaton College. Most married others from the evangelical and Scandinavian northern European subculture. Except for my aunt Gloria. She married Ralph Buscarelo.

Ralph was Italian. He was formerly Catholic, having met Gloria through InterVarsity Christian Fellowship. He was a lifelong Democrat. And he was outspoken, even to the point of being obnoxious. As a kid, I remember him well at family gatherings at my grandparents' home on Lake Geneva. He'd almost relish starting arguments.

"Am I the only one in the room who voted for Jack Kennedy? Do you all hate FDR even though he got us out of the depression?"

"Doesn't the Bible say we're saved to do good works? This isn't just about getting a ticket to heaven!"

Once, as we were sitting around the living room in this nice summer home on the lake, Ralph picked up a copy of *Better Homes and Gardens*. Paging through it, he suddenly got everyone's attention and declared, "I think this magazine is as pornographic as *Playboy*! It's worshiping materialism." Of course, some of the pictures in the magazine were not unlike the room where we were sitting.

But as a teenager, I loved talking to Uncle Ralph. He challenged me to think about issues and questions that other aunts and uncles would never raise. Those interactions helped me, and other family members, deal more honestly with my faith and its meaning for my life in the world.

The thing is, we all had to deal with Ralph because he was part of the family. We were bound together by those ties. It made us uncomfortable, to be sure, and sometimes Ralph made things worse by his poor judgment. Yet, he was part of us, and in the long run our life together was richer as a result.

In a denomination, we are put into relationship with people we would never choose. But God chose them. And part of how the Spirit works is to use the diversity of those called into the body of Christ for our mutual enrichment and our growth into "the full stature of Christ." That's why working to preserve and strengthen the ties that bind us is a deeply spiritual calling.

My story seemed to strike a chord. The decision about Rhem would remain, and play itself out. But the focus began to shift toward valuing the ties that held us together in Christ. Further, a study process was initiated, and eventually taken up by the Theological Commission, to clarify the uniqueness of Jesus Christ in God's work of salvation, while trusting the mystery and sovereignty of God's grace with respect to those of other religious faiths.

Our sense of unity was also deepened by "Spring Sabbath," which took place in St. Louis two weeks later. This arose from a desire to affirm pastors, and to gather them together for fellowship rather than for governance. I had noticed how well this worked in the Evangelical Covenant Church. About our size, the Covenant gathered 95 percent of its pastors each year for a "midwinter" conference focused on their enrichment and sharing. I thought we should try something similar.

Never having done this, we asked a team of pastors to plan the time, and wrote to all the consistories encouraging them to send their pastors. The weekend after Easter was chosen, and it was designed as a real Sabbath. We'd meet, worship together, listen to a speaker — Rich Mouw, president of Fuller Seminary, was chosen after we had unsuccessfully tried to get Garrison Keillor — enjoy our fellowship, explore St. Louis, and end with communion together.

Six hundred pastors came — more RCA pastors than ever had gathered, in our entire history, at the same place and time. They loved it. Their evaluations were off the charts. It was a simple idea, but it dramatically proved a point. To deepen fellowship, build trust, and strengthen bonds of unity, we needed to provide a nonlegislative setting for gathering together our pastors, and allow them to design it in ways they would find enriching.

My time leading the RCA was approaching two years, and my inward embrace of the call I sensed by the lake at Grandchamp, Switzerland, was finding deep confirmation.

April 12, 1996

    Spring Sabbath.

    I had the sudden, clear, and strong conviction — an affirmation — that "I am called to lead this church." I knew it, felt it, said it — from deep within. . . . Set forth the vision. Build the fellowship. Give myself — show an example. Clarify the questions, gather together those who need to find the answers. . . .

    This is what I was intended to do, what God had prepared — even from the start — that I am fulfilling, carrying out God's purpose for me, more than any other task or job. I know I have been shaped, molded, led to do this —

    To give leadership to this little church, and to be faithful to that task, is at the heart of my being.

More and more, I was realizing that carrying out my service as general secretary was not simply a matter of "doing." Despite a schedule that seemed filled with endless activities and tasks, the heart of my service depended on my "being." Who I was within, and what kind of presence I brought into a meeting or classis or board, was crucial, and even more important than the abilities involved in "doing" the work.

The first retreat of the General Synod Council had started a search to articulate a clear sense of our mission as a denomination, and a vision for our future. Having no precedent for this, and also dealing with full agendas, the council's work toward that end proceeded slowly. But they planned for another retreat in January 1997, this time at Rancho Capistrano, a retreat center owned by the Crystal Cathedral, in California.

Creative work went into their process. They arrived at language that attempted to capture the group's aspirations. Worship together was rich and inspiring. But when the council gathered for its final plenary session, some were uneasy about the draft language for the proposed mission and vision statement. It didn't seem compelling and wasn't fully capturing what had been intended.

The council then made a surprising and unanticipated decision. They approached me and said, "Wes, we want you to take what we've done and go off somewhere and provide your best effort at drafting what this should say."

Some members then added, "Yes, go up to the mountain and see what happens."

Not at all expecting this, I said if I did so, I would want to take others with me to engage in this discernment process together. From the time I was interviewed to be general secretary, the search for a clear vision for our future had been a dominant theme. Now, I wanted to create a process with others that could fulfill the RCA's expectation.

At the Carmel Retreat House, I often browsed through a book with pictures of various monasteries throughout the United States. One Trappist monastery particularly intrigued me — St. Benedict's, at Snowmass, Colorado. Situated on a high plateau surrounded by mountains, it seemed dramatically beautiful, and it welcomed retreatants. Remarkably, they had space during March, and I decided that we would go up to the mountain.

I chose a group including our General Synod president, Tony Vis, Vice President Chuck Van Engen, as well as Lou Lotz, John Chang, Shari Brink, Gloria McCanna, and Mary Clark. We arrived on a brisk, starlit evening; seen from 10,000 feet elevation under clear skies, the heavens truly declared the glory of God. Brother Chuck greeted us. Privately, I asked him one question that was on my mind. We were Protestants, I explained, and wanted to be sensitive to their understandings of the Eucharist, while also desiring to participate as deeply as possible in their worship.

He smiled. "Up here, we don't believe that Jesus served communion just to Catholics."

The monastic rhythm provided a structure to our time of discernment and work. We worshiped, prayed, shared deeply together, absorbed the effort passed on to us by the GSC, and then began testing images, phrases, and words. Snowmass became for us one of those "thin places." We found shared affirmation around common themes of missional engagement in the world. Our hopes and intuitions became enfleshed in words:

> The Reformed Church in America is a fellowship of congregations called by God and empowered by the Holy Spirit to be the very presence of Jesus Christ in the world.
>
> Our shared task is to equip congregations for ministry — a

thousand churches in a million ways doing one thing — following Christ in mission in a lost and broken world so loved by God.

Much more followed in a compelling picture that imagined what this vision might look like, and then how it would be lived out. All contributed to these words. The very last sentence came to me in the shower on our final morning:

> To live out this vision by consistories, classes, synods and staff, our decision-making will be transformed by a pervasive climate of worship, discernment, and biblical reflection. We will no longer do business as usual, nor our usual business.

Our time together at St. Benedict's felt holy. But it also touched on fears and anxieties. Several of us had dreams. And in one I remembered, a guillotine served as a deeply threatening image. I sensed it was conveying feelings about the potential cost involved in following what these phrases were saying.

These were not mere words. They were crystallizing a commitment, which we believed was inspired by God's Spirit, to engage all of the Reformed Church in America to follow Christ in mission, going wherever that led. Moreover, this mission statement was declaring that our central task was to equip congregations for their participation in God's mission. While that might sound benign, in fact it was radical, turning relationships upside down. Congregations didn't exist to equip the denomination's programs. The denomination, with its staff, structures, and resources, existed to equip congregations.

I was already thinking through the implications this statement of mission and vision could have for our staff and for our programs, our priorities, and our style of working. But none of us at Snowmass knew how, or whether, these words would be accepted by the wider church. Moreover, I had purposely decided not to invite any staff colleagues to Snowmass. My thinking was that any mission and vision statement had to be owned by the church and couldn't seem produced by staff. But that carried the risk of key staff not buying into a crucial initiative that they were completely excluded from creating.

The picture in my dream of a guillotine kept coming back to me. Committing to the full meaning of the mission and vision statement could carry serious costs. If the church rejected it, that could even mean my service as general secretary should end. We knew that this was serious, and that all of us should be ready to face the costs that could come from following this commitment. So we left Snowmass exhilarated, but also with a sense of apprehension.

I gathered my staff leadership team at the Carmel Retreat House to share our results, as well as the potential implications I could see for our work. They were curious, outwardly accepting, and open. But it was hard to convey the spiritual experience that had accompanied these words. And in truth, it took a full year for the whole staff to embrace the mission and vision statement, and see it as a foundational direction that guided and redirected our work. A few staff never really did so, and eventually left.

The crucial test, however, came at the GSC, which had commissioned me and then the others in this task, and had to claim these words as their own, or reject them. We were meeting in Newark, following an urban ministry conference. The Snowmass group explained our process, and then laid out the statement of mission, the vision, and the steps for carrying it out. It was what the GSC had been yearning to hear since the first retreat at Phoenix. They responded by singing the doxology.

The final step was to bring this to the General Synod in June at the Milwaukee campus of the University of Wisconsin. Since the RCA had never adopted a statement of mission and vision, some wondered why this was necessary. Others sought to critique the theology they saw implied in its words. In my report to the synod, I tried to make the case for why this was needed:

> The story of the Bible is the account of God's faithful initiative to redeem his people, calling them forth into a new community. Continually, God's Spirit instills vision — vision that reaches out beyond normal human boundaries, vision that challenges our narrow-minded anxieties, vision that enlarges our hearts, vision that calms our fears with a holy fear of God's presence, vision that expands our faith in the sovereign power of God's grace and love.

A biblical vision . . . is a compelling and sustaining picture of God's most desirable future. It places a people deeply in touch with God's clearest intentions for them. And it brings them to the brink, asking them to follow, to walk through the Red Sea, or cross the Jordan, or go through Samaria, or go to the ends of the earth.

A biblical vision also places the church face-to-face with the culture in which it lives and prays and witnesses. In every place and time the church stands in need of discerning how it should live out Christ's presence in the midst of its particular culture.

Delegates had the opportunity not only to debate the statement, but also to suggest editorial changes, which were given to a committee and then brought back to the plenary session. In its final consideration, most all the comments were strong in affirmation, and in expectation of what this could mean for the RCA. A few demurred. John de Velder, a retired, venerable missionary of the RCA, pleaded for the synod to delete the phrase "We will no longer do business as usual, nor our usual business." He felt it cast judgment on the past faithful work of the church. But John Chang then proposed that this sentence be given even more prominence, saying it was one of the most important parts of the whole statement.

In the end, after making some helpful editorial adjustments, General Synod warmly and enthusiastically gave its approval to the whole Statement of Mission and Vision. But few could imagine its eventual implications. For years following, those words have echoed in consistories, classes, committees, and institutions of the RCA. They became a marker in the changing journey of the RCA — a journey that has led its congregations into a fresh and creative missional engagement with the culture, revitalizing congregations, renewing communities, and transforming the lives of thousands.

A Second Chapter

I T WAS THE second chapter of my service as the RCA's general secretary. After we adopted a "compelling picture of God's desired future," which is the best definition of vision I know, the task was to seek its implementation. I guessed this would take four or five years. But I underestimated the obstacles and distractions that would arise.

No matters cause more sleepless nights, and more emotional and spiritual anguish, at least in my experience, than personnel issues. These began to erupt. A critical case involved our treasurer. Though well liked by most of the staff, he had a serious conflict with our investment manager. Because of other staff dynamics, the treasurer didn't have direct authority over him. In essence, the organization lacked a "chief financial officer." The treasurer had deep and serious reservations about our investment strategy and about how our investments were being handled.

Efforts at communication and mediation proved fruitless due to intransigence on both sides and a determined effort by our investment manager to have full control over his operation. Eventually trust was shattered, boundaries were broken, and outside groups were triangulated into the conflict. I came to the reluctant conclusion that I had to dismiss our treasurer. This would be one step in creating an integrated structure of financial management with a chief financial officer, including oversight for the millions of dollars held in our investments as retirement funds for our pastors.

I don't like firing people. I thought the staff I inherited as direct reports were the team that I'd work with into the future. This was another naive assumption. Especially in church organizations, our deep pastoral impulses would have us believe that every conflict can be resolved and anyone's failures can be redeemed. Certainly mistakes can be forgiven. But in the end, the mission of an organization is deterred by a hopeful belief that staff differences can always be resolved. Grace is not conflict avoidance.

The final conversation dismissing the treasurer took place on a Friday afternoon. I was emotionally depleted by the time it was over. Saturday morning was cold and rainy. Karin had wanted a small path cleared through the semiwooded brush in our backyard. I worked there for hours, becoming totally soaked and exhausted, trying to process and resolve my feelings.

Meanwhile, staff anxieties were already running high. They were trying to figure out the implications of the mission and vision statement and also, in many ways, trying to figure out me and my leadership style. I was pushing for change, with the mandate of the general synod, and was unwilling to simply "manage" the staff system as it was. Now, the firing of a valued and well-liked staff colleague became the catalyst for feelings of mistrust and anxiety to erupt.

We established a listening process for staff to anonymously share their feelings and concerns; these were then shared with me, in preparation for a staff retreat. I've learned since how any system will project its fears on to its leader, and also that the nature of a leader's response will either amplify or calm such fears. But at the time, this wasn't easy.

The conference call with the "listeners" from staff was one of my most painful moments as general secretary. I was told the staff did not trust me. They said that I didn't tell the whole story about firing the treasurer, that I lacked relational or listening skills, that I wanted only one agenda, that I didn't welcome criticism or other points of view, etc. There were clear reasons for these feelings. Yet, I felt that this fundamentally did not describe who I am.

Nevertheless, the atmosphere of fragile trust, and a climate where even some are fearful, needed to be addressed. We always — and I always — need to deepen trust, to listen more, to be present more. And with the staff this was especially crucial, especially now. I needed to hear and learn from my mistakes, my weaknesses. I needed to be open and nondefensive.

But fundamentally, I needed to be rooted in my identity with God, who calls me his "beloved," to use the words of Henri Nouwen. These words of his struck me: "As the Beloved, I can confront, console, admonish and encourage without fear of rejection or need of affirmation. As the Beloved, I can suffer persecution without a desire for revenge and receive praise without using it as proof of my goodness."

I would return to that quote from Nouwen countless times in the coming years. It helped me through this time as we gathered the various themes of staff concerns and made commitments to address them. We did away with the existing staff "administrative council" and devised a new structure of staff teams allowing for wider participation in our decision-making process.

More fundamental than structure, however, was staff "culture." Someone had given me an article from the *Harvard Business Review* titled "Changing the Way We Change." It argued, in studying three huge organizations, that the "800 pound gorilla that impaired performance and stifled change was 'culture.'" This was a first step for me in realizing that changing the "culture" of an organization was far more important in achieving lasting and desired changes than simply reorganizing structures. But it also was more difficult. Structural changes focus on who works with whom. Changes in organizational culture focus on the shared values undergirding all work done together.

I was also learning that this "second chapter" of my work as general secretary, and any hope for changes in staff culture, would require changes in me. My first three years were marked by a leadership style that was focused on a process to articulate the RCA's mission and vision. It took strong and persistent action to prompt the denomination to do something it had never done before. Beyond any doubt, many experienced my leadership as focused, resolute, and unwilling to be deterred. Since staff were largely excluded from the process, they had all the more reason to conclude that I had an agenda and was not open to listening to other voices.

But now the situation had dramatically changed. Implementing this mission and vision would require widespread participation and deep ownership. The process had to be open to all voices, drawing on their creativity and commitment, to figure out what it meant for the RCA to live out this vision. My task was to do all I could to invite and welcome all into the process, listening intently and allowing the outcome to be shaped by them. This required a different style in my own leadership. All this would take time, and it had to be based on strengthening trust, which is the "coin of the realm" in an organization like ours, and most others.

These same dynamics affected not just staff, but the whole denomination. Lofty words adopted by General Synod had to take on flesh in 950 congregations, forty-six classes, and eight regional synods, as well as numerous institutions and groups. A major communications strategy was launched. But more importantly, I realized my time and priorities had to be refocused.

I decided to visit each of our forty-six classes over the next two years. That seemed to be the best approach available to invite the whole church into a process of discernment on the mission and vision statement adopted by General Synod. This also provided an extraordinary opportunity to listen to the concerns of each classis. Often our General Synod president or vice president accompanied me.

The experiences of this year sharpened and deepened my understanding of what it meant to be general secretary. In the spring I returned to Dayspring, where Karin and I were married, for some days of writing and retreat.

April 31, 1998

In these days the theme which has kept recurring is that of being a shepherd. The Scripture from John 21 for Sunday — on the beach — "feed my sheep." Tend to the flock.

My thoughts and prayers after walking through the fields — that I have been called to this amazing position, and that the heart of it is to be a pastor — to be a shepherd — to tend to this flock, to nurture them, to offer direction.

It is this dimension of my work that has so deeply called forth important parts of who I am — my sense that I need to express leadership that is rooted in the Spirit; spiritual leadership, not merely administrative leadership.

Yes, of course there is the administrative side. And I enjoy that. Further, what I mean here by "spiritual leadership" is not simply being pastoral, although that is included and is important. Rather, it is bringing the dimension of spiritual attentiveness, discernment, community building, vision, prophetic sensitivities, call, centered conviction, and presence into the heart of what I do, and what we do together.

Another crisis was waiting that would test those words written in the splendid isolation of Dayspring. It came from New Brunswick Theological Seminary (NBTS) and its president, Norm Kansfield. Years earlier, when living in Geneva, our family took a vacation in Locarno, Switzerland, one of our favorite places. It's located in the southern, Italian-speaking area of Switzerland on Lake Maggiore, so it combines the charm of Italy with Swiss efficiency.

The long train trip back to Geneva cuts through the Alps. We sat in a European-style compartment, and as I walked by other compartments, a voice called out to me. It was Norm Kansfield. He had been attending a theological consultation in Rome. I hadn't seen Norm in years. He had been the librarian at Western Theological Seminary when I studied there, and Karin and I were friends with Norm and his wife Mary. Since then he had gone to Colgate-Rochester Divinity School. I introduced Norm to J.K. and Karis, and we had a wonderful conversation as the train wove its way toward Geneva and beyond.

But now Norm and I were drawn into a different, and difficult, encounter. As president of New Brunswick Seminary, Norm had announced the appointment of Dr. Judith Wray to a one-year position as professor of New Testament. Dr. Wray was an open and practicing lesbian in a long-term, committed relationship. News of the appointment had caused a firestorm in many parts of the RCA.

As in most denominations at that time, the RCA's official stance on homosexuality declared that the practicing homosexual lifestyle was contrary to Scripture, while at the same time it encouraged love and sensitivity toward such persons. As one of two RCA seminaries, with long, historic ties and denominational support, New Brunswick's proposed action threatened a major rift between the seminary and the denomination. The controversy could easily engulf the forthcoming General Synod.

New Brunswick Seminary's Board of Trustees met just days before General Synod, and I was asked to join them and speak to this controversy. I noted how this action would be seen as a major breach of trust by many in the church, given New Brunswick's role as a teaching institution of the RCA. Further, it would polarize and inflame debate, and likely prompt recrimination toward the seminary.

At the same time, the RCA needed a safe space for reflection and discernment around the issue of homosexuality. The formative policy positions had been written twenty years earlier, in 1978 and 1979. Calls since then for ongoing study, sharing, and reflection around the pastoral challenges involved, as well as for understanding the use of Scripture in addressing difficult moral and ethical issues, had gone largely unheeded.

I told the board I intended to propose a "moratorium" on policy debates and votes on homosexuality in order to create an opportunity for needed dialogue and reflection in a nonconfrontational environment. But much would depend on what Norm and the board decided to do with the appointment of Dr. Wray. The board's own dialogue was serious and intense. They made the decision to withdraw the appointment.

Yet, the tension and anxiety around how this matter would be handled at General Synod remained acute. On the eve of synod in Holland, Michigan, I went to St. Francis de Sales Church to pray. As an ecumenical gesture, synod would be meeting at this Catholic church a couple of nights later on Sunday evening, and John Bell from the Iona Community in Scotland would be our worship leader. But I was focused on what would happen when synod convened at Hope College in the morning.

In my report the next day at the start of General Synod, I set forth my three-year "moratorium" proposal: "[T]o instruct this General Synod to refrain from deliberative debate and policy decisions relating to homosexuality . . . and to urge this same action on the 1999 and 2000 General Synods . . . and to enter into a process of intentional discernment over the next two years concerning the pastoral challenges related to homosexuality."

The proposal also requested that no agencies, institutions, or assemblies of the RCA take action in contradiction to our policy during this period.

Debate was focused. Some from the "right" wanted synod to pass an official "rebuke" of New Brunswick Seminary. Other voices wanted guarantees protecting homosexuals in the RCA from any form of judicial action. But the vast majority of delegates embraced the moratorium proposal and its commitment to ongoing discernment and dialogue.

Norm Kansfield also made a gracious speech to the synod, saying: "When living at the edge, it is very easy to cross the boundaries of propriety and acceptability; that is very clearly what I did in the present instance. I apologize to you for what this action did to the peace and unity of our denomination. Neither New Brunswick nor I have ever thought to be an embarrassment or insult to the General Synod."

We avoided what could have been a bloody conflict, bought some time, and created some space for dialogue. Yet, as I said to synod, "it still leaves us as a church with a crucial and important question: how will we, the Reformed Church in America, choose to address this issue, not only in this situation, but in the future?"

My conviction has been that no legislative actions of General Synod will resolve the differences in perspectives and pastoral practices that exist in the RCA concerning homosexuality. No words of a General Synod will change a person's sexual orientation. As witnessed in other denominations, attempts at legislative remedies will simply serve to polarize, alienate, and ostracize groups on one side or the other, dividing the body of Christ. The challenge, in my view, is to create an atmosphere of trust that recognizes that certain differences need not be divisive. That becomes possible only when we find ourselves bound together in a common calling to God's mission.

The moratorium proposal opened the way for that synod, and several following, to devote a singular focus on implementing the mission and vision statement. I presented to the 1998 synod seven key priorities, confirmed by the General Synod Council (GSC), to shape our work accordingly, and the energy of the delegates rapidly gravitated to those ends. Further, the moratorium, adopted for three years, seemed to be automatically extended to the next six years as momentum around our missional calling kept gaining strength.

But the space for discernment, in nonlegislative settings, around the challenges of homosexuality wasn't widely utilized. Some thought the moratorium meant we weren't supposed to discuss the issues of homosexuality. The opposite was intended: we were to be talking with one another instead of voting. Ultimately, I hold myself at fault for not doing more to encourage the opportunity for such dialogue instead of expecting that it would simply bubble up from the grass roots.

With this missional trajectory of the RCA beginning to take hold, the staff and I wondered where it would lead, and tested ideas with the GSC. We were focusing on what should happen at General Synod in 2000, at the dawn of a new millennium.

I proposed that we hold the 2000 General Synod in Jerusalem. Staff colleagues thought I was crazy. Several had the self-confidence to tell me so. My thinking was that at this juncture in history, two millennia after the life, death, and resurrection of Jesus, we should return to the place of our faith's historic roots, and to where the church was founded. But the costs and logistics seemed prohibitive.

Instead we thought in more parochial terms of our history, turning to where the RCA was founded — New Amsterdam, in 1628, which today is New York City. A plan began to emerge for a unique gathering, wrapped into General Synod, which would help us discern the particular missional directions of the RCA in the twenty-first century. Representatives would come from every congregation and be exposed to the ministries and outreach of RCA congregations in New York City, as well as interacting with representatives of our global mission from around the world.

Moreover, we would hold this gathering over Pentecost weekend, capturing the themes of the Holy Spirit's institution of the church with those from all nations, and sending us into mission. Rev. James Forbes of Riverside Church would preach on Pentecost evening, and Dr. Robert Schuler, of Crystal Cathedral, and Dr. Arthur Caliandro, of Marble Collegiate Church in Manhattan, would also speak during the gathering. Moreover, Emilio Castro, former general secretary of the World Council of Churches who hired me to its staff, agreed to lead our Bible studies.

Central to this whole gathering, however, would be a process of discernment, listening to what the Spirit could be saying for the shape of our future mission and witness. In Reformed circles, "discernment" is not always a comfortable word. We are far more accustomed to "deliberation," "debate," and "decisions," preferring the orderliness of such a process.

But I was intrigued with other models for the church to engage necessary decisions and directions, and I was skeptical of the unquestioned wedding between a parliamentary process using Robert's Rules of Order and Reformed polity and governance. Further, my ecumenical experiences continued to expose me to a wide range of styles for church bodies to govern themselves, including a growing use of consensus decision-making in careful and impressive ways.

Charles Olsen, a Presbyterian minister, had written two books related to this search: *Transforming Church Boards* and *Discerning God's Will Together.* Chuck had met with the staff leadership group several months earlier, and we were impressed by his approach to the process of discernment, which used many ancient spiritual practices of the church to help a group discern a "common mind." So we asked him if he could facilitate this process for a group of one thousand.

We called the event "Mission 2000," and held it at Hofstra University in New York. General Synod delegates convened and then were joined by hundreds more from throughout North America and partners from around the world. Along with being exposed to a wide variety of missional outreach efforts, they also met in groups of about twenty-five. Each was led through a process of prayer and response to questions, and representatives from each group shared together to discover common themes. The result, facilitated by Olsen, was a "Pentecost Letter" to the congregations of the RCA that captured powerfully the yearnings of the thousand folks who had gathered. It was a remarkable model of discernment and a moving result that never could have been reached through our customary deliberative, parliamentary process.

The fruit of this time was then harvested by the General Synod delegates. One of several actions that had lasting results was the request to develop a ten-year goal that would specify the directions and desired results of the RCA's missional engagement into the future. The directional commitment of the mission and vision statement adopted three years earlier now needed to be crystallized into work that would shape and reshape the RCA over the coming decade.

MOST EVERY MONTH I kept my scheduled day at the Carmel Retreat Center and my talk with my spiritual director, Father Ivan. Ivan's probing questions, his wise insights, and his gentle advice were like fresh water for a thirsty soul. I'd leave after breakfast with Karin, taking a short, pleasant drive up the Ramapo Valley, and arrive home for dinner. But just those few hours would prove to be life-giving.

More of my focus went to building the staff. With a couple of retirements, and another painful dismissal, I was now choosing and putting into place the group of staff that reported directly to me. The team that was emerging, and the trust and commitment that were beginning to grow, was making a tremendous difference.

Relationships with peers in other denominations were also growing. One was Dick Hamm, president and general minister of the Disciples of Christ. We met early in my service when I entered a room of other "heads of communion" of denominations belonging to the National Council of Churches (NCC). Most there seemed at least ten years older than I except for a younger person at the end of the table, who also was the only one there using a laptop. I knew we'd have a lot in common.

Dick and I, along with other denominational leaders, would gather at governing board meetings of the NCC. But all our time and energy would be focused on the NCC's crisis *du jour*. The ecumenical organization was plagued during that time by shrinking revenues, strategic incoherence, and inept management, and we were consumed with trying to exercise some effective governance over this dysfunctional organization. What this did not provide was meaningful time to share with one another.

Dick proposed that this "head of communion" group gather separately for its own time of retreat, and I strongly agreed. We found a unique site at the College of Preachers facility on the grounds of the National Cathedral in Washington, D.C., and established the time in mid-December. A simple but startling agenda was proposed. We would spend the first afternoon and evening allowing each person to share his or her joys and sorrows of the past year. Then we would move into twenty-four hours of silence, during which we would pray for one another, reflect on Scripture, and simply rest in this unique gift of silent space. Following this, we would share together the fruits of our solitary time, and worship together. Finally, any ecumenical "business" would be conducted during a few hours the morning of our departure.

About ten or twelve of us who were leading denominations would participate each year, and this became a holy and treasured time. In December 1999, when this tradition was just beginning, the retreat provided me the open space to think and pray about where my call to the RCA was heading, what I could offer, and how long I should stay.

Early in the new year, reflecting on the duration of my call to the RCA, I had a conversation with Bruce and Vicky Menning when I was in Grand Rapids. They had been close friends since our days at Hope College. Bruce and I were in the same fraternity, and Bruce actually met Vicky when we went on a "double date" together — Vicky was my date.

Both were (and are) ordained pastors in the RCA, and had done creative and courageous ministry together. A few years earlier, I had asked Bruce to serve as the RCA's director of global mission, and he had become a key part of our staff leadership team.

Bruce and Vicky always spoke truth to me, and I wanted to talk with them about how long I should serve as general secretary. I knew other options would come. One, in fact, had already come and gone: I had been asked — actually recruited by its leadership — to be a candidate for general secretary of the World Alliance of Reformed Churches, but had turned this down. Further, I knew that in a year, the World Council of Churches would be searching for a new general secretary, and several people had spoken to me about this.

The three of us sat in the living room of their home following dinner, and Vicky shared with clarity her counsel and convictions. She challenged me to think about staying with the RCA for a longer period — perhaps ten years.

She said Barbara Brown Taylor sometimes tells married couples in trouble that they need to stay together in order to "grow up." It's the only way. And perhaps, by analogy, I needed to stay with the RCA long term in order to demonstrate or experience those growing places within me — to see the fruit of a long-term commitment, both within me and in the life of the church.

Vicky used another expression: "Sometimes you have to sweep up your own dust." In other words, not just stir everything up, but stay with it, work with the results, see through what has been started.

Ten months later, again at the year-end "head of communions" retreat at the College of Preachers, and following the tremendous success and impact of Mission 2000, I was still pondering my future, including the challenge that had come from Bruce and Vicky, which Karin also shared. I jotted down a simple prayer: "Dear God, are you calling me to a long-term commitment to the RCA? And what are you calling me most to do?"

I sought out Dick Hamm, and in a private sitting room in an alcove of the College of Preachers building, we reflected on my six years as general secretary and my future. Dick was less concerned about any long-term time commitment, and stressed more the importance of discerning and staying with the clarity of my call.

We talked about how I had reinvented my job and role, and needed to continue to do so. He said, "These systems without bishops yearn for some form of authority that is not rooted in hierarchy." Dick felt that I had figured out how to exercise authority and gain trust in ways not dependent upon rank or position — that I had learned to "exercise authority without claiming it." This takes a combination of spiritual integrity and vision, and I had been trying to learn how to do this.

Dick and I tended to agree that my role should be focused on vision casting, on being a "pastor at large," on holding the denomination accountable to our vision, and on being the ecumenical officer. The "stated clerk" and denominational "CEO" functions should recede (and be delegated more to others). I should keep thinking about how to "reinvent" how I carry out my role.

I was clearly thinking now about another new chapter in my work as general secretary, one that might be marked by a long and sustained commitment to this calling. But that would be tested by the possibility of returning to Geneva.

Hearing Our Call

———

CRAIG VAN GELDER, Pat Keifert, and I sat around the circular teak table in my New York office one morning drinking coffee. I was interviewing them to see if they were the right ones to do a "missional audit" of the RCA's structures. This was part of our effort to see how our governance structures, our staff organization, and the priorities of our work could all be aligned around the missional direction that had been embraced by the General Synod and now was being implemented. Audits were done by independent firms for financial integrity and also management effectiveness. So why not do an audit of our structures around their missional effectiveness?

Van Gelder was a Christian Reformed pastor and theologian who previously had taught at Calvin Seminary and now was teaching at Luther Seminary in St. Paul. His writing and work on the missional church were well known, and he obviously understood Reformed polity. He brought along Pat Keifert, also a professor at Luther Seminary. If the audit was to be done, it would take place through an organization called Church Innovations, and Keifert was its president.

Pat looked like a European theologian. He was an affable, stocky person with a gray beard and glasses who sat listening, and then would interject incisive questions. At one point in our conversation, he looked at my coffee mug, which came from the fly shop where I fished in West Yellowstone, Montana.

"Are you a fly fisherman?" he asked.

For the next twenty minutes the conversation suddenly veered to the Lamar Valley, cutthroat trout, Soda Butte, Slough Creek, browns and rainbows, the Madison, and the Yellowstone River. Van Gelder simply watched our conversation bounce back and forth like a tennis match.

Eventually we returned to the audit. We agreed that Church Innovations would do this missional audit of the RCA's structures. I'd work out the details with Keifert a few weeks later in the summer, when we'd meet in the dining room of the Mammoth Springs Lodge on the north end of Yellowstone Park. Both of us, we discovered, planned to be fishing there during the same week!

Two results came from that morning meeting in New York. First, the audit provided a helpful, independent look at our structures through a missional lens. Several recommendations it made were eventually implemented, including reorganizing the General Synod Council (GSC) as a smaller executive committee, drawn directly from the General Synod and able to give effective direction for implementing our mission and vision. Eventually, my own job description as general secretary was also rewritten and staff were reorganized into "clusters" that reflected the emerging priorities of our work.

Second, our meeting in the Mammoth dining room began a tradition of gathering a few pastors, theologians, and authors each summer at Yellowstone Park. Keifert would invite those working on missional church issues from three or four denominations. We'd gather in the morning for biblical reflection ("Dwelling in the Word") and discussion around common challenges, and then go fly-fishing in the afternoon and evening. We came to call it the "Ichtheology" gathering (a play on "ichthyology," the study of fish). I'd invite four or five folks from the RCA to be a part. For me this was almost heaven.

Shortly after starting as general secretary I had gone fishing with Dick Welscott on a cold November day in Michigan. Dick was an expert in new church development, working part-time on our staff and also with the RCA's Michigan Regional Synod. I wanted to persuade him to become the denomination's full-time director for planting new churches. We were fishing for spawning salmon in the Pere Marquette River with heavily weighted hooks.

"They've got only one thing on the mind — sex. You've got to hit them with the weights on their head to get their attention," he explained.

We fished well into darkness. I fell in and got soaked, chilled, exhausted, and frustrated. But by the morning at breakfast (I had eggs and bacon, and Dick had cherry pie), I convinced him to take the job. I also told him he had to learn how to fly-fish and come to Montana with me. It was more civilized, like an art.

Dick took to fly-fishing like, well, a fish takes to water. Before long, he was far better than I, always catching more trout. A few years before the encounter with Pat Keifert, Dick had convinced me to host three days of fishing in Yellowstone each summer with three or four laypeople who were, or could be, donors to the RCA. These encounters became priceless.

We'd have Bible study and devotions in the morning, fish through the day, and then gather in the evening to talk about the RCA. The guests would set the agenda, and I gathered tremendous wisdom from laymen who often were successful in business, loved the church, but felt that their voices were rarely heard in the governing bodies of the denomination.

When Larryl Humme became director of development, he joined Dick and me on these summer fly-fishing donor-cultivation trips. It was all new to Larryl, but he tried to be a good sport. He got a pair of waders from someone in the south Chicago suburbs where he lived. They were heavy, cumbersome, clunky, rubber waders more suited for putting wood piers into a Wisconsin lake than for fly-fishing in a Montana river.

We were fishing the Yellowstone River near Buffalo Ford, meaning this is a place where buffalo actually cross the river. The Yellowstone is wide, with a swift current, and holds beautiful cutthroat trout. Our guide had gotten Larryl and a couple of others, including Mark De Cook, across part of the river to an island to fish. Now they were coming back. Locking arms together, they waded into the deep, fast-flowing current that reached above their waists. Larryl's bad knees buckled and he fell in, with water pouring into his heavy waders. It was dangerous. Mark and the guide managed to hold on to him and finally got him to the shore.

I was at the picnic area grilling food as Larryl marched toward me, carrying his clunky waders. Red in the face, soaked, sputtering, and angry, he threw the waders at my feet and said, "Do I have to do this to keep this damn job?"

We bought him new waders, and he did keep his job for several years. He then became a member of the GSC, and told everyone that story.

For me, fly-fishing can be a contemplative experience. My love for the sport is far greater than my aptitude. I actually find time to fish only a few days a year, but each summer I get to Yellowstone either with an RCA group, and the Ichtheology gathering, or just with friends. Once in a great while, I do really well.

Fly-fishing in Yellowstone Park provided metaphors for the issues facing the RCA. In one General Synod report, I compared the tension between the mission of the church and the order of the church to the relationship of a river to its banks. While fishing on the Lamar River in the northeastern section of Yellowstone, I thought of how the current is always flowing, but it's directed by the banks. Without any banks, the water would simply dissipate and have no direction. Likewise, the order and polity of the church provide the framework for its mission to flow.

At the same time, the river is always shaping and pushing its banks. Riverbanks are never constant and stationary, and even the Army Corps of Engineers has trouble forcing a river into a predetermined course. The banks exist to facilitate the river's flow, and they shift with the changing flow and force of the river, just as mission should always influence and reshape the order of the church.

At times, I've arrived in the Lamar Valley to discover, much to my surprise, that the entire flow of the river at some point has completely changed, moving on a different path. What happened, I learned, was that the spring runoff of melting snow from the mountains was so powerful and intense that it burst over its established banks and established a new place to flow, creating fresh banks.

With pictures of the Lamar River showing on the screen, I explained to General Synod that sometimes the mission of the church becomes so strong and empowered by the Spirit that it can reconstitute well-established parts of the church's order. Even then, just as new banks are

needed to guide the river's new path, new forms of order become necessary to shape and undergird the church's mission.

The tension between mission and order began to emerge as one of
the foundational issues, often beneath the surface, that framed many of
the challenges and conflicts that the RCA began to face. I came to see
this as necessary, and even healthy, as long as the underlying issues
could be identified within this framework. This wasn't a conflict to be
solved, but rather a "polarity" to be managed.

The GSC had been given the task to establish a "ten-year goal." The
internal origins of this idea had come from an article describing the need
for organizations to have a "big, hairy, audacious goal," or a BHAG, to focus their energy and work. We stopped using that language, and some in
the church opposed the very idea of having such a goal as a corporate,
secular model imposed on the church. But General Synod had used the
language of a ten-year goal to clarify concretely where our mission and
vision statement would take us.

The GSC and staff used a variety of means to discern where our energies and focus should be placed, and what we believed God's desired future for the RCA might look like. I convened a "Think Tank," we had retreats, and the GSC experimented with various group process exercises
to find clarity and consensus.

Our plan was to have the language and content of a ten-year goal approved at the spring meeting of the GSC in 2002 for presentation to General Synod that summer. What we meant by "approve" was important.
Following Mission 2000, we had continued to work with different models
of discernment and decision making. In fact, a General Synod president,
Steve Vander Molen, and staff members Ken Bradsell and Jeff Japinga
had traveled all the way to New Zealand and Australia to watch how national church assemblies there were making all their decisions by consensus, and typically not using Robert's Rules of Order at all.

We were experimenting with these various approaches to decision
making. For instance, all the members of the GSC were given three cards
— green, yellow, and red. As issues were discussed, the moderator would
test "the mind of the house" by asking those in agreement with a given
view or proposal to show green cards, those who had questions to show
yellow cards, and those firmly opposed to show red cards. Then particu-

lar people would be called on to express concerns or questions. The discussion would flow in this manner, and the hope was to get to a point where all could be in agreement, or where those opposed were willing to "step aside" in view of a strong consensus.

GSC at that point still comprised sixty-seven members. The final version of the proposed language for the ten-year goal was being discussed and modified on the last morning of the spring meeting, with the moderator hoping to guide the body to a strong consensus. But adjournment was approaching, with planes to catch. For a final time, the moderator asked for cards to be raised. The great preponderance were green, but there were a few yellow and three or four red.

The officers gathered with me and staff colleagues Jeff, Ken, and Shari Brink to decide how to proceed. I had been determined to get the proposed goal to synod that year; in my view, the whole process had already taken too long. But others felt that the strong reservations indicated by the red cards, plus the few yellow, meant that we should not proceed, even though these were a small minority of the whole GSC.

The officers made the decision to postpone the action, feeling that would be true to the process the GSC was trying to learn. I was frustrated. That meant it would be another year before a ten-year goal could be presented to General Synod. But we were trying to change the way we did business, and nurture a different decision-making culture. Plus, this would offer more time to test the proposals with the wider church. It proved to be the right decision. Had we been operating under our traditional method of Robert's Rules, such an outcome would have been unthinkable.

The next year did provide for classes and other bodies in the church to respond to the proposed direction of the ten-year goal. I took part in several classis and regional synod meetings discussing where the RCA should be headed in the next decade. Themes such as a central priority for starting new churches and ways to effectively emphasize congregational revitalization found strong affirmation. Other aspirations were raised as well. And when the GSC met in the spring of 2003, it achieved consensus on what to present to General Synod.

But when General Synod began its consideration of the proposed language and content for the ten-year goal, it became clear that this would be contentious. A variety of concerns and agendas were raised, some of which were not really related to the proposal. Others objected to various phrases. Some said it wasn't ecumenical enough. Concerns were raised about making a false idol of numerical growth. Then various amendments were proposed, and synod found itself trying to be a drafting committee of 240 people.

In many respects, the debate was the occasion for some who had been disconcerted about the direction of the RCA ever since adoption of the mission and vision statement — and in some ways, since the time I started as general secretary — to express their anxieties, fears, and frustrations. A few questioned the need for such a goal at all. Others, on the other hand, were frustrated that any delegates could question an emphasis on extending the gospel to those unchurched, and expanding the kingdom. Debate and proposed amendments dragged on into the evening, and finally synod was recessed without any final action, which was postponed to the next day.

That evening I couldn't sleep. At 2:00 A.M. I was pacing in the Pine Grove on the campus of Hope College, and praying. It felt like the whole attempt to adopt a clear goal that would focus and direct our efforts over the next decade might go down in flames. Three years of work would come to naught.

But my deeper prayer became one of relinquishment. I had to fully trust God and trust the presence of the Spirit in the life of the delegates assembled together. This was one of those times when I needed to take all my effort, and that of many other colleagues, and simply turn it over to the mysterious providence of God. I couldn't control the outcome, and shouldn't even try. Rather, I needed to pray a prayer of abandonment.

I got back to my room and finally fell asleep.

The next morning as General Synod convened, I learned that a group of delegates were also up in the night, praying and working together. Several who had raised questions or reservations from various perspectives had come together and found common ground — perhaps even holy ground. They worked on a draft of new and revised language for the overall ten-year goal, taking into account the debate from the day before, and presented it to the General Synod:

Our Call

Following Christ in mission together, led by the Holy Spirit, and working with all the partners God provides, we believe that God is calling the Reformed Church in America over the next ten years to focus its efforts and resources on:

> *Starting new congregations and*
> *Revitalizing existing congregations,*

Thereby empowering fruitful and faithful ministries for the glory of God.

These two primary initiatives were to be supported by an emphasis on discipleship, leadership, and mission. Further, the GSC would be given the task of developing specific strategies to achieve these initiatives over the next decade.

This resounded with delegates. One after another began rising to voice not only their affirmation, but also their commitment to what was proposed. I remember so well Rick Veenstra, a pastor from Michigan, coming to the microphone and saying, "I can commit the rest of my ministry to working for this goal." A groundswell of affirmation was building.

Something had happened over the evening, and God's Spirit was at work. It wasn't just language that now seemed to connect with the delegates, but a sense of welcoming and embracing a future for the Reformed Church in America shaped by joining God's mission in the world in specific ways. The General Synod not only passed the proposal by an overwhelming margin. They then sang the doxology.

And in those twenty-four hours, I learned a huge lesson in relinquishment and trust.

I DON'T THINK I COULD have remained centered and helped guide the synod though a difficult but dramatically important time of decision making had I not withdrawn my candidacy to be general secretary of the World Council of Churches a couple of months earlier, in April 2003. I had set aside the most promising and, I can honestly say, tempting option to leave my service with the RCA. Remaining centered in my calling after nine years, taking other options off the table, and not looking elsewhere made a decisive difference in my leadership. People knew I was "all in."

Getting to that point, however, was an arduous journey of discernment.

On an early spring day in 2002, I was at the Potter's House in the Adams Morgan neighborhood of Washington, D.C., where years earlier I had worked every Friday night as part of a mission group in Church of the Saviour. Gordon Cosby was meeting me for lunch. At eighty-four, his body was frail but his mind was sharp and incisive.

Even though he had not seen me for years, he sat down and said, "Well, Wes, how is it going with your inner spirit?" Vintage Gordon.

The decision about whether to apply to be the WCC's general secretary was still months away, but ecumenical friends were already talking with me about it. I wanted to know what Gordon thought.

"So few people," Gordon said, "are willing to work for change in the long run. To stay committed to the depth of change that is necessary. Such change, such deep change, simply takes time."

Gordon was amazed at how much I had been able to achieve in what he said was a short time. A mission statement, now working its way into our life. A group of committed staff who seemed like a real team. But that just set the stage.

"Servant leaders are one thing. Servant structures are another, and that takes far more work," Gordon explained. He wasn't claiming a definitive discernment for me, but was sharing his own testimony and experience. His advice was clear.

But two months later I was near Helsinki, Finland, for the meeting of the WCC's Special Commission on Relations with the Orthodox. Shortly after arriving for our meeting in Jarvenpaa, a pleasant retreat site by a lake, Metropolitan Chrysostomos talked with me. The ecumenical patriarchate in Istanbul wanted me to know that if I were a candidate for general secretary, they would support me. They were impressed, he said, by my previous work with the Special Commission. We had a good conversation, and I told him it would depend upon a strong sense of call.

Later Rev. Dabba, head of the Mekana Jesus Church in Ethiopia, asked me to take a walk with him after dinner down to the lake. Several people had been talking, he said, and would like to see me be a candidate for general secretary. By the lakeshore near a sauna, we talked and prayed together. This pattern continued.

A couple of trusted WCC staff members and friends emphasized to me that what the WCC most needed now was spiritual leadership. Konrad Raiser had given great intellectual leadership, but people were "absolutely depleted," as one longtime staff person put it. "No one gets replenished. The challenge is spiritual revitalization."

That summer Karin and I were in Yellowstone. We sat on the small platform opposite Cliff Geyser, sipping wine and talking mostly about the WCC general secretary opening and our future. Karin had found some expression for her pastoral gifts at Ponds Church in Oakland, New Jersey, where we were living, and was considering how to pursue ordination. I poured out my heart about the urgings I'd been receiving, and my questions. We sensed that the future was open, and uncertain.

Back home, Karin was taking steps around her calling. She had found real clarity and affirmation in her pastoral work. One Sunday I watched her, from a distance through a window, sharing her call with the consistory, and she was so passionate, so energized, so alive. I felt her ministry must be given space to grow.

I didn't know how everything fit together, but I was trying to simply trust God.

The WCC Central Committee, of which I was a member, met in Geneva early that September. The list of those encouraging me to be a candidate was growing, with friends from Asia, Africa, and Latin America approaching me and saying that the colleagues from their region felt likewise.

I went out for a *fillet de perches* dinner with my two closest friends from among the leaders of U.S. churches there, Dick Hamm and Cliff Kirkpatrick. I shared the reactions I was receiving, but also Karin's journey desiring finally to establish a place for her pastoral ministry.

The conversation was rich and deep. Then Cliff looked me straight in the eye and said, "Your whole life has prepared you for this. You can do it. But it's not worth jeopardizing your marriage."

That fall I began a three-month sabbatical given to me after having served for eight years. I started this by taking a week at Our Lady of Solitude House of Prayer in Black Canyon City, Arizona. Hiking through the surrounding hilly desert, I prayed and wrote exhaustively in my journal. Names were given to places. A rise with a flat area above a canyon became the "RCA Plateau." It was the place where I prayed deeply and reflectively about the denomination. Climbing to the top of a nearby hill, I prayed earnestly about my calling, and named this the "Hill of Call."

September 27, 2002

I knew — on top of that hill — that I am beckoned and called, and that to be faithful, I must be open.

But I also know that this comes only from a place of relinquishment — of not having to do this, not needing it, and being willing to put my other call — my call to Karin — first.

September 28, 2002

I reached the top, again, and simply walked and prayed. And I asked again if I had heard correctly.

Yes. Karin is first. And that is right. I can serve on the RCA Plateau. It's a good place to be.

I asked again if I should simply close off the WCC as an option. No. I am to remain open.

But free from all personal desire or vain attraction or aggrandizement. . . . And simply open to call.

Then I heard this message — "Be not afraid." Simply trust that your life is in God's hands. Simply trust that God will use you, where God wills, as God wills. . . .

That word kept coming, and I sang it.

And then I broke into prayer, aloud, shouting on the top of the "Hill of Call." Bless you. Thank you. I love you Christ.

My arms were extended high, holding my walking stick in the air, as I exclaimed in words that just came from the heart — Thank you Lord. Bless you.

It was a moment of the heart's joy breaking forth. My inner self bursting into voice. A precious, peaceful time of exclamation.

Most of my sabbatical was devoted to writing a book, which became *Leadership from Inside Out: Spirituality and Organizational Change.* My friend Doug Fromm had made available a cottage on Cape Cod, and I spent several days there writing from morning to night. But I also kept reflecting on the WCC position, remembering the strong and clear sense of call that emerged within me toward the RCA at Grandchamp in January 1994. I knew that if I was to proceed with the WCC, I needed the same kind of clarity in my soul. But I didn't think it was quite there yet.

By the end of the year, again at the "head of communions" retreat in D.C., it seemed clear to me that I should hold this whole process lightly, with inner detachment. I proceeded with the application process and worked intently on a requested vision statement for the future of the WCC. But I also kept reminding myself that I was ready to relinquish it, and that, just as happened in my call to the WCC staff in 1988, I knew that Karin came first.

Further, another foundational issue troubled me. My vision for the WCC's future was clear. I believed that ecumenical relationships desperately needed to be broadened. Composed mainly of the world's historic Protestant churches and Orthodox churches, the WCC represented only one-quarter of Christianity. The Catholic Church cooperated on some issues but kept its autonomous distance through not being a member. The fastest-growing churches especially in the global south, largely evangelical or Pentecostal in nature, lived mostly in total isolation from the WCC and other regional ecumenical bodies. In my view, all that had to change.

Doing so would take a huge concerted effort. But the WCC was laden with factions and interest groups, pushing numerous agendas, all of which fought hard for shrinking resources as its revenues were declining. A fundamental shift in the council's energies and direction would not only be difficult, but might not even have the support of key leaders in its governing bodies.

Anna Marie Aagaard was a longtime ecumenist from Denmark who had been selected as one of the WCC's presidents. We had worked together well on restructuring proposals and on breaking down organizational and theological silos that prevailed in so much of the WCC's life, and we had gained one another's trust. On a Monday evening in March at a dinner in New York City, Anna Marie talked to me about the enormous effort it would take just to stabilize the WCC. And then she asked whether there would be space for something new. Would the investment be worth it? Might something new emerge in other ways at the global level that could carry hope for the future?

Later that week Karin and I flew to Daytona Beach for a board meeting of Call to Renewal, an initiative begun by Jim Wallis for a broad Christian witness around the issues of poverty and justice. I chaired its board and always looked forward to the formal and informal conversations we had.

On Friday evening, Jim, Karin, and I had a long conversation about my future. Our friendship, forged over many years, had remained deep and strong. He listened to Karin's concerns and also wondered if the WCC could be revitalized. Moreover, Jim stressed the growing role I had with other U.S. church leaders, and what that could mean for the future. I wrote in my journal on the plane flying home with Karin: "So it's all very very hard. The discernment does not seem clear. But it is pointing away."

At the Board of Benefit Services meeting a week later, I had breakfast with Steve Brooks. A gifted pastor from Colorado Springs who later died tragically from Lou Gehrig's disease, Steve had been General Synod president and was a trusted friend. And he was honest. Leaving the RCA, Steve said, would hurt the ten-year goal. He understood that the WCC wanted a "turnaround" person just like the RCA did. But he put it to me bluntly: "If we're asking folks to sign up for the next ten years, then you should be asked to do the same."

A trip to Taiwan and China with the current General Synod president, John Chang, followed. When I returned, I learned that my daughter Karis was having a difficult time at Hope College owing to personal issues, and Karin had been on the phone with her continually. Also upon returning, I opened an e-mail requesting that I come to Albania to be interviewed by the Search Committee for the WCC general secretary position. I was in turmoil.

It was Holy Week. I decided to go to Carmel on Saturday to seek final clarity. That Easter eve was spent walking, praying, reading through my journal for the past year, and writing pages of reflections. I could trace the deep and persistent questions that had remained unresolved.

April 19, 2003

Doubts remain around whether the investment of the next 7-8 years of my life to insure the organizational and institutional sustainability of the WCC is the way to best express my ecumenical vision and call. . . .

Further, throughout this time of discernment, I have frequently said and known that the RCA is a "good place to be." The "plateau" in Arizona. That I love being there — that my call was so real and profound, and that it endures . . . so much still to learn, to give, to do. . . .

So inwardly, as far as I know, I have a deep and clear sense that I need to withdraw from the search process for the next general secretary of the World Council of Churches.

I let that discernment rest over Easter and for a few days, and found peace. So I e-mailed key friends and colleagues and drafted a letter to Rev. Makke Masango in South Africa, moderator of the Search Committee, explaining my decision to say no.

Cliff Kirkpatrick, who was a member of the search committee, called me at home. My application was terrific, he said. Did I know that I was at that point probably the leading candidate? Was I sure? I shared with Cliff what I knew to be true. But I felt some real pain, and a deep sense of loss. Yet it didn't change anything. I was clear.

In late August I went to the WCC Central Committee in Geneva that elected my former colleague Sam Kobia as its next general secretary. Flying home on a Lufthansa flight across the Atlantic, I wrote this: "I am coming home. Home to New Jersey, home to Karin, home to Karis and J.K. . . . I was not called away from home — but rather called to stay home. And I know that for now, this is where I belong. . . . For the sake of the RCA. We can see this denomination move into new expressions of life and faithfulness. . . . For the sake of what is happening, for what God is doing — yes, for this denomination that I have come to love."

Mission Comes First

I'D LIKE TO PASTOR a church in the Lincoln Park neighborhood of Chicago. About two miles north of downtown, the neighborhood's wooded streets are lined with stone row houses and small apartment buildings, many of which have become condos. Young professional women and men, with music playing in their ears from iPods Velcroed to their arms, jog to Lincoln Park and the lakefront. Some have dogs jogging with them on leashes. More have dogs than have babies, from what I observe.

Clark Street is filled with ethnic restaurants and bars, crowded at night with the changing, younger, upwardly mobile demographic of the area. Wrigley Field is a mile or two straight north. Whenever I'm there, I think about the people I pass on the street. They are on the go, making money — often more than they know what to do with — and trying to establish their professional and personal lives. And the vast majority have nothing to do with the church. That's why I'd like to pastor there.

The Cenacle Retreat and Conference Center is nestled into the midst of the Lincoln Park neighborhood, on West Fullerton near Clark Street. It's a curious presence there, and home for a small community of Cenacle Sisters, a Catholic order. Like many such communities, dwindling numbers have turned it into a ministry of hosting retreats and conferences, both to carry out its adherents' vocation and to build sustainable revenue. We found the Cenacle to be an inexpensive location for small RCA gatherings.

In May of 2004 I convened a "Think Tank" at the Cenacle. My conviction was that space had to be created for some of the most perceptive minds and strategic leaders in the RCA to gather together and try to envision the future, and the challenges we faced. This was an experiment to provide creative, innovative thinking that then could be shared, sifted, and appropriated by our governing bodies.

Having adopted "Our Call" and set clear directions for the RCA in the next decades, I hoped gatherings such as this "Think Tank" could clarify concretely what it means to be a "missional church," anticipate the challenges we could expect in coming years, and affirm the distinctive qualities of Reformed identity in a missional context. While drinking a latte the first morning at Caribou Coffee on Clark Street, I thought, in a way, this was like asking, "What would it take to start an RCA congregation in Lincoln Park, and what would such a congregation look like in this subculture?"

I invited Pat Keifert to join us as a consultant at this meeting, and our group included Dennis Voskuil, then president of the RCA's Western Theological Seminary, some members of the General Synod Council (GSC), and other perceptive people in the RCA. We developed a consensus around the major points of tension we would face in this missional movement of the RCA:

- *The creativity and contextualization of new churches.* Baptism, its relationship to the Lord's Supper, approaches to worship, and other theological issues would pose challenges to established RCA understanding and practice.
- *The outlook and expectations of younger generations.* Shifting values on participation rather than membership, and on practical demonstrations of faith as opposed to dogmatic declarations, would pose increasing challenges.
- *The growth of non-Anglo, racial ethnic, and multicultural congregations.* Differing cultural understandings of decision making, styles of meetings, and equal use of languages other than English would create a new set of expectations for what is "normal" in the RCA.
- *The avenues and means for the education and formation of pastors.* The needs of diverse, growing congregations would require far more

flexibility in our present, seminary-based models of preparation for ministry.

On this last point Pat Keifert put the challenge to us well. He asked, "Can you de-link issues of class and educational level from ministry?" In his view, that would be crucial for our future missional outreach.

We also focused on what was at the core of Reformed identity. As we looked to the major commitment for planting new churches that was envisioned in "Our Call," some asked whether these churches would clearly say, "We are Reformed." More importantly, just what would that mean?

At General Synod a month later, I offered a tentative summary of what the group thought was essential to Reformed identity:

- *We believe in God's radical, sovereign grace.* The RCA's three confessions, and the heart of the Reformed tradition, affirm the powerful, providential, liberating initiative of God's grace, calling us into the one body of Christ.
- *We are governed by collegial decision making.* Neither hierarchical nor congregational, we live our life together by trusting communities of decision making.
- *We seek to integrate the Word with the world.* God's truth is whole, never segregated to only the church; it is capable of transforming the world.
- *We are nurtured in worship and prayer.* We believe worship roots our life as God's people, even while we celebrate the diversity of styles in which worship is expressed.

The searching discussion during those days at the Cenacle, both during our formal times and while strolling around Lincoln Park on pleasant May evenings, actually proved to be a precursor to our future. In the seven years that followed, "Our Call" kept pushing the church into an ongoing dialogue around what it means to be both missional and Reformed.

Some had sharp critiques of "Our Call" from the beginning. In general, these followed four points. First, it sounds like a business model inappropriate for the church. Second, there's too much stress on numbers, which quantifies the mysterious work of the Spirit. Third, it seems like a top-down, centralized approach. Fourth, it seems to go against dimensions of our polity.

A group of loyal RCA pastors primarily from churches in the East formed the "Chicago Invitation." They sought to raise a series of theological questions and historical perspectives that challenged trends they saw in the RCA. In their view, core understandings of our polity and traditional practice that were essential to a Reformed identity were being threatened. They engineered a few overtures (proposals from a classis or regional synod) to the 2004 General Synod expressing some of their concerns, but none gained any real traction with delegates. Yet, they consistently sought to remind us that you go "through tradition into mission."

Meanwhile, "Our Call" was being embraced in many parts of the church. The regional synod executives and key GSC staff agreed to become the "guiding coalition" for the ten-year goal, and we began focusing our work cooperatively on the arduous task of congregational revitalization and the ambitious goals set for planting new churches — 400 by the year 2013. But more than this, we focused on the systems, structures, and values that would be needed to sustain such a movement.

The heart of it all was a simple but radical declaration: "mission comes first." We invited consultants and authors who could help congregations navigate the journey to becoming truly driven by participating in God's mission in the world. Increased focus was placed on how our forty-six classes were functioning. Many felt they were perpetually consumed by narrow, inward-looking management and administrative concerns, and lacked both missional vision and strategic, courageous leadership. Experiments in changing the style of classis meetings, and even rewriting bylaws around the initiatives of "Our Call," began to spring up, particularly in the Midwest and West.

In all this, we were beginning to align our priorities, our resources, our staff, and our structures with the directions General Synod had embraced in "Our Call." This was the hard part. It would take years. Yet, momentum had been generated. Reading Jim Collins's book *Good to Great* as part of a task force on "missional structures," we resonated with several of his analogies. We were getting "the right people on the bus" in terms of key leadership, and we could sense that "the flywheel was beginning to turn." The commitment to becoming a truly missional church was being slowly but persistently embedded in our denominational DNA.

THE 2004 GENERAL SYNOD took an action, proposed by a delegate from Canada, affirming "that marriage is properly defined as the union of one man and one woman, to the exclusion of all others." It was prompted by concerns expressed by pastors in Canada regarding pressure that could be placed on them to perform same-sex weddings. While several, including myself, felt that those concerns were exaggerated, the statement was consistent with General Synod's actions for the past three decades, and not a great deal of attention was given to it.

A few weeks later my close colleague, Ken Bradsell, came into my office and asked if I had heard about Norm Kansfield's action. I hadn't. Ken told me that in late June — actually a couple of weeks after synod — Norm had married his daughter Ann to a woman. I was surprised, but quickly started to think through the implications. If Norm had gone to Massachusetts to perform a quiet civil ceremony marrying Ann to her partner, many in the church who heard of it would disapprove, but they would understand a father's love for his daughter.

But Ken then filled in more of the details. This was a religious ceremony, held in a church in Massachusetts (where same-sex marriage was legal at that time) and apparently using the RCA liturgy. Further, Norm shared this after the fact with others, including the board of trustees of New Brunswick Seminary, where he was president.

As word spread, so did anger in many parts of the RCA. Norm was not only president of one of the RCA's seminaries. He was also a "professor of theology." In the RCA, this is called the "fourth office." In addition to ministers of Word and sacrament, elders, and deacons, the RCA calls a few to this office as "teachers of the church." Moreover, these professors of theology are directly accountable to the General Synod in matters of theology and practice.

By the fall it was clear that we were facing a full-blown crisis. Congregations and classes were demanding that formal disciplinary action be taken against Norm — most insisting that he be removed from office. Others spoke of withholding money from the seminary. While a few voices expressed support for Norm, the weight of opinion was that Norm's action had clearly violated the RCA's position and could not be allowed to stand. To put it simply, a professor of theology and teacher of the church, who also was president of a seminary, knowingly disobeyed what the General Synod had declared only two weeks earlier.

The situation was complicated by two levels of accountability. As president, Norm answered to the board of trustees. As professor of theology, Norm was accountable to the General Synod. Moreover, discipline exercised by the synod would have to come through an actual trial, with the synod delegates as the jury. No one could even remember if and when General Synod had conducted a trial of one of its professors of theology. To me, that seemed like a nightmare.

Discussions with Norm and steps toward bringing official "charges" began in the fall. In January 2005, I found myself in a hotel conference room with New Brunswick's board, discussing Norm's fate. His contract was up that June, and Norm had been hoping for a brief extension. Board members were concerned, and some were angry, not about the wedding per se, but about the whole way Norm had handled it, and the resulting conflict with the church. More than that, the finances of the seminary were in poor shape, and several board members were losing trust in Norm's ability to preserve the financial security of the institution.

The board ended up "reprimanding" Norm for "taking a controversial public action while President by officiating at the same sex marriage of his daughter in Massachusetts without prior Board discussion or approval." They announced that his contract would not be renewed and thanked him for his service. Private feelings of board members were stronger than their public statement.

The board's action, however, didn't satisfy those in the church who were demanding that disciplinary action be taken against Norm in his role as professor of theology. They were insisting on a trial at General Synod. Further, Norm seemed ready and willing to defend himself. But I wanted to explore every avenue to avoid a trial.

Attempts at mediation proved fruitless. At one point I considered taking an administrative action and dismissing Norm as a professor of theology because his service at New Brunswick had ended. The conservatives called this the "nuclear option," because it would prevent the synod from deciding on Norm's guilt or innocence. Further, Norm was not going to step down on his own from his service as professor of theology.

When General Synod convened at Union College in Schenectady, New York, we entered into a trial of Dr. Norman Kansfield. While working for weeks with Ken Bradsell and attorney Bruce Neckers to see that we had a fair process, my real feeling was that simply going to trial was an awful outcome. And of course, the media was fascinated. Paul Boice, our new communications director, had a hundred calls and inquiries from the press.

Norm and his attorney put forth a strong defense. In essence, they put the RCA's position on homosexuality on trial. Ann was put on the stand and testified courageously to her homosexual orientation, and her love of God, her marriage commitment, and her call to the ministry. A few summers earlier Ann had worked in my office as an intern, and I had strongly encouraged her desire to attend seminary. It felt tragic to see her now in this situation.

But the facts of the case were simply too hard to refute. Whatever one's views on the issues of homosexuality, Norm had taken a public action directly contrary to the General Synod, which he served. Delegates found him guilty.

In our peculiar judicial process, the General Synod also was responsible for the terms of discipline. They decided, first, to remove Norm as a professor of theology, but then also to suspend him as a minister of Word and sacrament in the RCA. That meant he couldn't preach, baptize, or perform communion in RCA congregations.

The severity of the sentence was deeply shocking to many. When we departed the assembly room where our proceedings had been held in closed session, several nondelegates lined the hallway, kneeling, dressed in black, and holding candles in silent protest and mourning. They included my daughter, Karis, who was at synod to help in the bookstore.

In my room at the Holiday Inn that night, I had never been more worried about the future of the Reformed Church in America. The scars left by this trial were very deep. It wasn't just the issue of homosexuality, but also the high-profile judicial action that was only deepening divisions, emboldening factions, and sowing a spirit of mistrust and mutual recrimination.

I feared for what would happen if the RCA continued down that path. It would not be a denomination in which I would want to serve as general secretary. Our long and promising effort to focus our energies on our missional calling in our society would get obliterated. Energy instead would go into conflicts that wouldn't get fully resolved but would alienate groups and keep us distracted from responding wholeheartedly to the challenge of "Our Call."

The next morning I was to give my annual report. I had left some paragraphs unwritten pending the result of the trial, and now, in the middle of the night, I was struggling and praying over what to say. It felt to me that there were forces threatening to hijack the focus and direction of the RCA. Those who had pressed for the prosecution of Norm Kansfield would now try to amend our Book of Church Order, as overtures to this synod were proposing. The result would be an ongoing fight in each classis over what should be stipulated constitutionally. To me, that not only seemed unnecessary but also guaranteed that we would be engulfed in this conflict, that it would find no unifying resolution, and that we would lose our cohesion around common mission.

The next morning I implored the General Synod delegates not to take actions that would set us on a course of ongoing constitutional conflict. Taking that path, I told the delegates, would be saying

> that the presence and participation of gay and lesbian persons in the RCA will be resolved by judicial fiat rather than by pastoral responsibility. . . . Moreover, any controversies then become endless legal fights. I, and you, have seen this happen in other denominations, where their national gatherings are known publicly by rancorous legal fights over cases and regulations applying to homosexuality. The actual outcome matters less because divisions are institutionalized, the climate is poisoned, and common mission becomes virtually impossible in the presence of such divisiveness, mistrust, and hostility. Brothers and sisters, we do not want to go there.

Having rendered its verdict on Dr. Kansfield, synod could trust the church's other assemblies to deal with these issues and could take steps to encourage dialogue, understanding, and the healing of divisions that had become so painfully evident. Our focus could then be placed on the pastoral challenges faced by congregations. "We have not the right," I suggested, "to close our hearts and our doors to those on society's margins whom Jesus would invite to dinner."

That evening Peggy and Tony Campolo addressed the synod. I knew Tony through the board of Call to Renewal, and Karin and I had enjoyed rich times with Peggy and him. They did not agree on the issue of homosexuality. While both were evangelically committed Christians examining Scripture, tradition, and experience, Tony held to a more conservative stance such as that officially supported by the RCA and Peggy held to a more inclusive position, believing there was room for Christians to live in committed, monogamous same-sex relationships. But those differences didn't divide their marriage. More important commitments bound them together and nurtured respectful dialogue between them.

Tony and Peggy had spoken to various church assemblies, sharing openly and thoroughly where the two of them agreed and disagreed in order to demonstrate how these differences did not need to divide the body of Christ. When it seemed inevitable that General Synod was headed for a trial, I called Tony and Peggy to ask if they could speak at this synod.

They readily agreed, despite their complex schedules and existing commitments. (Tony, in fact, could get there only on a private plane, which we then privately financed.) Their presentation that evening was passionate, earnest, humorous, and enlightening. It helped reduce the anxiety of synod delegates and encourage us in the path ahead.

Before General Synod adjourned, it authorized an official three-year dialogue in the church around the questions of homosexuality. Such calls had been issued before, but with little result. This time, however, resources would be available for a coordinator and steering committee to guide this effort. The point would be to listen carefully to the variety of experiences, understandings of Scripture, and pastoral wisdom around these questions existing in the RCA.

Synod also adopted visionary and expansive objectives for congregational revitalization and church multiplication, the main initiatives of "Our Call." Further, responding to recommendations in my report, an initiative to explore what it would truly mean for the RCA congregations to embrace a multicultural future was adopted. Further, a process of "missional reflection" that would evaluate and suggest changes in our existing structures was also begun. Delegates wanted to return our focus to our mission.

Proposals to seek further amendments to the Book of Church Order related to the issues at Norm's trial were turned aside. Following synod, the officers and I sent a letter to all RCA congregations, echoing perspectives I had shared in my report. We explained that our historic position regarding homosexuality was unchanged, but that we were engaging in dialogue over the presence and participation of gay and lesbian persons in our congregations: "Because of our unity around Christ's mission, our relational culture, our evangelical convictions, and our ecumenical engagements, the Reformed Church in America has the opportunity to model a different way for a denomination to address the controversies in the church over this matter. It would be a gift to ourselves and to others in the Body of Christ to do so."

That has continued to be my hope and conviction. In the end, the church's debate over homosexuality revolves around a very narrow question. If a couple of the same sex are committed publicly to a monogamous, lifelong relationship, should they, in the privacy of their bedroom, be celibate or sexually expressive? I understand that there are different convictions around that matter. But what I don't understand is why those differences should rupture fellowship between brothers and sisters in the body of Christ.

It seems completely mistaken that this narrow ethical difference should become a church-dividing matter in the Anglican communion, or should alter how Rome has fellowship with historic Protestants, or should cause Lutherans to break their bonds of communion with one another, or should cause anyone to question whether they can maintain their vow to fellowship and unity in the Reformed Church in America.

The Bible has over 2,000 verses dealing with poverty and wealth, but we don't make those overwhelming biblical instructions a matter that defines our fellowship with one another. In fact, the Bible has stern warnings against lending money for interest, supported in much of the pre-Reformation history of the church. But we don't exclude bankers from fellowship because we recognize the modern ethical complexity of those questions.

In the years leading to the Civil War, some pastors in the RCA argued strongly from Scripture that slavery was justified and was God's will, while others argued that such treatment of other humans was an offense to God. But, unlike in some denominations, even this conflict did not cause the Reformed Church in America to divide.

In the years since the Kansfield trial, the RCA has been able to follow the counsel found in that letter sent to all congregations. Difference and tensions, of course, remain. But we have learned the wisdom and the power that come from knowing that mission comes first.

"Keep Your Hands on the Plough, Hold On"

R CA STAFF COLLEAGUE Ken Bradsell and I were having breakfast at a hotel in San Diego in late January 2006. We were sharing our reactions to the gathering of the RCA's new church planters and spouses that we had just witnessed. Both of us were overwhelmed.

Years ago Dick Welscott had begun gathering the pastors and spouses who were doing new church starts for a time of retreat, encouragement, and renewal. He started, I think, with three couples. Now in San Diego the hotel's conference room was packed with committed, creative, energetic men and women from throughout North America who were planting new RCA churches.

Their worship together was thrilling. Their enthusiasm was contagious. Their commitment was inspiring. Their creativity was amazing. And their hope was humbling. It was there in San Diego, looking out at this group that I was about to address, that I realized the RCA no longer had a new church development "program." We now had a church multiplication "movement." It was building its own, Spirit-led momentum, gathering energy and reshaping our future.

That's what Ken and I were talking about at breakfast. At one point Ken said, "This is a part of the RCA that a lot of friends of mine simply don't know." We began dreaming about how to share the new reality of what was happening in our church multiplication efforts with the wider RCA. These retreats for new church planters were happening every other year. Ken wondered, what if all our commissions, boards of agencies, racial-ethnic councils, task forces, advisory bodies — in short, those groups that meet annually anyway — could be gathered at the same time and place as the new church planters retreat?

On January 24, 2008, I looked out at a crowd of 800 people gathered at the Marriott Hotel by the River Walk in San Antonio for the RCA's One Thing event. It was the culmination of that conversation begun two years earlier in San Diego. But more important, in the faces of those gathered I caught a glimpse of the future of the RCA.

In addition to the various organized boards and groups who had agreed to meet together, we had been intentional in inviting emerging young leaders, women in ministry, and those from non-Anglo racial backgrounds. We had sought to gather both those in established places of leadership and those whose presence and voices would be critical in shaping our future. Our new church planters had their retreat at the center of things, along with pastors of congregations that were planting or "parenting" new churches.

Groups involved in congregational revitalization also had a key presence in San Antonio. Led by staff colleague Ken Eriks and his team, this work was beginning to blossom, with hundreds of RCA pastors joining networks of covenantal accountability, transformational learning, and mutual support, undergirded by a generous grant from the Lilly Foundation. Many congregations were using Natural Church Development, a tool for assessing congregational health, and we were beginning to discover the power of coaching to assist those in the process of congregational change. Our practice was showing us that congregational revitalization and church multiplication were mutually dependent, enriching one another.

Together, all who gathered at One Thing began to experience what the RCA was becoming. Author Reggie McNeal spoke to us each evening. His missional heart and passion struck a nerve that resonated deeply. The title "One Thing" came from our Mission and Vision Statement a decade earlier: "a thousand churches in a million ways doing one thing — following Christ in mission in a lost and broken world so loved by God." More and more this phrase seemed to describe what was now actually happening.

When the RCA adopted this statement, it also included a section that imagined the changes that could result. One phrase said this: "Imagine . . . a denomination that prays in many languages and beholds the face of Christ in every face." The faces at One Thing were evidence of our movement toward a multiracial future. But this was not without its obstacles.

Brad Lewis was serving as General Synod president for the year ending at the 2007 General Synod. A professor of economics at Union College in Schenectady, Brad had been a very active leader in many parts of the RCA. In his year as president, Brad wanted especially to strengthen the RCA's commitment to a multiracial future.

One of the president's responsibilities is to select the preacher or preachers for General Synod. Wanting to find speakers who both practiced and would demonstrate multiracial leadership to the synod, he selected Rev. Andres Serrano, a dynamic RCA pastor in California from the Dominican Republic (not to be confused with the controversial artist of the same name), to lead opening worship and Jacqui Lewis, pastor of Middle Collegiate Church in New York, to preach at daily worship each morning. An African American and an outstanding preacher, Jacqui also played a leading role on the RCA's task force on multiracial congregations.

Middle Collegiate was a thriving congregation in the East Village area of lower Manhattan. Years earlier Gordon Dragt had taken it from a withering band of a dozen members to a congregation of several hundred who were very involved in the creative, artistic community of the area. This also meant that Middle Collegiate was one of a handful of RCA congregations that welcomed and affirmed gay and lesbian persons.

Middle took this part of their identity seriously, advocating for gay and lesbian causes, even while recognizing that it stood against the official positions of the RCA. As the pastor who had recently succeeded Gordon Dragt, Jacqui fully supported the congregation's inclusive commitments. But Jacqui's deep passion was to build a multiracial congregation and expand that vision throughout the RCA.

Brad had consulted me, and I had agreed that Jacqui would be an exceptional preacher, helping the synod to see the biblical and practical challenges of living as a multiracial church, witnessing to Christ's reconciling love. Neither of us anticipated the firestorm that this choice would create. While assuming that some would dislike the choice of Jacqui

Lewis because of her congregation's stance on gay and lesbian issues, I thought those delegates would understand and accept that Brad had selected her to preach on the gospel's call to racial reconciliation. And I was foolishly wrong.

E-mails, letters, and phone calls came pouring into my office, especially from conservatives as word began to spread that Rev. Jacqui Lewis had been selected as one of the General Synod preachers. Most demanded that this choice be rescinded. Brad, I, and the other officers conferred, and felt that the original reasons for the selection of both preachers remained valid. Brad even talked with Jacqui and received the biblical texts and themes for her preaching. She never intended even to mention the issue of gay and lesbian persons. We communicated this to all who protested.

Synod began with opening worship Thursday evening, with Andres Serrano preaching as delegates gathered at Third Reformed Church in Pella, Iowa. Friday morning the synod convened in the field house of Central College. Our first activity was to be morning worship. But a delegate came to a microphone and raised a "point of order," and then offered a motion that Jacqui Lewis be prohibited from preaching and that Brad Lewis and I offer a formal apology to the General Synod. One delegate from Canada angrily shook his finger in my face condemning this choice as I was offering an explanation of our procedures and a defense of our president. Meanwhile, Jacqui Lewis and the worship team were waiting to lead in the worship of God.

We had to call a recess for two or three hours, convene a special committee of synod delegates representing a fair range of views, and then meet to decide how to proceed. It was a difficult discussion. Brad offered again his rationale for how all the worship services and preachers had been selected. Several supported him. Finally, I shared my grief over synod having come to such a painful place over, of all things, worship.

We stated again that this choice in no way implied an approval of Jacqui's views or her congregation's practices regarding gay and lesbian persons. Meanwhile, Jacqui was at the Monarch's Restaurant in Pella's Royal Amsterdam Hotel with Bruce and Vicky Menning wondering whether, in fact, she would preach the sermons she had prepared. A person of less grace, after listening to a debate over whether or not she should be allowed to preach, would have been on a plane heading home.

The committee agreed to a resolution that recognized the president's prerogatives in this matter, and clarified that this selection was made solely on the basis of addressing the challenge of our multicultural future. Jacqui then delivered three sermons to the synod that constituted some of the most outstanding biblical preaching on this theme that I have heard.

When I came to give my report, however, I felt that the mood of the synod had been soured, almost poisoned. It was as though I had to push through a fog to convey the spiritual conviction of my words. Never before had I experienced that kind of resistance.

When we delved into the business of the synod, controversy continued. The Missional Structures Task Force begun two years earlier came with its report and several recommendations pushing for more flexibility and experimentation in our structures, and envisioning basic changes in our governing bodies. Representatives particularly from our three eastern synods were alarmed. They saw this as a potential assault on parts of our polity that needed to be safeguarded, and felt that these recommendations were coming without sufficient listening or a trustworthy process.

So a synod that began with conservative members in an uproar over the choice of a preacher now saw its more "liberal," eastern representatives distrusting a process aimed at structural reform. Several of the task force's recommendations were defeated or modified; this was one synod where it was hard to find a center that would hold. But the underlying concern of the task force continued through an initiative that would examine over the next three years what it means to be both "missional" and Reformed.

The turbulence of this synod demonstrated, among other things, that I and others had to be more intentional in listening carefully to all the voices in the church. Brad Lewis and I agreed to meet with the Illiana Classis, a classis spanning the border between Indiana and Illinois, just south of Chicago, which had registered some of the strongest protests over the choice of Jacqui Lewis. That session of the classis, held at Springs Community Church on a cold winter evening, was beneficial and built trust. I also determined to pay more attention to people in the East who were concerned about nurturing the roots of our identity. Times spent with pastors there in honest dialogue proved to be mutually beneficial.

Continuing to center on the challenge of "Our Call," however, put these other points of tension and conflict into perspective. One September evening in Michigan, when the regional synod executives and key General Synod Council (GSC) staff were meeting together, we invited ten area pastors to have dinner with us and answer a simple, honest question. "What difference has 'Our Call' made in your ministry in the past four years, and what challenges remain?" We didn't know what to expect but wanted to hear.

The result was stunning. One after another, these pastors — men and women, black and white, from diverse churches in the area — testified to how "Our Call" had inspired them, grounded them, provided essential support and encouragement, and opened new expressions of mission and ministry in their congregations.

A few weeks later the GSC met, and its agenda included my performance review. Their affirmation of me was an overwhelming gift. Despite the difficulties of the past synod, they were more positive than ever in their evaluation of my leadership.

On a retreat day after GSC, the words of an African American spiritual, sung on a CD by the group Chanticleer, came to me: "Keep your hands on the plough, hold on." Clearly, that was my task. So by the time those at One Thing gathered in San Antonio the following January, it was clear we were back on track, and the missional momentum of the RCA was moving us forward.

THE MOST DIFFICULT MOMENTS of the 2007 General Synod didn't come from the controversies and mistrust that seemed to arise from all sides. Rather, this came when Karin called me to say my mother was taking a downward spiral in her struggle against cancer and its related effects. Karin went to Chicago to be with her. A couple of days later she said, "If you want to be with Mom while she is still living, you should get here soon."

As a young adult I had to work hard to establish a close relationship with my mother. That began changing after my marriage. After my father's death, Karin and I had invited my mom to spend the Christmas season each year with us in Switzerland. In 1993 she came with a box of Marshall Field chocolates given to her by Bob Smith. Bob had lost his wife, and they lived in the same retirement home.

They discovered a wonderful love for each other, and my mom asked me if I would marry them. The service was held at Lake Geneva, Wisconsin, on a sunny Saturday at the end of summer. And responding to a dare from her younger brother Ken, my mom and Bob each went parasailing on the lake following the reception. We recorded this and later showed the video to Mom and Bob's astonished friends at the Windsor Park Manor, their retirement home near Wheaton, Illinois.

My mother kept growing, intellectually and spiritually. Before marrying Bob, at the age of seventy-five, she took a trip with World Relief to Burkina Faso in Africa, to view efforts to fight poverty and empower women. She would always ask me questions about politics and religion, and tell me the latest books she was reading. She became a "social justice democrat" living in a bastion of evangelical conservative Republicans.

Mom and Bob counted their anniversaries in months rather than years. And they enjoyed many. Then colon cancer struck my mother, with an operation and ongoing complications following. On Mother's Day weekend, my brother Ron and sister-in-law Jan, my sister Marcia and brother-in-law Ralph, and Karin and I took Mom and Bob on a final trip to Lake Geneva. It was a glorious time at the place she had loved all her life.

Just a few weeks after that, she was slipping toward death. I left General Synod early, before closing communion, and joined Karin at her bedside. Mom was alert and even rallied. For the next four to five days, with family members coming and going, she maintained contact. Her faith was incredibly strong, as it had been her whole life.

But on Monday morning, with only Karin, Bob, and I there, her breathing began to change in a way recognized by the hospice nurse. Karin suggested that Bob lay beside her, which he did. And then Karin spontaneously began singing a song, "Turn your eyes upon Jesus. Look full in his wonderful face. And the things of earth will grow strangely dim, in the light of his glory and grace." She sang the chorus a second time, and Mom's breathing softly stopped. Her life had passed on into God's hands.

We returned home to Michigan that evening. I was to give the meditation at the funeral service. Next to Mom's bed in their condo were the journals she had begun keeping a few years earlier. I took them home with me. Wondering what to preach, and now beginning to deal with my grief, I put on the Brahms *German Requiem* and started paging through her journals. Her words were filled with such steady faith, deep insight, and constant compassion; it was at once so powerful and sorrowful. Repeatedly, I burst into tears and sobbed.

Then I came upon this entry:

My thoughts are turning more and more to the life to come. It is a struggle though, because although we know we have a home in glory, we still cling to life here. The words of so many of the old gospel songs come to my mind. Do I really believe these wonderful promises about the life to come? If so, why do I worry about the future, and fear death?

"Turn your eyes upon Jesus
Look full in His wonderful face
And the things of earth will grow strangely dim
In the light of His glory and grace."

In her last journal entry, Mom shared this:

This is a weekend never to be forgotten. Here we are at the Geneva Inn, overlooking the beautiful lake with sun sparkling on the water, accompanied by my Bob and three wonderful children and spouses, enjoying God's creation in my favorite place on earth. If this is so great, what will heaven be like? As I look at my shrinking body I wonder how long Lord. But I have no reason to worry or to fear. I am so grateful. . . . "To God be the glory, great things he has done."

The sermon became obvious. I would let Mom's own words from her journal speak of her faith and hope. And I knew as never before the way my mother had passed on to me a legacy of faith so deeply rooted in God, and continually growing.

From Park Ridge to Selma

T HE WORD *sankofa* refers to an African symbol of a bird with its head turned backward taking an egg off its back. It symbolizes taking what is good from the past and bringing it into the present to enrich our understanding of today. From this metaphor we took the name of our journey, a three-and-one-half-day pilgrimage that intended to look back into pivotal moments in the history of our nation's civil rights struggle in order to look forward into the RCA's multiracial future.

At 4:30 P.M. on Wednesday, April 22, 2009, thirty-four participants boarded a bus at the Evangelical Lutheran Church in America building near O'Hare International Airport in Chicago, Illinois. Half of us were African American, and the other half were "white." Most of our regional synod executives as well as several key General Synod Council (GSC) staff members were making this journey; each person was partnered with another participant of the opposite race. My partner was James Seawood, who was serving as vice president of the General Synod and pastor of Brighton Heights Reformed Church in Staten Island, New York.

My childhood home and the farm bought by Big Daddy were just five blocks away in Park Ridge, which was a typical all-white suburb when I grew up. So for me, this trip felt really personal. I had never before made the journey from Park Ridge to Selma, Montgomery, and Birmingham, either geographically or psychologically.

We set out on our all-night ride to Selma. Before we fell asleep, we watched the movie *A Time to Kill,* based on John Grisham's novel of racial inequality and violence in the South, and shared our reactions with our partner. By then it was after midnight.

I awoke at 5:00 in the morning when the bus stopped because a cooling hose had burst. By about 7:00 we made it to a truck stop in Tennessee where the bus could be fixed, and we stopped for breakfast. The black friends at my table just laughed when I asked for an English muffin; this was grits country.

Selma, Alabama, was the site of a voter registration march in 1965; March 25 is remembered as "Bloody Sunday." The conflict occurred when marchers tried to cross the Edmund Pettus Bridge over the Alabama River. We now walked across the bridge together and then looked at the monuments commemorating leaders of that effort, including John Lewis, who is presently a member of Congress. Then we were on to Montgomery, visiting the Civil Rights Memorial Center, before arriving in Birmingham that evening.

I will never forget Carolyn McKinstry's statement about the African American experience: "We understood terrorism before 9/11." We met with Carolyn at 7:30 A.M. Friday after a welcomed bed and shower at a hotel. Carolyn's story is remarkable. She is a lifelong member of Sixteenth Street Baptist Church in Birmingham, holds a master of divinity degree, and is active as a leader in several Birmingham community service organizations.

In 1963, Carolyn was fourteen. She was at Sixteenth Street Baptist Church on Sunday, September 15, to help with Sunday school as usual. Around 10:20 A.M., she answered the phone in the church office and heard a voice say, "You have three minutes." Shortly after that, a bomb exploded in the church. Four young girls, Carolyn's friends, were killed.

This was three weeks after Martin Luther King Jr.'s "I Have a Dream" speech at the Lincoln Memorial. It was seen as the Ku Klux Klan's response to desegregation. Two of the perpetrators were not brought to justice until thirty-three years later, in 2002. We ended our time with Carolyn in a circle of prayer, and then moved on to the Civil Rights Institute, a compelling presentation of this chapter in our nation's history.

Our *sankofa* journey continued to Atlanta and then Chattanooga before heading home to Park Ridge. We tried to process what we had seen and experienced along with way — in my case, with James Seawood. The bus rides included videos on the same themes, making this an intense, rolling seminar.

We learned of the *sankofa* journeys from the Evangelical Covenant Church in America. A denomination similar to the RCA but from historic Swedish immigration, the Covenant has focused its energies on church planting and racial reconciliation. They made rigorous efforts to address racism and create a fellowship that was genuinely multicultural. And they have been succeeding. Over 20 percent of their congregations are non-Anglo, and unlike most denominations, the Covenant has been growing numerically in churches and members for the past several years.

The *sankofa* journeys have been one of the tools used by the Covenant to address issues of racial justice, and Earl James, the RCA's coordinator for multiracial initiatives and social justice, began to pioneer this approach in the RCA's life together. In my own life, that *sankofa* journey was the single most powerful and change-producing antiracism experience that I've ever known.

The General Synod prior to this journey, in 2008, had added "a multi-racial future freed from racism" as a "sixth element" of "Our Call." Halfway through this ten-year goal, we were recognizing that the future intended by God was reflected in Revelation 7:9, where a multitude "from every nation, from all tribes and peoples and languages," would be "standing before the throne and before the Lamb." That vision was being embraced and was breaking into our life. We could see this in our new church plants; of the 400 we were committed to start by 2013, over one-third were to be of racial and ethnic backgrounds different from our white majority.

This meant we had to be far more proactive in confronting the sins of racism within our own life, as well as in our society. So our Commission on Race and Ethnicity was prompted, along with others, to propose that this new dimension be added to "Our Call." Most of the GSC felt instead that this commitment should be embedded in all we did around church multiplication and congregational revitalization, supported by discipleship, leadership, and mission.

I agreed with the GSC, maintaining that our antiracism commitment should be woven throughout our life. But I was wrong. That wasn't enough. Sometimes, when you argue that a concern should be present everywhere, it becomes easy for it to be diminished and barely present anywhere. General Synod had this debate, and eventually agreed to adopt a new, distinct element in our ten-year goal that made explicit our commitment to a multiracial future freed from racism. That provided a new mandate for a variety of antiracism initiatives such as the *sankofa* journeys.

But by far, the most decisive step in confronting the challenge of racial reconciliation was the RCA's encounter with the Belhar Confession. In 1995, the General Synod met in Mahwah, New Jersey. It was my first synod since being installed as general secretary a year earlier. Representatives from the Uniting Reformed Church in Southern Africa met with us — Leonardo Appies and James Buys. I had known Leonardo from my time with the World Council of Churches, and seeing him at Mahwah was an unexpected reunion. He and James presented the Belhar Confession formally to the General Synod. They termed it their gift to us, and challenged us to study, reflect, and determine what it would mean for the RCA.

The Belhar Confession emerged from the church's role in the struggle against apartheid in South Africa. Named after the town where it was adopted, the Belhar is a powerful statement of Christian faith that focuses on the biblical call to racial reconciliation, unity, and justice. Along with the other historic Reformed confessions, the Belhar became a founding confession for the Uniting Reformed Church in Southern Africa. The RCA had forged a strong partnership with that church years earlier in our solidarity against apartheid.

When we received the Belhar as a "gift," we weren't sure what to do with it. It was referred to various commissions for study, attracted attention for its solid biblical grounding and strong statement of faith, but more or less remained in limbo for a few years. We wondered how seriously to take this gift.

Doug Fromm, my colleague and friend who served part-time as associate for ecumenical work, while pastoring an RCA church in Ridgewood, New Jersey, had worked with the Belhar and the Commission on Christian Unity from the beginning. At one of our breakfasts when we reviewed ecumenical work, Doug wondered just where this was going. The underlying question was this: Could the RCA ever adopt the Belhar as a fourth confessional standard?

The idea was huge, even breathtaking, which is probably why it hadn't been engaged earlier. As a confessional church, the RCA had three historic Reformed confessions, the Belgic Confession (1566), the Heidelberg Catechism (1563), and the Canons of Dort (1618). These are foundational for our life, declaring what we believe, and are part of our constitution. No confession had been added for almost four centuries.

But as Doug and I talked, it seemed right to engage the RCA with this challenge. The only way the content of the Belhar would ever be taken with the seriousness that it deserved was to propose it as a fourth confession. Knowing it would take years, with an outcome highly uncertain, we decided to move down that path and encourage the Commission on Christian Unity to design and begin such a process.

In the years that followed, a study guide was painstakingly prepared and then widely shared. Theologians at our seminaries were engaged in penetrating reflection on the meaning of confessions, and the content of the Belhar. General Synods were given time to learn and discuss the significance of this confession. Mitri Raheb, a Lutheran pastor from Palestine, came to synod and addressed the significance of the Belhar for churches in the Middle East, and Israel Batista did the same for the churches in Latin America.

In my own thinking, I began to see a convergence, which I believe was totally providential, between the RCA's consideration of the Belhar and our experience in living out "Our Call." The Belhar would undergird our missional engagement and provide a confessional foundation for our commitment to a multiracial future freed from racism. For the same reason, many in our church multiplication movement, including Tim Vink, our gifted and visionary coordinator, came to affirm the Belhar's contribution to our contemporary witness to the gospel.

I once stated that the RCA's three existing confessions "didn't contain a missional comma." It was an exaggeration not appreciated by a couple of our seminary professors. But I was trying to make a point. The Belgic Confession was written from a context where emerging Reformed faith in the Netherlands was being persecuted. The confession sought to explain the basics of Reformation belief and clarify that it was no threat to the civil order, unlike the threat of the Anabaptists. The Heidelberg Catechism, the most beloved of our confessions, was written as a warm and accessible instructional presentation of Christian doctrine. The Canons of Dort were written to resolve a famous theological dispute dealing with the nature and scope of election, atonement, and grace.

The church's calling to participate in the mission of God in the world was simply not a contextual or theological concern when these three confessions were written. That doesn't distract from their remarkable qualities, but it does highlight, in my judgment, the need for a confession like Belhar, dealing with the meaning of the gospel for the issues of reconciliation and justice in the world.

Early in the process, we realized that we didn't really know how the RCA would adopt a new confession since we had not done so since our founding in 1628. Al Janssen, perhaps our foremost authority on church order, Gregg Mast, Doug Fromm, Ken Bradsell, and I met in my office to try to figure this out. At one point Al wondered if we should call a special General Synod just for this purpose.

Eventually we decided that adoption could take place through amending the Book of Church Order, but we would schedule one vote by General Synod for "provisional adoption" and then another vote two years later. If approved both times, then it would have to be approved by two-thirds of our classes, as with any change to our Book of Church Order, before being finally adopted.

The first vote came at the 2007 General Synod and went relatively smoothly. The crucial vote, however, was 2009. The debate over the Belhar was one of the richest I had ever witnessed at a General Synod. Moving and passionate speeches in favor were given, including those by several younger pastors and seminarians. Some said it was the prospect of adopting the Belhar that had brought them to the RCA. Thoughtful speakers in opposition raised two concerns. The first was whether the Belhar was not just a persuasive statement of faith rather than an actual confession of the church. Did it rise to confessional status?

The second concern was whether a phrase in the Belhar could be interpreted in such a way as to argue for changing the RCA's position on homosexuality. Even though the Belhar was never intended to speak in any way to such issues, such fears were real in some parts of the church. During synod, a clause was even added to the introduction of the motion to adopt the Belhar clarifying that no relationship was intended between the Belhar and the RCA's official stance on homosexuality.

The rich debate ended with a vote in favor of adopting the Belhar, by a margin of about 2 to 1. We later learned that the live stream of the synod's consideration and vote was watched not only by RCA members in North America but also in South Africa.

But now approval by at least thirty-one of our forty-six classes was required. Despite the actions of synod, this was in no way a foregone conclusion. A Belhar Team, headed by Harold Delhagen, chair of the Commission on Christian Unity, was set up to be in touch with each classis, offering any resources requested, and to monitor the voting process. We tried to respect the line between providing assistance and lobbying. But for me and all those on the team, the issue was clear: we needed thirty-one positive votes by March 31.

As each classis met and voted, the outcomes were surprising and unpredictable. Some classes considered sure things narrowly defeated it. And others assumed to be opposed ended up approving. I kept a chart with me wherever I went, tracking the votes and doing the math. It was going to be very close.

And in my view, so much was at stake. I thought of the seminarians I had met with at synod, who were universally in favor of the Belhar and were depending on it for their future ministry. Our non-Anglo racial ethnic groups had come to see this vote as a litmus test of the RCA's commitment to racial justice. Our commitment to a multiracial future would lose all its credibility if, in the end, Belhar was not adopted.

Our friends from southern Africa were also watching with nervous hope. Our action would impact their witness and ongoing relationship with the Dutch Reformed Church, which had historically been deeply involved in the policy of apartheid, mandating a separation of races. Further, as far as we knew, this was the first time that a confession written by Christians in the global south would be adopted by a church in North America.

As we neared the deadline of the end of March, the total was thirty in favor and fifteen against, with one classis yet to vote, Central Plains. Its churches were mostly in Oklahoma, Texas, Nebraska, and Kansas. Because of geography and cost, the Central Plains Classis met face-to-face only once a year, in the fall; at their fall meeting they hadn't acted on the Belhar. In lieu of a face-to-face meeting in the spring, they would vote on constitutional questions, including the Belhar, over the Internet.

I called Dale Assink, the regional staff person who worked with the Central Plains Classis. Dale and I had attended a multiracial strategy coalition meeting earlier that year with Earl James in Chicago, where the Belhar had been a constant theme of discussion, and Dale was committed to its adoption. I told him that all now likely depended on how Central Plains voted.

It seemed deeply ironic but, in the end, perhaps appropriate that the fate of the RCA's fifteen-year process of engaging the Belhar Confession now depended upon thirty or so faithful pastors and elders sitting behind computers in their homes and farmhouses on the plains of America's heartland. Dale was enormously helpful, and also was in touch with the classis clerk, Charlotte Foreman, who was carefully and methodically collecting the votes.

March 30. My cell phone rang as I was at the airport en route to Louisville for an ecumenical meeting. It was Dale. The final votes were in and tallied. Central Plains classis had approved the Belhar.

I got to the Hampton Inn in downtown Louisville. The heads of the Christian Reformed Church, Presbyterian Church (USA), United Church of Christ, and the RCA, with our ecumenical officers, were meeting to try to reach an agreement between our Reformed churches and the Roman Catholic Church on the common recognition of our baptisms. I found Doug and suggested we get a glass of wine before dinner. Then I told him what I had just learned from Dale. Doug had given years to this effort from the very beginning, and now we'd see the result we had hoped and prayed for.

It turned out later that one classis, Nassau-Suffolk from Long Island, which had initially, and surprisingly, voted against the Belhar, met again to reconsider their vote a few days after I had heard from Dale. Their reconsideration ended up with a positive vote. So in the end, when General Synod met at Northwestern College in Orange City, Iowa, thirty-two classes had voted in favor. With representatives of the Uniting Church of

Southern Africa worshiping and celebrating with us, we took the final action declaring that the Belhar Confession was a fourth confession of the Reformed Church in America.

My only regret was that Ed Mulder's plane had been delayed, and he couldn't be with us for this moment. As general secretary during the time of the RCA's engagement against apartheid, Ed had led the RCA in courageous witness. He had worked with the Belhar team, traveling and speaking to classes, and encouraging many in their decision making. When he finally did arrive, we found a moment for Ed to share with the synod his feelings of personal gratitude. In many ways, the adoption of the Belhar was the completion of a witness that God's Spirit had placed on Ed's heart during his first visit to South Africa decades earlier.

From Jerusalem to Antioch

P REPARING FOR General Synod, I was searching for a way to help the RCA understand the challenges, tensions, and opportunities we now faced as we looked toward the completion of "Our Call." In the 2004 General Synod, the year after "Our Call" was adopted, I told the synod that we had 50 new churches under way, with 4,000 people worshiping in them. Now at this synod in 2010, I would tell the delegates that there were 250 new RCA churches under way, with 17,500 experiencing the grace and love of God in those places.

Similar growth was occurring in our efforts in congregational revitalization. We could count 479 pastors in seventy-seven network groups designed to support them in their process of leading congregational change. Training of coaches for pastors and congregational leaders was rapidly expanding. So many promising initiatives had now gained real traction and were becoming embedded in our life.

Yet we faced serious tensions. People worried about whether our new churches were truly Reformed. The use of commissioned pastors, who served in specific congregations but were not ordained as ministers of Word and sacrament, was making some nervous and concerned. Others worried about the fidelity of some pastors to the RCA's understanding of infant baptism. And the new "city classis" in the Synod of the Far West, an experimental nongeographical classis linking congregations engaged in fresh ministry and new church starts in major urban areas, was causing some to warn that the basic nature of classis was being altered.

Such tensions — and there were many — were predictable and even healthy in some ways. Yet, they could also sow the seeds of distrust, gossip, and derision that could become spiritually debilitating and deadly.

The previous October, I had gone "up to Jerusalem" with Jerry Dykstra, then executive director of the Christian Reformed Church, some of his colleagues, and our General Synod president James Seawood, his wife Emra, and our vice president Don Poest. We were making a pilgrimage there, led by RCA missionaries Marlin and Sally Vis.

We were following an ancient tradition. At the time of Jesus, the temple, rebuilt by Herod, made Jerusalem a major center of pilgrimage in the world. Jews would dream of going to Jerusalem, and thousands did, including the family of Jesus, during the three religious festivals observed each year.

Marlin and Sally took us to a high corner of the city that might have been the area where the disciples were gathering and hiding, after the ascension, when the Spirit came at Pentecost. So the whole church can trace its roots back to that place in the city of Jerusalem. It's the fountainhead of our faith.

But what I realized in new ways during my time there was that Jerusalem did not become the center of the early church's mission in the world. Controversy and persecution faced these first believers. After Stephen's stoning, many early followers of Jesus fled Jerusalem, and some traveled as far as Antioch. I tried to imagine this. Antioch was 300 miles away, a journey of about ten days on foot. But Antioch was not only separated geographically from Jerusalem. Culturally, socially, politically, and religiously, it was a different world.

Antioch was the third-largest city in the Roman Empire, after Rome and Alexandria, with up to 500,000 inhabitants. In stark contrast to the Palestinian Judaism of Jerusalem, Antioch was a city of Hellenistic culture, including its various deities and religious practices. Up the river fifteen miles from the sea, it was also a center of trade and interchange throughout the empire. Antioch was highly cosmopolitan, with Syrian, Cypriot, Egyptian, and Persian influences, as well as a Jewish population. Its main street was paved with marble and lighted at night.

It was in Antioch that the gospel, brought by those fleeing Jerusalem, took root and flourished. The gospel was proclaimed to Greeks, and many came to faith as this young church grew. This fellowship was not dependent upon continuing observance of Jewish law or worship in the synagogue, but solely upon embracing the message of Jesus, acknowledging him as the Christ, and living in the power of the Holy Spirit.

The amazing, incarnational power of the gospel of Jesus Christ, the Word that was made flesh in the Jewish culture just outside Jerusalem, now became incarnate within this foreign, cosmopolitan Greek culture of one of the empire's leading cities. The church at Antioch became the crucible for the missional imagination of the Christian church.

Of course, we know the conflict that followed. The church in Jerusalem — made up of those apostles and others who maintained a presence as the "headquarters" of the church — was unsettled by what was happening in Antioch. They sent Barnabas to investigate. Described as the "encourager," his first question seemed to have been, "What is God doing here?" Acts says that "when he came and saw the grace of God, he rejoiced, and he exhorted them all to remain faithful to the Lord with steadfast devotion" (Acts 11:23). Many more believed, and the church continued to grow.

Still, the conflict persisted and wasn't resolved until the Council of Jerusalem, recorded in Acts 15. Those in Antioch, recognizing that they were affirmed in their fresh expression of the gospel, respected the reasonable requests from the founding church in Jerusalem. Upon listening to the experience of what God's grace was doing, the church in Jerusalem empowered and affirmed the church at Antioch. Antioch became the first missional church, the center of the early church's mission in the world, sending Paul and Barnabas to Cyprus and the world beyond.

This prepared the way for Christian faith to transform the known world. If Barnabas had given a negative report, or if the council of Jerusalem had reached a different conclusion, the Christian church as we know it would not exist today.

That is what I decided to share with the General Synod in 2010. My conviction is that it's this journey from Jerusalem to Antioch that defines the church's life today. Our most critical challenge is continuing the transition from being a settled denomination to becoming a missional church.

It is easy and tempting to draw dichotomies and to play tradition and mission over against each other. But that's a great danger, one that does not serve us well, nor does it draw the appropriate lessons from the biblical account of the early church.

Much of the conflict in the church today, in my view, reflects the tension between Jerusalem and Antioch. The journey between Jerusalem and Antioch was a two-way street. Those in Antioch knew that Jerusalem was the wellspring of their faith, the source from which the gospel message had first emerged. Those in Jerusalem affirmed what God's grace was doing and subsequently had to wrestle with how it changed their understanding of the gospel message. Through sending Barnabas, Jerusalem began by asking the right questions: What is God doing in Antioch? Is this the work of the same Spirit? How can we listen, learn, and encourage, as well as guide and instruct?

Most denominations, including the Reformed Church in America, have their contemporary Jerusalems and Antiochs. The account in Acts shows a climate marked by honesty and transparency, and by deep commitment and openness to discovering the ongoing work of God's grace in their midst. This climate allowed the early church to grow, and to transform the known world. We need that climate today, between all those who have leadership and responsibilities in today's Jerusalems and all those addressing the realities and challenges of today's Antiochs.

I offered this biblical metaphor to the Reformed Church in America in 2010. It seemed to resonate. I remain convinced that navigating the dynamics of change driven by our missional engagement in the world will require the wisdom and the quality of relationships demonstrated in the early church's journey from Jerusalem to Antioch.

There was a poignancy in my heart as I communicated those words to the General Synod of 2010, for I knew I was entering my last year of service as general secretary of the Reformed Church in America.

Earlier in the spring, Karin and I had taken a week's vacation in Taos, New Mexico. We decided to visit Ghost Ranch, the well-known Presbyterian conference center in a dramatically beautiful setting captured by Georgia O'Keeffe's paintings, who had lived nearby. While there I noticed that the Monastery of Christ in the Desert was only a few miles away, and we decided to visit.

At the end of a canyon, reached over twelve long miles of a winding dirt road through stunning rock formations, the monastery looks as if it grew out of the surrounding landscape. Realizing that it accepted those coming on retreat, Karin insisted that I come back there in May. Each year prior to General Synod I try to take an extended retreat, and I agreed that this would be welcoming space. I checked, and they had one room available for the dates that had been blocked in my calendar.

Before leaving for the Grand Rapids airport on May 24, I looked at my journals on the shelves of my study. A blue three-ring binder contained my preparation for my interview for the position of general secretary in 1994 and the remarks I made to the General Synod before being confirmed and installed. I took the folder with me, along with my most recent journals.

I'd been pondering for some time just how long I should continue serving as general secretary. Sister Laura, my wise and wonderful spiritual director, had listened often to my musings and offered solid counsel. I'd usually conclude that I'd keep serving for another two or three years. But that pattern seemed to be repeating itself, even as another year or two would go by.

Arriving at the monastery, I settled in to the familiar rhythm of walks, worship, prayer, journal reading, and writing. After a while, I picked up the blue binder and began reading. I was struck deeply by what I found. Those pages expressed the expectations of the church, and the aspirations and commitments I made to the General Synod in 1994. As I read and reflected, it became clear that what was identified then had been worked on, addressed, and in many cases largely accomplished.

The themes of discovering a vision, clarifying our mission, nurturing a sense of spiritual renewal, engaging the culture evangelistically, living into our ecumenical commitments, caring for pastors, expanding new church starts, broadening our cultural diversity — all these, I found, were expressed from those early days. And a unifying conviction was captured in my words to that General Synod: "The church is formed in response to God's mission in the world."

At one point on my first evening I wrote in genuine surprise, "My God, it looks like I've done all the right things!"

I spent the next two days in a combination of startling discovery, genuine anxiety, and probing questions. I read through my journals for more clues, wrote down differing options and timetables, and kept asking if I was hearing now a clear word that my time of service had come to a close. I hadn't come expecting to hear anything that definitive, but I was, after all, on retreat, and hoping to listen to what God's Spirit might say.

As usual, I had taken the General Synod workbook with me — the massive binder containing all the work, papers, studies, and materials for synod. Usually on this May retreat I read it from cover to cover. But not this time.

May 27, 2010

Clarity.

After a walk down the road to a point overlooking the Chama River and a tributary, I came to a greater sense of clarity.

But first — I had decided after lunch to read the GS Workbook. After about an hour, I suddenly felt — this was crazy . . . on a retreat, I don't have to do that — it was getting my mind and spirit out of the retreat mode. So I came back to my room, and then walked down the road, in a new direction.

And so these things came clear.

I really am over — or, to put it better, I have done what God called me to do at the RCA. I have completed the task that God has given me, and done so well. It just feels like I have this sense of completion. So now, what's remaining? It is to make this transition. And it does seem that a July announcement makes sense.

I then gave this time to "settle," and to see if I could rest with it. Coming back from vespers, I felt a deep contentment, and peace.

My thoughts turned to my future, and also to the conversations immediately ahead to see if this discernment found confirmation — most especially first with Karin. I decided to leave a half-day early and get home sooner. Karin's first response, in full affirmation, was that she really wasn't surprised.

The call that had first come to me on that snowy January day in

Grandchamp had remained steady and sure through sixteen years. Now, it felt that I was being released from that call. For what purpose, I wasn't clear. But before I left the Monastery of Christ in the Desert, I wrote this:

May 27, 2010

I can't expect God to write the next chapter in my life if I don't open the page.

A Vision from St. Mary's

_____

TWENTY-SEVEN OF US gathered at the conference center at St. Mary's College and Seminary outside Baltimore on September 7-8, 2001. The gathering, hosted by Cardinal William Keeler, comprised Christian leaders from the full spectrum of denominations and theological traditions. John Busby, national commander of the Salvation Army; Bob Edgar, general secretary of the National Council of Churches (NCC); Jim Wallis of Sojourners; elected leaders of historic Protestant denominations; representatives of Orthodox churches; evangelical and Pentecostal leaders; Ron Roberson from the ecumenical staff of the U.S. Conference of Catholic Bishops; and others had agreed to attend this off-the-record retreat.

We gathered to evaluate the state of ecumenical relationships in the United States and to explore whether there was a need for something new.

Ecumenical life in the United States was hopelessly lodged in separate silos. The NCC was made up of the "mainline" Protestant denominations, the historic black churches, and the Orthodox churches. Its thirty-six member churches totaled about 45 million people. The National Association of Evangelicals (NAE) had fifty-two member denominations as well as independent congregations and parachurch bodies, representing several million Christians. The Catholic Church in the United States, to which one in four Americans belonged, was organized through the U.S. Conference of Catholic Bishops with its large budget and staff. Some major denominations such as the Church of God in Christ (with about 4.6 million members) and smaller denominations like the Evangelical Covenant Church were not members of either the NCC or the NAE.

Several quiet conversations had prepared the way for this retreat at St. Mary's. Bob Edgar, a Methodist minister who had served as a Democratic member of Congress from Philadelphia and as president of the Claremont School of Theology, had become general secretary of the NCC in 2000, taking over an organization that was floundering financially and organizationally. Bob and I explored the possibilities for a wider ecumenical fellowship that could include the churches of the NCC, evangelical and Pentecostal churches such as those in the NAE, and the Catholics. In my view, as long as those groups remained segregated and separated from one another, any claims of ecumenical progress in the United States were hollow and barely credible. Further, some models were emerging around the world where national ecumenical bodies were being reformulated to include Catholic, Protestant, and evangelical participation. We wondered if something similar could happen in the United States.

Kevin Mannoia was the president of the NAE. He and I had also met and talked about how to build broader avenues of fellowship. One of the lamentable realities was an NAE bylaw that prevented any denomination from joining if it was a member of the NCC. Kevin wanted to see that changed. He was also eager to explore new relationships that would bring the NAE out of its ecumenical isolation.

For some time I had been convinced that the RCA was a potential bridge between the evangelical and ecumenical communities. As a founding member of both the NCC and the WCC, the RCA's ecumenical credentials were unassailable. But we also nurtured a strong evangelical spirit, particularly in the midwestern and western regions of the church. From the time I began as general secretary, I had described the RCA's character as being both evangelical and ecumenical.

Therefore, through the Commission on Christian Unity (CCU), we decided to apply to join the NAE, while making clear that we would faithfully maintain our membership in the NCC. That would also be a means for the NAE to consider changing its bylaws. Our application was sent to the NAE with Kevin Mannoia's support.

New overtures were also being extended to the Catholic Church. At an informal meeting of church leaders at the Cove, the Billy Graham Training Center near Asheville, North Carolina, I approached Cardinal Keeler, a preeminent Catholic leader in ecumenical matters, for a private discussion over a meal. Sharing some of the openness in new leaders like Bob Edgar and Kevin Mannoia, and drawing on the precedents of Catholic participation in councils of churches in other parts of the world, I asked the cardinal if the time was ripe for a new conversation. He was completely open and supportive, desiring to see such an initiative. And he offered St. Mary's as a site for hosting such an encounter.

Father John Hotchkin had been serving as the executive director of the U.S. Conference of Catholic Bishops' office of ecumenical affairs for three decades. He was highly respected as a dean of ecumenists. Bob Edgar; Cliff Kirkpatrick, the stated clerk of the Presbyterian Church (USA); and I went to Washington, D.C., to meet with Father Hotchkin and some key Catholic bishops during their fall conference. We shared emerging ecumenical possibilities. Hotchkin knew the politics of these matters within the U.S. Catholic Church better than anyone, and he was ready to cautiously take some steps forward.

I invited Edgar, Mannoia, and Hotchkin to jointly address the delegates at the RCA's 2001 General Synod on our ecumenical hopes. They agreed, and the result was an impressive public display of affection. Earlier, Hotchkin had accepted Edgar's invitation to meet with the NCC executive committee. Patterns of dialogue and exploration were slowly being established.

Then, a couple of weeks after our General Synod, on June 24, 2001, Father John Hotchkin, at sixty-six years of age, died suddenly from a severe bronchial infection. A short while later, Mannoia was removed as president of the NAE. His support of the RCA's application and proposed change in their bylaws had created an internal controversy, and their finances had become unstable, due in part to Kevin's decision to move the NAE offices to Los Angeles. Those factors combined to allow board members dissatisfied with Mannoia's farsighted leadership to force his resignation, and put the RCA's application on hold.

Bob Edgar called me and asked if appearing before the RCA's General Synod portended an ill fate, and wondered what would happen to him.

The range of participants coming to the St. Mary's retreat was as broad as we had hoped, however, and I approached this encounter with keen anticipation. At a minimum, this was an opportunity to begin to build relationships between church leaders who functioned in different ecclesiastical silos and rarely interacted with one another.

The conference center at St. Mary's was ideal. It was located in a quiet setting with comfortable accommodations and a pleasant room for meeting. The time was designed with an open and flexible framework for conversation with simple questions. We first addressed what was working well in ecumenical relationships. Then we asked, what were our dissatisfactions? A list of concerns, which we called "laments," quickly came to the surface:

- The lack of common witness
- The appearance of disunity to society
- Our actual lack of unity
- "Dividing walls of hostility" among us
- No one structure that represented even one-half of the churches in the United States
- Doing mission in a disunited way
- The misunderstanding and judgment of one another
- The way our disunity impeded our work for social justice
- The lack of a common voice on issues of human dignity
- Our inability to impact the public square
- Our lack of dialogue with one another
- Our broken relationships that have not been made whole
- The split between theology and service

It was a revealing, and even stunning, summary of our dissatisfaction with the state of relationships between the various groups and traditions of Christianity in the United States.

Then we asked ourselves if we believed there was a need to create something new. And we found ourselves in unanimous agreement.

The group went on to dream and envision what this might be like, and even formulated an initial draft of what we hoped for.

> An ecumenical table or forum with the broadest possible representation of the Christian churches in the United States, for the purpose of dialogue and witness, with the following objectives:
> - Enhancing fellowship and mutual support
> - Speaking to society with a common voice
> - Understanding our differences and our commonalities
> - Serving the needs of society
> - Mutual prayer together
> - Providing a witness for Christ in the world

This was the genesis of Christian Churches Together in the USA (CCT). It would take several years to implement this vision, and the mission and purposes would be further clarified. But those September days outside of Baltimore gave birth to a new and historically unprecedented fellowship expressing the unity of churches in the United States.

The architecture of this new body began to be drawn up over the next year and a half, and included several unique features. CCT would be organized around church "families," including the historic Protestant churches, the Catholic Church, the evangelical and Pentecostal churches, and the Orthodox Church. We knew of only one other ecumenical body organized in this fashion, the Middle East Council of Churches. This seemed to be an intriguing way to represent the realities of church life. No major decision could be made by CCT without the approval of each of the families, and the steering committee and governance structure were established on this basis.

All our decisions would be made by consensus. This broke with the traditional reliance on Robert's Rules of Order and a parliamentary style that dominates most denominational structures and other ecumenical organizations. Skeptics about this procedure became convinced it could work as Sharon Browning, an organizational consultant recommended by Bob Edgar, facilitated the process in our organizational meetings, using versions of consensus decision-making at each step.

We also agreed to include Christian organizations among the participants in CCT. Such a step was more significant than it might initially seem. Traditionally, ecumenical bodies like the NCC, the WCC, and even state and local councils of churches are made up only of churches, or what Protestants call denominations. But when one examines the realities of the Christian community in the United States, so-called parachurch organizations like World Vision, Young Life, InterVarsity, and hundreds more have extensive influence. This is especially true in the evangelical and Pentecostal world.

Therefore, if CCT was to attempt to adequately represent the realities of the Christian community in the United States, such organizations had to have a place at the table. At the same time, we realized that they could quickly dominate CCT's life, so it was agreed that they should be limited to 20 percent of overall membership. This provision has allowed Bread for the World, World Vision, Habitat for Humanity, the American Bible Society, Sojourners, Evangelicals for Social Action, and the National Hispanic Christian Leadership Council to play active and influential roles in CCT along with thirty-seven denominations representing the spectrum of the Christian community.

From the start, those founding CCT were convinced we needed a new organizational model with as "light" an infrastructure as possible. Worried about the heavy bureaucracy and perennial financial stress of the NCC, no one wanted anything similar. More fundamentally, we were committed to see that the "work" of CCT would be carried out by the efforts of those in its participating churches and organizations, with minimal staff and budget for CCT itself.

When a group of thirty-six church leaders met in the spring of 2002 to outline our way forward, John Busby, national commander of the Salvation Army and moderator of our steering committee, announced that he was retiring, and thus we would need new leadership for this emerging organization. The group asked me to take over this role from John. For the next five years, until CCT was launched, this became my primary ecumenical activity. At times it felt like a second job, and I think my staff shared those feelings.

Bob Edgar and the NCC Executive Committee were fully supportive of this process in these early, formative years. The Executive Committee even formally adopted a motion made by Bruce Robbins, the ecumenical officer of the United Methodist Church, stating in effect that the NCC was ready to explore any options, including ending its present institutional life, in order to become part of a new ecumenical body. The goal was to expand and strengthen fellowship and common witness with the widest possible range of Christian churches.

Edgar and I talked candidly about the possible ways forward. We looked to the experience of councils of churches in Great Britain, Australia, and elsewhere that had gone through fundamental transformations. In some cases their existing national council was closed down to allow a new, more inclusive ecumenical body to emerge.

Edgar saw this as a real option, as did I. An NCC proposal for funding to the Lilly Foundation was made with this scenario in mind. Bob even spoke confidentially about moving out of 475 Riverside Drive in New York and establishing the headquarters of the new organization in a place like Baltimore.

Yet in Bob's thinking, such an option, while very dramatic, represented the way in which the NCC would evolve into a more inclusive ecumenical body, with evangelicals, Pentecostals, and Catholics. Many of the core staff and functions of the existing NCC, such as Bible translation, education, faith and order, and justice advocacy, would remain, embedded in the new organization.

In January 2003, fifty-seven church leaders gathered at Fuller Seminary in Pasadena, California, to adopt a proposed organizational plan for Christian Churches Together. Several important decisions were made, but by that time it was beginning to become clear that a simple evolution of the NCC into a new organization was not likely to happen. On the one hand, evangelical and Pentecostal representatives exploring participation in this new fellowship were highly sensitive to the NCC's involvement. The old wounds between the evangelical and ecumenical worlds were still not healed, and these participants didn't want to join a newly morphed version of the NCC.

Further, nearly all the participants exploring this emerging initiative were clear about establishing a new organizational model. No one wanted a heavy, staff-driven bureaucracy. CCT had to be owned by the churches and organizations themselves, which had to have the ability to carry out most of its functions. Networking and connection between its participants would shape the organizational paradigm, rather than membership in an institution that implemented all its work through a central office.

These discussions proceeded. A few months later, Bob Edgar and I met for lunch and a focused discussion at the Le Monde restaurant on Broadway, a few blocks from 475 Riverside Drive. When Bob had seen the model for minimal staff, he realized things were moving in a different direction than what we had originally hoped. In its beginning years, CCT necessarily would be established as a completely new and fully independent fellowship. Bob's support continued to be unabated. He was committed to seeing this happen for the sake of the wider ecumenical cause.

At the same time, each of us wanted to be sure that the NCC and CCT would not become competing organizations; that would injure both. Establishing a broader ecumenical table in the United States was essential, but that would not diminish the need for the NCC's work with its member churches, nor, for that matter, the work of the NAE. We committed ourselves to doing all we could to prevent others from trying to play these two groups against each other. Edgar wrote to all the NCC member churches explaining how he and the NCC's executive board "viewed the two organizations as complementary," adding that "your participation in Christian Churches Together is important in order for this new ecumenical table to gather all the voices needed for its effective witness."

The 2003 Pasadena meeting also raised the issue of establishing a fifth "family" in the formation of CCT — one that would represent the historic black churches. The compelling rationale was that American church history, through the struggle against slavery and the Civil War, witnessed the emergence of the black churches, such as the African Methodist Episcopal Church, the African Methodist Episcopal Zion Church, the Christian Methodist Episcopal Church, the National Baptist Convention (USA), the National Baptist Convention of America, the Progressive National Baptist Convention, and others. These churches, in American religious life, constitute a distinct reality, as do the Orthodox, Catholic, historic Protestant, and evangelical/Pentecostal churches, and therefore should be one of the founding "families" of CCT.

CCT's steering committee basically agreed with the proposal, establishing "racial/ethnic churches" as a fifth family that would form its constitutional basis. A few African American church leaders had been involved in the earliest explorations of CCT, but the historic black churches, along with other groups, were not adequately represented. Following the Pasadena meeting and the decision to form CCT on the basis of these five families, efforts to engage leadership from the historic black churches became far more intentional.

In 2004, Bishop Earl McCloud Jr. was elected to head the Office of Ecumenical and Urban Affairs of the African Methodist Episcopal Church. Early in his tenure he questioned the need for CCT. When we were together at an NCC Executive Board meeting, and I gave a report on CCT, Bishop McCloud said we had too many meetings and ecumenical organizations, and doubted what good CCT could do.

In further discussions, it became clear that Earl and others were concerned that CCT would weaken the NCC, despite the assurances and commitments that had been made. Moreover, the historic black churches felt, for good reason, that the NCC had provided an important platform for their witness and concerns, which they did not want to see diminished.

Bishop McCloud also alleged that CCT included right-wing conservative evangelicals who were unsympathetic and resistant to the concerns of the black churches for justice. (That was putting it politely.) In conversations with Earl I tried to point out that the right-wing religious groups he was concerned about wanted nothing to do with CCT, and that most of the evangelical and Pentecostal groups involved in CCT evidenced strong commitments to racial reconciliation and social justice. But for whatever reasons, Bishop McCloud had made up his mind.

Others shared reservations as well, including Thomas Hoyt, bishop of the Christian Methodist Episcopal Church, who was also serving at that time as president of the NCC. At a breakfast meeting in Chicago, Bishop Hoyt explained carefully his hesitations, while also making it clear from his point of view that he didn't want to prevent CCT from being established.

But the tone of discussion around CCT didn't always remain that civil. I and others began hearing charges and allegations about CCT and our supposed lack of interest in anything other than building cozy friendships. It became clear that a couple of people with ecumenical responsibilities were working behind the scenes to actively undermine CCT and its leadership, alleging insensitivity to racial justice, as well as other attacks. In all my ecumenical experience, this was among the most depressing and distressing events I have ever witnessed.

Given the history of race in America, and the persistence of enduring racism in our society and in our churches, addressing issues like those involving the relationship of the historic black churches to CCT inevitably has multiple layers, touching on acute sensitivities and strong perceptions. It requires patience, repentance, and careful listening to resolve them. But we were committed to doing so.

Meanwhile, CCT continued to emerge. At Camp Allen, a spacious Episcopalian conference center about an hour and a half outside of Houston, we met in January 2004 to experiment with what CCT would actually be like if and when it was officially established. Two subjects would be discussed — prayer and the changing face of global Christianity. Again, over fifty church leaders came; by that time about twenty-five churches were officially in the process of deciding to be founding participants of CCT.

Sometimes the simplest areas of focus become the most profound. We chose to share about prayer, asking representatives from each of the five families to explain the understanding and practice of prayer within their traditions. Then we divided into small groups composed, as much as possible, with the diversity present at the meeting. We invited them to discuss their reactions and then, if they wished, to pray together.

The result was moving and memorable. Several participants cited this time of praying together as the most significant in the entire meeting, because of the range of traditions. Some Orthodox participants said they had never prayed with a Pentecostal. Evangelical participants shared never having prayed with a Catholic priest, much less a bishop. Simple encounters like these demonstrated both the depth of spiritual separation between these families and the openness and hunger for a deeper encounter with one another.

The Houston meeting also established June 2005 as the official "launch" date of CCT, by which time bylaws would be approved and this new body would legally become a reality. A public worship service of celebration was planned at the National Cathedral in Washington, D.C., in September 2005. Former president Jimmy Carter was at the top of the list of those we would ask to preach.

All this assumed, however, that we would have sufficient participation by each of the church families by that time. A major question remained whether the Catholic Church would join. The U.S. Conference of Catholic Bishops (USCCB) would make that decision at their meeting in November 2004.

From the start, Catholic bishops had been faithfully involved in CCT's development, particularly Bishop Todd Brown from Orange County, California, and Bishop Stephen Blaire from the Sacramento area, who each successively chaired the Committee on Ecumenical and Inter-religious Affairs. Staff from the ecumenical office of the USCCB had been very supportive. But they all emphasized that no one could predict how their vote would come out.

The Vatican had no objection, leaving the decision to the U.S. bishops. Cardinal Keeler, who hosted the first meeting at St. Mary's that cast the vision for CCT, spoke strongly in favor. When the vote was taken, the ratio of bishops that approved joining CCT was over 2 to 1. This marked the first time that the Catholic Church in the United States had officially agreed to join an ecumenical fellowship.

The *New York Times* the next day took note of this development, and news quickly spread. Had the Catholic bishops not approved, CCT in all likelihood would not have been established. This was a historic step, and now momentum around CCT continued to grow.

The next CCT gathering occurred in June 2005 at a Jesuit retreat center in Los Altos, California. Various discussions with representatives of the historic black churches had continued, but their reservations remained. Bishop Thomas Hoyt came to the gathering to politely explain his church's hesitations. Other black churches were only beginning to become engaged and requested more dialogue.

We were faced with a dilemma. With the Catholic Church making its decision, and strong representation from the other families, the expectation was that CCT would be officially established at this time. But no historic black church had committed itself. We had created a separate family for these churches, and now their decision not to participate was threatening to veto the entire process. Our commitment was that all five families had to agree to all major decisions.

As moderator I proposed that we wait another year, allowing more time for dialogue. We came to consensus that we shouldn't establish CCT without making every effort to secure the participation of at least some churches from the historic black church tradition. The service of celebration that fall was canceled.

Other steps forward emerged from our time at Los Altos, however. We began discussing what CCT would "do" when it became officially established. All affirmed and treasured the building of bonds between us. But Rich Stearns, president of World Vision, put it this way: "Being here with CCT is like being on a cruise ship. I'm having a wonderful time being together with others. But I wonder, where are we going?"

The evangelical/Pentecostal family group, of which Rich was a member, proposed that CCT address the issue of domestic poverty. If this were an area where the breadth of church leadership in the United States could find common ground, then CCT could have a powerful impact. The whole group agreed. That set up a process, over the next two years, involving staff from the U.S. Catholic conference, Sojourners, Bread for the World, Evangelicals for Social Action, and various denominations in producing a common statement on the causes of and solutions to domestic poverty, with specific calls to action.

More immediately, however, dialogue with the historic black churches became a matter of highest priority. Don Williams, a staff member from Bread for the World and steering committee member for CCT, played an important role in keeping conversations going.

Dr. Stephen Thurston was serving as president of the National Baptist Convention of America, one of the nation's historic black Baptist denominations. He was pastor of a church on the south side of Chicago, and we met at a restaurant close to the Loop for lunch and a long, rich discussion about his denomination, ecumenical relationships in general, and CCT. He had been exposed to CCT and appreciated the emphasis on worship and sharing, as well as its recent commitment to address domestic poverty. Following our lunch, he assured me that he and his board would seriously consider being a part of CCT.

Dr. William Shaw, president of the National Baptist Convention

(USA), one of the largest historic black churches, had been in ongoing discussions with others about CCT. Dr. Shaw pressed the issue of how participation would address and help rectify the largest concerns of his churches, such as poverty and economic justice. Ron Sider was one of the CCT steering committee members who was in conversation with him.

After his careful process of inquiry, Dr. Shaw announced that the National Baptist Convention (USA) would join CCT. Dr. Thurston shared the news that his denomination would also become a part of CCT. That meant there would be at least a beginning representation of historic black churches. And with that development, CCT was ready to be officially established.

At the end of March in 2006, we gathered at the Simpsonwood Conference and Retreat Center outside of Atlanta. All the pieces had finally come together. Thirty-four denominations and Christian organizations, representing over 100 million Christians, had committed themselves to be a part of Christian Churches Together, making this the most inclusive fellowship of churches and organizations in the United States. Together, we stood and read our purposes and commitments, and then sang the doxology.

In the evening, I sat on the porch of one of Simpsonwood's cottages, drinking a glass of wine with Jim Wallis and Ron Sider. We thought back to where things were in 1976 when the Chicago Declaration was issued, and what had happened in the churches to bring us now to the birth of CCT, and its potential for a resonant Christian witness in our society.

That moment was five years in the making, but only marked CCT's official starting point. Its work on domestic poverty continued. When Barack Obama was elected president, representatives from CCT met with members of his transition team, prior to the inauguration, to share CCT's comprehensive statement on domestic poverty and press for specific commitments from the new administration.

In January 2008 Dick Hamm, former president and general minister of the Disciples of Christ, was installed as CCT's first executive director (part-time), and the Orthodox church leader Leonid Kishkovsky replaced me as moderator of the steering committee. CCT was beginning to establish an organizational culture and structure that would strengthen its sustainability.

In addition to maintaining its focus on domestic poverty, attention was also turned to evangelism. The 2010 meeting was held in Seattle, in part because the Pacific Northwest is known as the "none zone." A remarkably high number of people in this region, when asked for their religious affiliation, respond "none." Those from the five families shared and compared their particular approaches to sharing the gospel of Jesus Christ. Writing a report afterward, I said, "This dialogue on evangelism is the richest I've experienced in so broad a gathering. Major ecumenical organizations like the National Council of Churches and the World Council of Churches rarely put this topic on their agendas, and the evangelical/Pentecostal community, though it focuses heavily on evangelism, discusses mostly within its own ranks, so this was a fresh encounter."

The following year, in January 2011, we went to Birmingham, Alabama, to focus specifically on the issues of race, and its relationship to poverty. Part of our work was to write an answer to Dr. Martin Luther King Jr.'s famous "Letter from a Birmingham Jail," written in 1968. We tried to frame what the churches today would say in response to the questions and challenges raised at that time by Dr. King.

What always touches my heart during these CCT gatherings is the worship. Each of the five faith families leads a time of worship in a style of its choosing. So in Birmingham, for instance, we went to an Orthodox church to take part in their Epiphany liturgy. The local Catholic bishop brought a choir to our hotel meeting room to lead morning worship. The Protestant family led a solid liturgy with classic hymns, accompanied by an organ, in the Episcopal Cathedral. Bert Waggoner, national director of Vineyard, U.S.A., flew in a songwriter and band members to lead in a high-octane, Pentecostal worship one evening, and Stephen Thurston preached a closing sermon the last morning. All of us seem to find a way to enter into all these forms and styles of worshiping God. And that gives me hope.

CCT is a bold ecumenical experiment in the United States. I'm convinced it's a fresh pathway in the search for unity in Christ's body, and a promising paradigm for the future. Several of the "laments" from the retreat at St. Mary's are being addressed, while others still remain. But in the decade since that time, the vision from St. Mary's has begun to take hold, creating a new way in which divided families of faith can seek to live, work, and pray as those who belong to one Lord.

The Evangelical Lutheran Church in America has its headquarters on Higgins Road in Park Ridge, a few blocks from where I grew up. From its conference room on the eleventh floor, looking north, one can see my home, as well as the subdivision that Gundersen and Sons built on what had been farmland west of Mary Seat of Wisdom.

I was there for a meeting of CCT. Archbishop Wilton Gregory, who served a term as president of the U.S. Catholic Conference of Bishops, was with us; he and I both were serving as "presidents" of CCT, and I had gotten to know him well. So I told him the story of how my grandfather had bought the farm, and after wrestling with the decision, sold the desired parcel to the Catholics.

"That is remarkable," Archbishop Gregory said to me. "Mary Seat of Wisdom, there on Cumberland Avenue, is where I served, years ago, as a priest." What, I wondered, would Big Daddy say now?

The Heartland and the Frontier

————

I N 2005 ABOUT seventy church leaders from throughout Africa gathered at a pleasant church conference center in Lusaka, the capital
city of Zambia. All parts of Christ's body came together, including representatives from Baptist, Anglican, Pentecostal, Reformed, Roman
Catholic, Orthodox, Seventh-Day Adventist, evangelical, and Lutheran
churches, as well as people from the All Africa Christian Council, the
Association of Evangelicals in Africa, the International Fellowship of
Evangelical Students, the World Student Christian Federation, World
Vision, the United Bible Societies, the African Theological Fellowship,
and various national councils of churches. Also included were the Afri-
can Instituted Churches — those church groups originated in Africa by
Africans, rather than being started by missionaries from Europe or
America.

Why was this so important? Simply because it had never happened
before. The church in Africa suffers from the same kinds of divisions that
afflict the body of Christ elsewhere in the world: "mainline" historic Protestant churches, often with Orthodox churches as well, form councils of
churches or other ecumenical organizations. Meanwhile, evangelical
churches form their own, separate fellowships. Pentecostals are often
separated again in their loose-knit associations. The African Instituted
Churches add to the complexity with an organization of their own.
Finally, the Roman Catholic Church, in the African situation, stands

264

apart from all these groups, although in some cases they are members of national councils of churches.

So we're confronted by a church that is deeply divided, and those divisions are reinforced by institutional structures. In Africa, this is all the more serious for two reasons: (1) the overwhelming needs on the continent that call out for a unified response, and (2) the fact that the church is growing faster there than anyplace else in the world. In terms of numbers, growth, and vitality, Africa is the new "center" of world Christianity.

We started this Africa regional meeting of the Global Christian Forum (GCF) in Lusaka in a remarkable way. Each participant was asked to take about five minutes to share the story of his or her personal journey with Christ. That ended up taking a day and a half. The stories were rich and compelling, rapidly breaking down the stereotypes of evangelical, Catholic, mainline Protestant, Orthodox, and Pentecostal followers of Jesus.

The group then quickly identified several areas of social and political concern that were widely shared, beginning with the HIV/AIDS crisis. Nearly everyone there knew someone personally who was HIV positive or who had died of AIDS. Attention also turned to the challenges of good governance, corruption, and economic justice. It was refreshing to see the natural way in which these leaders embraced the necessity of the church to be involved in "social action," while also giving clear attention to personal evangelism and spiritual renewal. There really was no serious controversy over those issues, despite the wide diversity of churches and organizations that was present, and even though many had never met with one another before.

The Lusaka gathering was filled with the accounts of Christianity's explosive and unprecedented growth in the continent. "Ecumenical" and "evangelical" voices shared freely even as many of these leaders were encountering one another for the first time. Many Pentecostals present had never been in an "ecumenical" gathering before.

At the end of the meeting, Rev. Ekow Badu Wood of the Ghana Pentecostal Council put it this way: "This has been a beautiful opportunity for churches that have been marginalized to be given the opportunity to speak." Rev. Daniel Bitros, a pastor in the Church of Christ in Nigeria and former general secretary of the Evangelical Fellowship of Africa, said, "A stone has been moved from off the top of the hill, and now it is rolling. There is no other ecumenical body that could have brought us together in this way. Now we have to make this concrete."

But I was particularly interested in what Bishop Silas Yego would say. He headed the Africa Inland Church, which for twenty-five years has been an RCA partner in mission in Africa. This church emerged from the Africa Inland Mission, and that missionary effort had a tradition of a strongly conservative, evangelical posture. The bishop told me they never would have associated with the World Council of Churches (WCC) or other "ecumenical" bodies. But at the end of the gathering, he told the group that he had never been in a meeting like this and that he was filled with gratitude. He was determined to build similar bridges with other Christian bodies in his own context.

Even though the vision of the Global Christian Forum was launched as early as the WCC's 1998 Harare Assembly, its development has been slow and deliberate. First, the coordinating group had to determine if evangelical and Pentecostal leaders would actually be interested in participating. A meeting at Fuller Seminary with representatives from around the world tested that question, and the response was positive, particularly when it became clear that this newly imagined global fellowship would not be controlled by the WCC.

The strategy then was to test this model in various regional settings. Asia was first, with a meeting held in Hong Kong. Richard Howell, president of the Evangelical Fellowship of India, described that Asian regional encounter this way: "The Global Christian Forum is the best thing that could have happened to the Christian church in Asia. It gave an opportunity for those from different traditions to listen. We discovered one another. And we discovered Christ at work within our different traditions."

Within India, the national council of churches, the evangelical fellowship, and the Catholic conference of bishops began meeting together to create a new "forum," which started speaking to common issues in their country. This was a prototype of what the Global Christian Forum hoped to encourage around the world.

The Asia and Africa meetings were followed by a European gathering, held in Warburg, Germany. It was hosted by Metropolitan mar Gregorios Yohanna Ibrahim of the Syrian Orthodox Church, a strong supporter of the Global Christian Forum, at their monastery, which was purchased from the Dominicans in 1996. The presence of immigrants in Germany belonging to the Syrian Orthodox Church was just one of numerous examples we encountered during the Warburg meeting of how immigrant communities are transforming the landscape of European churches. A Latin American regional meeting followed, held in Santiago, Chile.

The response from all these regional gatherings, plus the similar experience of Christian Churches Together in the USA, was overwhelmingly positive and enthusiastic. About half of the participants at these meetings were from evangelical and Pentecostal groups, who had previously had virtually no ecumenical interaction with the historic Protestant, Orthodox, and Catholic participants also present. A new experience of fellowship was being discovered, grounded in the sharing of personal journeys with Christ, or "testimonies," which was shaping the emerging culture of the Global Christian Forum.

Sam Kobia, by then general secretary of the WCC, asked me to represent the WCC on the committee that was guiding the Global Christian Forum, and this deepened my engagement with a process that stirred my heart and focused my ecumenical passion. The committee itself was an ecumenical marvel. As it evolved, its members officially represented the World Evangelical Alliance, the Pentecostal World Fellowship, the Roman Catholic Church, the Ecumenical Patriarchate (Orthodox), the WCC, all the Christian world communions — including the Lutheran World Federation, the Baptist World Alliance, the Anglican Communion, etc. — the Organization of African Instituted Churches, the Moscow Patriarchate, the International Fellowship of Evangelical Students, and more. The Vatican's Pontifical Council for Promoting Christian Unity has been a member since the beginning. All this was historically unprecedented. And I have found it to be an absolute joy. It makes my soul sing.

The Global Christian Forum is not just responding to the entrenched historic division between the "evangelical" and "ecumenical" wings of the church. Much more fundamentally, it's a response to what Lamin Sanneh, Yale Divinity School professor of church history, calls the gulf between the "heartland" and the "frontier" in world Christianity.

Christianity today seems divided in new ways. On the one hand are those churches, largely in the north, and rooted in the heritage of the West, that have a deep sense of the historic Christian tradition and an ecumenical commitment to what the Nicene Creed names as "the one holy catholic and apostolic church." Historically, this has been Christianity's "heartland." But these churches find themselves struggling to maintain a resonant and vital witness amidst their modern or postmodern cultures. Their numbers and their cultural influence are in decline.

On the other hand are those churches, located largely in the south (but moving through migration into the global north), that exhibit a vital, even explosive spiritual power, and are propelling a Christian resurgence within their societies and regions of the world. These places feel like the new "frontier" of world Christianity. Yet, in their creative contextualization, links to the historic Christian tradition can seem tenuous, and the sense of belonging to the wider, global church, in all its expressions, is minimized or forgotten in their focused and frequently sectarian enthusiasm. Often, the expressions of Christianity from the frontier seem unsettling, threatening, and at times almost incomprehensible to the Christian heartland.

Building bridges across this contemporary chasm in world Christianity is the most urgent ecumenical challenge facing the church today. At its core, that is what the Global Christian Forum is trying to do.

That task is even more complicated because the "center" of world Christianity in terms of numbers of believers and resurgent trends of growth has shifted from the heartland to the frontier. Those who call themselves "nonreligious" are the fastest-growing religious group in the United States, now constituting 15 percent. Europe has become increasingly settled in its secularized cultural identity. But a Christian, postcolonial presence has grown remarkably in Africa, Latin America, and many places in Asia in what Lamin Sanneh describes as a "post-Western Christian awakening."

The Christian population in Africa, only a few million at the beginning of the twentieth century, is now over 360 million people and is projected to grow to 633 million by 2025. By that same time, 640 million Christians will be in Latin America and 460 million in Asia. The contemporary face of Christianity in today's world is a woman from a Kenyan village or a Brazilian favela.

This shift in Christianity's global foundations is not only geographical, but also confessional. Modern Pentecostalism, for example, recently celebrated its birth 100 years ago at Azusa Street. Today it boasts about 580 million adherents, or one of four Christians in the world, constituting one of the most dramatic stories of modern Christian history. Further, this number alone exceeds the total membership of all the churches that belong to the World Council of Churches. If growth continues at its present pace, by the middle of the twenty-first century the world will be home to one billion Pentecostal Christians.

The rapid growth of the church in the global south has changed the contours of modern evangelicalism as well. A few decades ago, 70 percent of the world's evangelical community lived in the global north. Today it is the opposite — 70 percent are in the south, where context shapes a witness that is becoming more holistic, integrating personal evangelism and social justice.

The Catholic Church as well is experiencing the pervasive changes brought by these shifts in the tectonic plates of world Christianity. In the first quarter of this century, Catholicism is projected to lose 20 million members in Europe but to gain 140 million members in Latin America, 100 million in Africa, and 50 million in Asia. Similar dynamics are having an impact on the Orthodox Church.

To carry out our vision, the committee guiding the Global Christian Forum decided the time was right to move beyond the successful regional meetings and host a truly global gathering. The dream was for this to reflect the incredible variety and complexity of world Christianity, both geographically and confessionally. The frontier and the heartland would be gathered together.

This never had been done. As inexplicable as it seems, never in recent Christian history have the recognized leaders from evangelical, Pentecostal, historic Protestant, Catholic, and Orthodox churches and global organizations, from around the world, been brought together in such a global encounter. But this is what had been imagined when the vision of the Global Christian Forum was first shared.

We knew this gathering had to be held in the global south, amidst the new "center" of world Christianity. So we chose a conference center in Limuru, Kenya, outside of Nairobi. The letters of invitation went out, and those invited came — 226 Christian leaders from seventy-two countries representing the full breadth of world Christianity, and virtually all the major global Christian groups, from the World Evangelical Alliance to the Vatican.

I had persuaded my good friend James Leggett, bishop of the International Pentecostal Holiness Church, to come to Limuru. Bishop Leggett and I were serving as presidents of Christian Churches Together in the USA (CCT), and he was also chairman of the Pentecostal World Fellowship and a board member of the National Association of Evangelicals. He treasured his time with CCT, but was initially cautious about the Limuru gathering of the Global Christian Forum. He had never participated in this kind of global ecumenical meeting.

The first evening in Limuru, Bishop Leggett came up to me and asked, "Do you think that the general secretary of the World Council of Churches would be willing to meet with me?"

It was both an honest question and a courageous request. The head of the World Pentecostal Conference and the general secretary of the WCC typically had no contact with each other, and their constituencies were deeply suspicious of one another.

But I told Bishop Leggett that I was certain Sam Kobia would be delighted to meet him, and the next day the three of us had lunch together. Bishop Leggett learned how Sam's father had been a Pentecostal preacher in Kenya, and the two formed a relationship that was a first step in building a bridge between these two constituencies. Stories like that occurred literally hundreds of times during these days in Limuru.

Following the practice of the Global Christian Forum, we began our time by meeting in groups of thirty to share the stories of our journey with Jesus Christ. Papers on theological or social issues are usually presented first at formal ecumenical meetings, followed by debate, as attendees search for areas of agreement. But in Kenya we were drawn together first through sharing our common experience with Christ.

In my group, for instance, an evangelical leader from Great Britain shared how reading *Mere Christianity* began his journey of faith, while a Catholic bishop told how Vatican II, which took place just when he began serving as a priest, led him into deep encounters with the Bible, using *lectio divina* as a way to encounter Scripture. A Salvation Army officer told how he left his law practice following a call to ministry, and a Seventh-Day Adventist leader from Uganda explained how an invitation to attend an Adventist congregation led to his conversion.

An Anglican bishop from Canada described how, at the age of fifteen, she experienced a "visitation" by Christ, who told her, "You will be a priest, and I will never leave you or forsake you." This was before her church ordained women. And the general secretary of the council of churches in Chad recalled how both his parents died when he was age two, but he survived and met Jesus Christ in a Sunday school class when he was eight.

A church leader from Indonesia left a successful career in the oil business because he clearly heard God's call into ministry. The archbishop of the Church of the Lord Aladura, one of the most vibrant and fastest-growing African Instituted Churches, based in Nigeria, was called into ministry and leadership of this church while being a computer consultant and politician living as an immigrant in Germany. And a leader of the Laos Evangelical Church related how while most Christians had fled the country, the tiny church that he stayed with, which had 26 members, experienced a revival in 1990 and now includes 7,000 believers. A priest from Malankara Orthodox Syrian Church in India explained how his faith journey had been enriched by experience at both an evangelical seminary and a Catholic university.

We spent most of a day simply listening to one astonishing and inspiring story after another. Maybe it sounds simple, but these kinds of encounters, among such a broad range of Christian leaders at a global level, really haven't happened in this way before. One participant put it plainly and clearly: "What we have heard is that God in Jesus has come to us in different ways." Another added, "We have now seen the people who are behind the badges we are wearing."

Our time continued with presentations in plenary sessions, Bible study, reports on new ecumenical models from specific countries, and discussion about what this newly emerging fellowship could and should do together. By the end, participants were expansive in their joy and affirmation of this time.

Peter Sleebos, a Pentecostal leader from the Netherlands, put it bluntly when he said that the Global Christian Forum had "created an environment where we feel safe enough and not intimidated by historic mainline churches."

Mel Robeck, a member of the Global Christian Forum committee and expert on the Pentecostal movement who teaches at Fuller Seminary, proclaimed, "I am stunned. What we have here might be described as a new Pentecost."

Bishop Brian Ferrell, secretary of the Vatican's Pontifical Council for Promoting Christian Unity, underscored the sixty years of ecumenical efforts that had helped prepare the way for this event, and added his church's emphatic "Yes" to the Global Christian Forum.

By the end, Bishop Leggett told me how these days at Limuru, Kenya, had forever changed his understanding of the global body of Christ. Many echoed those views, and observers called this meeting "a watershed in Christian history."

Sam Kobia, addressing the gathering, put it this way: "Some would have said that this event was not possible. But here we are, and the world wonders what will come next." He later added that there was nothing like this in ecumenical history.

The single person most responsible for making all this possible was Hubert van Beek. An engineer by training, this Dutchman served with his wife Ria as a missionary to Madagascar before joining the staff of the WCC. When I was doing consulting work with the U.S. board of the Vellore Christian Medical College and Hospital, an extraordinary institution started in India by Dr. Ida Scudder, an RCA missionary, I came across a booklet on the "ecumenical sharing of resources." It was part of a WCC effort led by Hubert to provide a framework for how economically rich and poor churches can relate together in equitable and mutually enriching ways.

Struck with the wisdom in the booklet, I not only shared it with the Vellore board but also got in touch with Hubert. Learning he was coming to New York, I set up a dinner with him at a Japanese restaurant and began a working relationship and friendship that has lasted for decades. He helped introduce me to the WCC, and when I later joined its staff we collaborated on countless projects.

Toward the end of Hubert's long service with the WCC, he was virtually the only staff person working consistently on the WCC's relationship with evangelicals, Pentecostals, and other nonmember churches and groups. Following the 1998 Harare Assembly, Hubert launched the initial explorations of the Global Christian Forum. When he then retired from the WCC, he took on this work full-time, while living mostly on his retirement and pension funds.

The apartment that he and Ria share is in Versoix, Switzerland, next to Geneva, with a balcony that affords a view of the lake and Mont Blanc in the distance. In a small study he works endlessly at his computer, planning the details of consultations and building a modest but growing infrastructure of names, churches, and organizations that has now become the most creative and promising global ecumenical initiative since the founding of the WCC. It was Willem Visser't Hooft, another Dutchman, who led the establishment of the WCC at its first assembly in Amsterdam in 1948. Hubert van Beek has followed in those footsteps.

One of the ironies, however, is that the Global Christian Forum has now picked up an ecumenical calling that the World Council of Churches has been unable to fulfill. I have served and loved the WCC as a staff member and governing board member for over two decades, but it has become painfully clear to me that the task of creating an ecumenical fellowship inclusive of all the major Christian "families," and building a bridge between the "heartland" and the "frontier," is beyond the WCC's present ability.

Like other major ecumenical organizations established a half-century ago, the WCC faces constantly shrinking resources and an inability to strategically prioritize its work. When I dropped in on its Central Committee meeting in Geneva in February 2011, I listened to the report of its Finance Committee. Its chair noted that because of decreasing revenues, its program budget would be cut by the equivalent of $1.2 million, and then added that this would require "a prioritizing of its work." I've heard and personally echoed the call for setting priorities to guide the WCC's work for over twenty years, but to no avail.

A staff sharply decreased in number confronts a wide range of programmatic expectations that are impossible to adequately fulfill. Staff morale constantly suffers, and those in its unwieldy governance structures are frustrated in their ability to make meaningful decisions. Further, there's little sense of any practical spiritual solidarity motivating the core of its mission. Bureaucratic politics and narrow agendas supported by distinct and often competing constituencies define far too much of the WCC's culture.

That's not to diminish the value found in the WCC's many programs, consultations, and relationships. Further, no one can deny the remarkable ecumenical achievements that have been made over the past sixty years, facilitated by the WCC. Its present general secretary, Olav Fykse Tveit, from Norway, brings the kind of spiritual clarity and expansiveness of vision that is sorely needed. But redirecting the goals, energies, and direction of the WCC toward bridging the chasms today in world Christianity — particularly the theological, ecclesiological, and geographical gulf between the heartland and the frontier — would require a deep shift in its culture and take years to accomplish. There's no sign that the WCC is prepared to make the strategic priority commitments required to do so.

The WCC's problem is complicated by the allergic reaction to it by the vast majority of the world's Pentecostals and evangelicals, along with the Vatican's decision not to be a member and to participate only selectively in its life. That effectively leaves only one-quarter of world Christianity fully in the fellowship of the WCC.

The great ecumenical irony of our time is that an initiative that for the first time in recent history has brought the leadership of all the families of world Christianity into a meaningful fellowship was engineered by one person behind a computer in Versoix, and assisted by a steadfast committee of church leaders all volunteering their time. Its annual budget then was around $100,000, with the Nairobi gathering costing about $250,000. Meanwhile, the WCC, with an annual budget of about $30 million supporting over 150 staff, provided some moral support and $25,000 annually, but then mostly looked on, often in amazement.

Following the stunning fruitfulness of the 2007 global meeting in Limuru, Kenya, the Global Christian Forum began charting its future. Its history and work were officially evaluated by three different independent research groups, and a New Delhi meeting of the GCF's steering committee along with major stakeholders charted a plan for the next three years. Regional gatherings would be continued and deepened. National expressions encompassing the breadth and style of the GCF would be encouraged. Plus, discussion began around what issues the GCF might address on a world level. Further, a second global gathering, building on the precedent in Limuru, was planned for October 2011 in Indonesia.

The only major region not to host a gathering of the Global Christian Forum is the Middle East. The fractious church politics of the region, which had virtually crippled the Middle East Council of Churches, made implementing the vision of the GCF formidable. Attempts to organize a regional gathering were rebuffed, in part because of very deep-seated tensions between Orthodox and Pentecostal or conservative evangelical groups over issues of proselytism. Intra-Orthodox conflicts also complicated matters.

The GCF committee decided instead to make a "team visit" to the region; a group would visit as many church leaders as possible, simply sharing the intentions of the forum and striving to build trust. I joined this extraordinary group of six, and in June of 2009, right after our General Synod, we traveled through Egypt, Lebanon, and Syria, visiting twenty-five church leaders in ten days.

My colleagues on this team were Metropolitan Makarios, Greek Orthodox archbishop of Kenya and Africa; Rev. Pirjo-Liisa Penttinen from the World Young Women's Christian Association and the Evangelical Lutheran Church of Finland; Rev. Fr. Gabriel Hachem, from the Greek Catholic Melkite Church and appointed by the Vatican; Fouad Youssef from the Evangelical Fellowship of Egypt; Rev. Dr. Prince Guneratnam, secretary of the Pentecostal World Fellowship and pastor of a 4,000-member Assemblies of God congregation in Kuala Lumpur, Malaysia; and Hubert van Beek, our coordinator.

Our group represented the diversity and vision of the Global Christian Forum, and it felt like we were on a diplomatic mission. Meetings in the formal reception rooms of the heads of Orthodox churches and Catholic "eastern rite" churches were mixed with encounters with Baptist, conservative evangelical, Christian Missionary and Alliance, and Seventh-Day Adventist leaders in the region. The gulf between these parts of the church was obvious; some did not even know each other.

Our continual sharing of the GCF's purpose, and our patient listening to the questions of church leaders from the region, was beneficial, building bridges of understanding.

For Prince Guneratnam, all this was new. As a major Pentecostal leader from Malaysia, he had never been exposed to such an array of "hierarchs" from Orthodox churches as well as the expressions of the Catholic Church in the Middle East. But he entered into the process with a sense of wonder and deep commitment. Well into our trip, as we rode in our minibus over the mountains from Lebanon toward Damascus, Syria, I asked Prince what he thought of the trip so far.

His response was immediate. "Why did it take us so long to do this?" Throughout this trip, I grew in my friendship and respect for this Pentecostal brother.

Every three years the Pentecostal World Conference gathers major leaders and three to four thousand from around the world for a global meeting. In August of 2010, this gathering was held in Stockholm. As president, James Leggett had invited me to come on behalf of the Global Christian Forum. Further, he told me that Prince Guneratnam would likely be elected to replace him. Moreover, Bishop Leggett had taken the historic step of inviting the new WCC general secretary, Olav Tveit, to address the gathering — an invitation that had its roots in the lunch at the Limuru, Kenya, global gathering.

Coming as an observer, I felt drawn into the electric, energetic worship each evening, and the preaching by noted Pentecostal personalities like Jack Hayford, Reinhard Bonnke, Dr. Young Hoon Lee, pastor of the Yoido Full Gospel Church in Korea, and many others. I had come a month after announcing my decision to retire as general secretary of the RCA, and my heart was full of questions and wonderings about what this meant, and what might come next.

Prince gave the main talk one evening; it was based on renewing one's strength like an eagle, from Isaiah 40:31. His theme was "How to Reinvent Yourself," and he drew on how an eagle goes into seclusion, plucks out all its worn, damaged, or broken feathers, and waits for forty days for new feathers to grow. That's how an eagle renews its strength, and it's a metaphor for us.

His talk moved me deeply. Afterward, as is the Pentecostal practice, he led those gathered in a moving time of prayer. For me, this brought about one of my life's more unexpected spiritual surprises.

August 25, 2010

I think I spoke in tongues today. It was after Prince Guneratnam's talk about being renewed like an eagle . . . to say "yes" to the next thing God is asking. In the prayer time following, I was praying continuously, "Lord, I need your guidance at this time," thinking about what will come after the RCA. I was praying that almost like a chant, and then I started saying continuous words that were like babbling utterances, and seemed to come uncontrollably. . . . I wasn't seeking this, it just happened. And it definitely felt out of control. I had to work to quiet it down and stop when the prayer time came to a conclusion . . . there was no special spiritual ecstasy, just this experience of these semi-automatic utterings that came forth naturally in this time when my whole body was in that kind of prayer. So I just want to let this settle.

The Global Christian Forum had brought me to the Pentecostal World Conference in Stockholm. And there, my personal spiritual journey was traveling in new ways on the bridge between the heartland and the frontier.

Epilogue

A T FIRST REFORMED CHURCH in Schenectady, New York, in February 2011, I sat with a group of about forty folks from the RCA who had joined me in the church parlor on Sunday for a three o'clock "fireside chat." This was one of numerous gatherings held in all parts of the church during my final months as general secretary. Pastors and congregational leaders met to hear reflections on my seventeen years of service and ask questions about the RCA, the future of the church, and the state of Christianity in North America and the world.

A thoughtful, gray-haired woman in the back of the room raised her hand and asked, "Is the church an organism or an organization?" That perceptive question stayed with me for weeks. It crystallizes so many of the issues facing denominations and the institutionalized expressions of Christianity in our culture.

Organization or Organism?

It's true, of course, that this question is as old as the church. There's always, at some level, a tension between the established, institutionalized expressions of the church and newly emerging forms of Christian community and spiritual practice that are outside organizational boundaries. But I believe we are entering into a time when this tension will become acute, and seriously strain both the present structures and the theological understandings of the church.

Several factors are increasing this tension. First, a younger generation simply relates differently to the present institutionalized church. Data from surveys demonstrate that about 27 percent of young adults, when asked what their religious affiliation is, respond "none." That number is growing. Further, those who do embrace faith, or find themselves on a spiritual pilgrimage, are less and less likely to express this through the "organized" church.

Such young people find and create new ways to build community with those on a similar spiritual journey. This takes place in part through electronic means of communication and connection, where many of this generation perpetually dwell. Consider this: 23 percent of newly married couples met online. If the means of social networking are used to establish the most important relationship in one's life, it should not be surprising that increasing numbers of people turn to forms of social networking to nurture their spiritual lives.

Of course, this doesn't replace the yearning for face-to-face community where words are made flesh. But it does change the forms of those communities. They are more episodic and organic. Moreover, those in this younger generation who are seeking faith draw on spiritual resources from a virtual religious smorgasbord. They may watch one of Rob Bell's "noomas," find a Web site with prayers from the ancient desert fathers, include hard rock songs from bands on their iPods that have creative Christian content, periodically attend a Bible study group, and spend a week in Malawi on a mission trip that a friend told them about.

Asking people like this to "join a church" is like asking a scuba diver to take snorkeling lessons. Why would I need to do that, they wonder, when I'm already finding effective ways to nurture my spiritual pilgrimage? Moreover, they are likely to have serious reservations about the churches they are asked to join.

This new generation has little tolerance for religious hypocrisy, and they see a lot of it. They tend to discount what a church says about its beliefs if those are not being practiced in authentic ways. It's expected that those in a church will be demonstrating what they say through making a difference, even in small ways, in the world. Moreover, most youth and young adults experience multiracial settings in their schools and workplaces. They expect and value this cultural diversity, and are turned off when it's not present in a church.

Established churches and denominations necessarily have clear ways of defining what a church is and prescribing its necessary features. Further, most function with a membership model. You are expected to sign up and join. Doing so presupposes that you agree with a set of dogmas. This is an entrenched paradigm taken for granted by those of us in the institutional church.

But for growing numbers of people who will be shaping a religious future, this paradigm doesn't connect or make sense to the way they live their lives, or to their pathways of spiritual practice. So this presents a dilemma to those who assume that the church is a body of believers who gather to hear the Word preached and to celebrate the sacraments, and who are organized and governed by deacons and elders, with a minister of Word and sacrament.

My concern as I imagine the future is that it just won't work to try to persuade those whose lives are wired and lived differently to fit into present organizational forms of the church. We are moving into an era where the church as an organism will have far more connectivity to pilgrims searching for a spiritual home than the church as an organization. This poses not just a practical challenge, but a serious theological one.

How do we make room, within our definitions of the church, for those who find vital Christian community on the fringes, or outside of established religious institutions? How can those in the leadership of the organized church create imaginative, hospitable space for others to walk together in their journey of faith, knowing that they won't fit neatly into our categories and structures? How do we think creatively about the ways in which social media are redefining how we nurture relationships, learn, and build community? How might that reshape our models of being the church?

For these reasons I'm encouraged by what I see in the "emergent church" movement. While that term has an elastic interpretation, meaning different things to different people, what I observe when I'm with such groups gives me hope. Often, the combination of ancient Christian practices with an open and participatory style of worship that involves all the senses — what you see, hear, smell, and touch — creates a fresh environment that welcomes those who are spiritual seekers as well as those whose faith is firmly planted in their lives. My hope is that the established church will experiment with ways it can offer hospitality to organic, emerging models of religious practice and community without trying to define and control them.

Social networking is changing the paradigm of belonging. As it did in other pivotal times in history, technological developments are dramatically altering the social and cultural landscape. The church has to rearticulate its forms and functions for the gospel to find expression in the midst of these changing realities. But this can happen. It is the capacity of Christian faith to constantly take on flesh within changing cultural and social contexts that enables it to continually reform itself and thrive.

This isn't to say that church as we know it will somehow wither away. Not at all. Congregations with approved pastors who preach and celebrate sacraments, governed by elders and deacons, will certainly endure. That's not the point. But I've come to believe that in their present form, such congregations will be limited in their ability to connect to the spiritual aspirations of many within the coming generation. A simple look at the average age of those in most congregations today provides empirical evidence of this reality.

For that reason, we should focus our spiritual imagination more on viewing the church as an organism and less on seeing it as an organization.

Settled or Sent?

Visiting hundreds of congregations has brought me to one conclusion. The most important question is whether a congregation's focus and energy are directed outside of its doors, following the call to join God's mission in the world, or whether they are directed inside, to sustain its internal life. I've found that it's possible to sense fairly quickly where the primary energy of a congregation is directed.

It turns out, at least in my view, that this has little to do with theology. I've seen externally focused congregations that are highly conservative in their theology and others that are on the left edge of the theological spectrum. Similarly, I've been with congregations that pride themselves on their progressive, liberal theology but put most of their energy into solid worship, excellent music, and lively social fellowship. Likewise, it's unfortunately easy to find congregations with highly conservative theology whose energy goes into protecting themselves from the world rather than engaging in the world.

The clearest way I've found to describe this difference is to ask if a congregation feels primarily "settled" or primarily "sent."

Of course, I need to add the caveats to address points that professors and pastors might quickly raise. This isn't an either/or. An externally focused congregation needs a solid foundation of worship and discipleship. The internal life of a congregation, as it nurtures members to be more faithful followers of Jesus, matters. And so forth.

It's helpful to think, as Pat Keifert does, of four movements in the life of those who become part of the body of Christ. First, they are *called*. They are responding to a call that has addressed their lives through the life of Jesus Christ. Then they are *gathered*. Christian faith is personal, but never individualistic. Being called to Christ means belonging to a community that is an expression of Christ's body. Next, they are *centered*. The community of believers grounds, shapes, and forms the faith of its members. But then, they are *sent*. Becoming part of Christ's body means following Jesus in mission in the world. That's where Jesus leads, that's what the Spirit empowers, and this is what God intends.

The first three movements — calling, gathering, and centering — lead to the fourth, sending. At least that's the design. Joining in God's mission in the world is not an option just for some, or a program to carry out, or simply an annual trip to dig wells in Zambia. It's the expected outcome of hearing the call to follow Jesus, and responding.

All this is the foundation for becoming a missional church. As I said earlier, *a missional church places its commitment to join in God's mission in the world at the heart of its life and identity.* In my journey, I've come to believe that learning what it really means to live as a missional church is the most important challenge before congregations, and for any denomination. We are to live as those who are sent.

The temptation to remain settled is enormous. So many congregations know how to gather people and then work on centering them, meaning doing a variety of classes, groups, social activities, and "Christian education" programs. But these easily evolve into attempts to keep members engaged in the church rather than to equip them for being sent out. The subtle goal becomes keeping people involved in church activities and preventing them from leaving.

I can describe a typical congregation like this. It has a rich history, going back to the 1700s. It's situated in the center of town, across from the post office. Chimes play from its steeple. Members are deeply loyal, boasting a long history with the church. The preaching is solid. The occasional infant baptism is done well. Adult baptisms are virtually unknown. A small group of young people are confirmed and then tend to disappear.

The social life of many of its members, especially senior ones, revolves around each other. People enjoy being with one another; some take trips together, or regularly see each other during the winter in Florida. A small choir keeps going with faithful members. While money is tight, the church meets its budget, including donations to the community soup kitchen.

Meanwhile, the community is changing and growing. New families are moving in. The typical problems of drugs and alcohol affect junior high and high school students. Although it is a relatively affluent community, poverty still stalks those on the margins, and immigrants, whose legal status is unknown to others, look for jobs cutting grass.

This picture can describe thousands of congregations in typical suburban settings. The church's members will say they are glad to welcome newcomers. But they assume such people will simply show up if they are interested. They are generally aware of problems with youth, and the presence of underprivileged groups, but they assume agencies and social workers will address them.

For them, the church is there to meet their needs, providing a place of worship and fellowship. They are internally focused and comfortable being a settled congregation. The Word is preached, the sacraments are performed, and the life of the church is properly governed. But they have little sense of actively participating in God's mission in the world.

However, I've seen congregations exactly like these turned inside out as they grasp the calling to be a missional church. The focus is shifted to the congregation's impact in the community. A safe place for kids to gather after school is provided. Mentoring relationships are established. Church members think creatively about how to welcome the many new families moving into the community, and learn how to speak comfortably about their faith in Jesus Christ. Initiatives are established relating to those in the community who are disadvantaged. In time, the energy and focus of the congregation shift outside of itself, and this movement is supported by inspiring biblical study, intentional preaching, and prayer.

These movements of transformation, beckoning congregations to change from being settled to being sent, are critical for the church's future. Even more important, they are critical for a vital witness to the gospel, and for the growth of God's kingdom. When followed faithfully, the commitment to become a missional church leads us to radical forms of discipleship, confronting political and economic powers that always prefer the church to be comfortably settled.

I shared earlier in this memoir about my experience with Church of the Saviour four decades ago. In the wide experience of church groups I've encountered, lived with, and led, both here and around the world, its model of being the church remains the most compelling and instructive for me.

Church of the Saviour was a high-commitment congregation organized around "mission groups." Every member belonged to one, and these groups were defined by their outward, missional call. Members joined them by responding to the call that came from each group's mission. That might be working on Jubilee Housing, or hospitality at the Potter's House, or a health and healing ministry with low-income people, or any number of missional callings.

The mission group also provided the accountability and support for one's inward spiritual journey with Christ. What always struck me was how fellowship — *koinonia* — was created not for its own sake, but in response to mission. It was in Church of the Saviour that I discovered the pathways and support to deepen my inward journey with Christ. And it was there that I experienced how that flows into an outward journey that works for the transformation of one's community and ultimately of the world.

When a congregation reclaims its missional identity, it recognizes that its very life is shaped to be an agent of God's change in the world, and to become a revolutionary force for good. That is what happens when congregations make the transition from being settled to being sent.

What about Jesus?

When I was four years old my mother asked me what I would do about Jesus. More than six decades later, I'm still asking myself that same question. What does it mean to say that my life will be defined by his?

After Big Daddy bought the farm and sold a section to the Catholics, his subdivision included a new home on Knight Avenue for our family. In seventh grade, when I was leaving that home in the morning to walk to Lincoln Junior High School, my mom would pray with me each day at the front door: "Dear Father, help Wes today to put Jesus first, others second, and himself last."

It's a prayer I've often dissected, and never forgotten. The various paths I've traveled since then are ways that I've wandered and searched to discover what to do about Jesus. The evangelical subculture in which I was raised was infiltrated by pernicious racism, captured by right-wing nationalism, absorbed with rampant materialism, and defended by haughty self-righteousness. But it taught me to ask the right question. What about Jesus?

Early in my journey, my responses to that question began to challenge my subculture's answers. The ensuing dialogue, however, echoed my mother's prayer: What does it mean to put Jesus first? Our problem is that we have domesticated Jesus and lost the radical challenge that question poses.

The central task of North American congregations, denominations, and Christian institutions in our day is to resurrect who Jesus is. We need to hear anew the call of what it means to be a disciple of his in this time and place. And then we must create and nurture communities of those who are claimed by this call and are willing to follow, traveling to unexpected destinations anticipated only by God's providence.

Frequently people ask me if there's a future for denominations, or specifically for the Reformed Church in America. Every decade or so a new crop of speakers and consultants discovers that denominational leaders will actually pay them a lot of money to come speak at church conferences about the demise and death of denominations. The best answer I ever heard to this question came from George Anderson, when he was presiding bishop of the Evangelical Lutheran Church in America. "People ask me if denominations will survive," he said, "and I say, have you ever tried to close a single church?"

Denominations, in one form or another, will endure. That's certain. The real question is whether they will do things that are useful and good. To do so will require their transformation. Their purpose and structure will be realigned around equipping congregations for their missional calling, rather than functioning as regulatory agencies and benefit services providers.

This will depend on recovering a radical sense of what it means to follow Jesus, and then creating structures that connect, strengthen, and resource communities of disciples called to participate in God's mission. The question isn't, "What about denominations?" It's "What about Jesus?"

My journey to resurrect the person of Jesus was helped by the pilgrimage I took a couple of years ago to where he lived, died, and rose. It was no ordinary Holy Land tour, but rather a deep exposure, through hours of hiking, reflecting, and praying, to the places that shaped Jesus' life. This was interwoven with the biblical narrative and the historical realities happening in that land today.

It turns out, for instance, that Nazareth at the time of Jesus was a town of only a few hundred people, and Jews had settled there as part of a movement to establish their presence and culture in this area. So it was not unlike Jewish settlements today on the West Bank.

I always wondered why the people of Nazareth wanted to push Jesus off a cliff after his inaugural sermon in Luke 4. There I learned it was, most likely, because of his references at the end of that passage of how God had blessed, healed, and used non-Jews for his purposes. Jesus was condemning the narrow nationalistic and ethnic exclusivity of his hometown, and the people became furious. That made it clearer to me where a follower of Jesus should be led in our current debates around immigration, and our perpetual appeals to nationalistic pride.

I sat at the pools of Bethesda recounted in John 5. The lame and the invalids were there, hoping for healing, because they were refused entrance into the temple. And Jesus chose this route to the temple to make a point about the worthy sons and daughters of Abraham who were being excluded from fellowship and worship because of cultural prejudices and unloving attitudes. It reminded me of how the church often treats gays and lesbians.

Such epiphanies were revealed throughout those days in Israel and Palestine. They reawakened a hunger within me to know the life of Jesus of Nazareth in order to follow him more faithfully as my Lord and Savior. To decide what to do about Jesus, we don't need to know a theological formula; rather, we need to know about Jesus.

This simple but radical call to follow Jesus gets beyond the last half-century of Protestant warfare between evangelical and ecumenical worlds, or the gospel of conversion versus the social gospel. This dichotomy has been widely decried, yet some institutions on each side still find it in their fund-raising interests to perpetuate this false conflict.

Personally, I have no time for those building a new form of fortress Christianity, attaching a right-wing political ideology to new expressions of biblicism, and highlighting hot-button issues like homosexuality. Ironically, the essential failure of these folks is that they ignore Jesus of Nazareth. Likewise, I am disillusioned by seminaries whose fascination with textual criticism and academic prowess replaces the simplistic faith of their students too often with cynicism, or even no faith, rather than a mature attachment to the person of Christ.

What excites me in seminaries, parachurch movements, campus ministries, and congregations is a fresh fascination with Jesus, as a radical servant leader of a transformational movement, embodying the fullness of God's love. In other words, God incarnate. I see those in a younger generation drawn to this authentic presentation of Jesus and challenged to live as his disciples, knowing that this means working for God's justice in the world. This also means learning the spiritual practices that create the space in one's life for the work of God's Spirit to transform our inner being. The old dichotomies are left behind as we decide what to do about Jesus.

Following this Jesus leads us to the frontiers of world Christianity. For those of us in North America, being his disciples beckons us to look beyond the framework of our national and cultural life. So much of the peculiar baggage we carry from American culture obscures the startling challenge that comes from saying Jesus is Lord. It's the non-Western world today that is witnessing the explosive power of the gospel and the expansive growth of the church. In some of those settings, putting Jesus first leads to persecution or even martyrdom. But in those crucibles of discipleship we catch unique and holy glimpses of the resurrected power of Jesus.

Enriched by the privilege of listening to the stories of Christians from around the world, my journey continues as I ask what to do about Jesus. I don't know when I was born again — whether at four, or twenty-four, or both of those times and many more. All that is safely in God's hands.

What I do know is that the gospel took on flesh. In each of our lives, grace tries to intrude continually, attempting to shape our story into an infinitesimal but uniquely valuable part of God's story. God can certainly do very well without any one of us. That's a message that the Reformed heritage has proclaimed with vigor. But God also delights in each one of us. When we ask what to do about Jesus, we are invited into an inner, transformative journey that allows the unique combination of DNA that shapes our being to be joined with the foundational movement of God's love. This seeks to shape the world into the home of God's glory. And for any one of us, that is a story worth telling.

Index

Index

Index

Index